W9-AWP-634

Other Titles in the Smart Pop Series

Taking the Red Pill

Seven Seasons of Buffy

Five Seasons of Angel

What Would Sipowicz Do?

Stepping through the Stargate

The Anthology at the End of the Universe

Finding Serenity

The War of the Worlds

Alias Assumed

Navigating the Golden Compass

Farscape Forever!

Flirting with Pride and Prejudice

Revisiting Narnia

Totally Charmed

King Kong Is Back!

Mapping the World of Harry Potter

The Psychology of The Simpsons

The Unauthorized X-Men

The Man from Krypton

Welcome to Wisteria Lane

Star Wars on Trial

The Battle for Azeroth

Boarding the Enterprise

Getting Lost

James Bond in the 21st Century

So Say We All

Investigating CSI

Literary Cash

WEBSLINGER

WEBSLINGER

Unauthorized Essays on Your Friendly Neighborhood Spider-Man

EDITED BY

Gerry Conway

WITH **Leah Wilson**

BENBELLA BOOKS, INC.

Dallas, Texas

THIS PUBLICATION HAS NOT BEEN PREPARED, APPROVED, OR LICENSED BY ANY ENTITY THAT CREATED OR PRODUCED THE WELL-KNOWN CHARACTER SPIDER-MAN.

"Horror in Long Underwear" © 2006 by Darren Hudson Hick
"Peter Parker's Penance" © 2006 by Lawrence Watt-Evans
"Superman vs. the Amazing Spider-Man" © 2006 by Keith R. A. DeCandido
"Raimi vs. Bendis: Reimagining Spider-Man" © 2006 by Robert B. Taylor
"The Tangled Web We Weave" © 2006 by Lou Anders
"The Perfectibility of Spider-Man" © 2006 by Richard Hanley
"Spider-Man: Class Straddler as Superhero" © 2006 by Matthew Pustz
"The Friendly Neighborhood of Peter Parker" © 2006 by Michael A. Burstein
"Spinning a Web of Shame" © 2006 by Joseph McCabe
"Spider-Man: Ultimate Loner—Ultimate Partner" © 2006 by Robert Greenberger
"Spider-Man No More: Moral Responsibility, the Morose Hero, and His Web of Relationships" © 2006 by Brett Chandler Patterson
"The Absent Father and Spider-Man's Unfulfilled Potential" © 2006 by J. R. Fettinger
"J. Jonah Jameson: Just What the Heck Is That Guy's Major Malfunction, Anyway?" © 2006 by Adam-Troy Castro
"Power, Responsibility, and Pain: The Price of Being Spider-Man" © 2006 by Paul Lytle
"Secrets and Secret-Keepers" © 2006 by David Hopkins
"Spider-Man Saves the World" © 2006 by Robert Burke Richardson
"Inner Demons, Outer Heroes, Outer Villains: A Look at Monstrosity in *Spider-Man* and *Spider-Man 2*" © 2006 by Michael Marano
Additional Materials © 2006 by Gerry Conway
Photos © 2006 by Nomi S. Burstein

All rights reserved. No part of this book may be used or reproduced in any manner whatsoever without written permission except in the case of brief quotations embodied in critical articles or reviews.

BenBella Books, Inc.
6440 N. Central Expressway, Suite 617
Dallas, TX 75206
www.benbellabooks.com
Send feedback to feedback@benbellabooks.com

Printed in the United States of America
10 9 8 7 6 5 4 3 2 1

Library of Congress Cataloging-in-Publication Data

Webslinger : unauthorized essays on your friendly neighborhood Spider-Man / edited by Gerry Conway with Leah Wilson.
     p. cm.
   ISBN 1-933771-06-2
   1. Spider-Man (Fictitious character) I. Conway, Gerry. II. Wilson, Leah.

PN6728.S6W43 2006
741.5'973—dc22

2006032613

Proofreading by Julia Whitehead and Jennifer Thomason
Cover design by Laura Watkins
Front cover design by Big Time Attic
Text design and composition by John Reinhardt Book Design
Printed by Bang Printing

Distributed by Independent Publishers Group
To order call (800) 888-4741
www.ipgbook.com

For special sales contact Yara Abuata at yara@benbellabooks.com

Contents

INTRODUCTION

Turning Point

I T'S HARD TO remember these days, with our friendly neighborhood wall crawler seemingly omnipresent in the pop culture *Zeitgeist*, but there was a time when Spider-Man existed solely in the pages of a single bi-monthly comic book, published by a small, second-class comic-book house.

That's when I fell in love with him.

I started reading Spider-Man when I was eleven years old, sometime around issue seven or eight, long after I'd become a fan of his predecessors, the Fantastic Four. (I began reading their adventures in *The World's Greatest Comic Magazine* with issue four.) To say I was swept away by this new hero, whose inner life seemed so much like my own, would be more than an understatement. I was hooked from the very first page. Peter Parker, Liz Allan, Flash Thompson, Aunt May—they were immediately as real to me as the members of my own family and the kids I went to school with. As someone who'd always felt like a bit of an outsider, and who'd recently moved into a new neighborhood where I was still trying to find my way, I identified totally with Peter Parker—the eternal outsider, the ultimate alienated superhero. I didn't just want to read about him, I wanted to be him. In some ways, I thought I was him. (Without the webslinging, wall-crawling, super-strength and spider-sense, of course.)

Less than eight years later, I got the chance to fulfill that preadolescent dream.

I *became* Spider-Man.

Okay, not exactly. I became the *writer* of Spider-Man's adventures, the first permanent replacement for his co-creator, the masterful Stan Lee. (Roy Thomas had written a few fill-in issues, but considered the assignment purely temporary.) At the age of nineteen, in early 1972, I took over as writer and (at first) co-plotter (with John Romita) of *Amazing Spider-Man*, but in a real sense, with that assignment I became Peter Parker...or maybe more accurately, Peter Parker became me.

I started writing comics a few years earlier, in my mid-teens, at first scripting "horror mystery" stories for DC Comics. A year or two before I got the best writing assignment of my life, I shifted from DC to Marvel Comics, where I cut my teeth writing superheroes on such titles as *Iron Man*, *Sub-Mariner*, *Daredevil*, and *The Mighty Thor*. During this time, Stan Lee moved from being Marvel's top writer and editor-in-chief to being its publisher, overseeing a tremendous expansion of the company's publication line-up. Roy Thomas, my friend, mentor, and patron, became the new editor-in-chief, and one of his first decisions as editor was to make me Stan's replacement on Marvel's flagship title.

Now, as I said before, there was a time before Spider-Man was an icon of the pop culture *Zeitgeist*, and in 1972, when I started writing his adventures, his moment hadn't quite arrived—though it was close, very close. Sure, he was the most popular character published by Marvel Comics, but in the early '70s, Marvel was still technically just a second-tier comic-book house sitting in the shadow of the richer, more well-established DC. Outside of our readership (and the handful of viewers who'd seen the late '60s Spider-Man cartoon show), Spider-Man was probably best known as the star of a one-issue "anti-drug" comic that had gotten some play in the media a year or so before. He was not ubiquitous as he is today; there were no toys, no books, no television shows, no movies, no trading cards, and no other magazines featuring the web spinner (with the exception of Marvel Team-Up, which had only begun appearing a few months before).

He was, in short, a character in a comic book. A very popular comic book, granted, with very devoted fans, but in the larger scheme of things, pop culture-wise, he had yet to make much of an impact.

Then I killed his girlfriend.

Her name was Gwen Stacy. She was beautiful, kind-hearted, not particularly bright (at least as far as you could tell from the way she acted in the stories), and she was in love with Peter Parker. And he was in love with her. And they were a couple, destined for great things, their union filled with joy and happiness and unbounded promise. A golden duo touched by the grace of the gods themselves....

Yada-yada, blah-blah-blah.

In retrospect, Gwen Stacy's relationship with Peter Parker has gained a stature it never seemed, to this longtime reader, to have at the time. She was a babe, nice enough, but not particularly interesting, and in no way suitable—in this writer's opinion—as the love of Peter Parker's life. For me, destiny already announced Peter's soul mate the day Mary Jane Watson appeared on his doorstep and told him, "Face it, tiger. You just hit the jackpot." MJ was forthright, dynamic, gorgeous, as much a wiseacre as Peter himself, and so obviously right for him I always assumed Peter's relationship with Gwen was just a temporary diversion from the true path fate had laid out for him. (Just as, earlier, Liz Allan—Peter's heartthrob in high school—gave way to Betty Brant, his heartthrob at the newspaper where he sold his photos, the *Daily Bugle*.)

So, when I got the chance, I killed her.

I can't say it was totally my idea. John Romita and Stan had discussed killing off one of the series's main characters before I arrived on the scene. They were leaning toward Aunt May, but I thought she was too important to the structure and mythology of Spider-Man to ever leave (it would be like killing off Alfred for Batman). Gwen was their second choice, and it's the choice I campaigned for, and with the permission of all involved, she's the one we decided to do in.

Which seems to have changed comics forever, and perhaps, in some small way, contributed to the rise of comics as an art form to (apparent) domination of modern American pop media.

See, it wasn't just the fact of Gwen Stacy's death that made that particular comic-book story a turning point for Spider-Man as a character and comic books as an industry; it's the way she was killed. In trying to save her, Spider-Man himself became (partly) responsible for her death. (Read the story if you want to know the details; it's been reprinted endlessly, and retold more times than I'd care to count.) He didn't just fail to save her. He unwittingly contributed to her murder.

Nothing like this, to my knowledge, had ever been done before in comics.

It was, in a sense, the story in which Spider-Man, and maybe all of us who read (and wrote) comics, lost his innocence.

That loss of innocence echoed a similar loss of innocence in society as a whole. As a country, we were dealing with the realization that superpower has its limits, and can backfire on those who choose to wield it. In 1973, when the story appeared, we were coming to the end of the Vietnam war, a futile and agonizing recognition of the limits of national power; in 1973, we were just beginning to hear about Watergate, which would lead to the resignation of a President, and a further display of the limits of power; and a few months before, in late 1972, we launched the last manned mission to the moon, Apollo 17, yet another reminder that all dreams come to an end.

With the death of Gwen Stacy, and the repercussions that followed, Spider-Man became firmly hitched to the social *Zeitgeist*—for the first time in his ten years of existence. Before that story, he was an all-too-accurate reflection of adolescent angst and alienation. After that story, he became a mirror to a generation confronting its unspoken fear of life's futility.

And all I wanted to do was write an entertaining story that would give me a chance to develop the relationship between Peter and Mary Jane.

Instead, it seems I helped Spider-Man (and comics) begin to grow up.

So now we come to the book in your hands. Thirty-odd years after Gwen's death, our favorite neighborhood web spinner is indeed a pop culture icon. What follows is an exploration of that iconic status, its causes and influences, the ramifications for our society and ourselves. These seventeen essays are an attempt by some of science fiction and comicdom's best and brightest to understand the impact of the webslinger on all of our lives.

I had fun reading what they had to say. I'm sure you will too.

Gerry Conway
Los Angeles, California
September 2006

DARREN HUDSON HICK

Horror in Long Underwear

Was Amazing Spider-Man in 1962 secretly a horror comic in disguise? That's the intriguing premise of Darren Hudson Hick's essay and it does indeed provide food for thought. (Of course, in a true horror tale, like, say, a zombie film, "food for thought" has a very different and, shall we say, cerebral connotation.)

On a personal note, Darren's description of Fredric Wertham's impact on comics brings to mind something that happened to me in the late 1960s, when Dr. Wertham appeared on a local New York television talk show hosted by Joe Pyne, an early Jerry Springer/Rush Limbaugh provocateur. Wertham was on Pyne's show to promote his latest pop-culture theory: television as a cause of juvenile delinquency. (I'm unfairly oversimplifying the man's thesis, but oversimplification is a technique he himself used to great effect.) Several of us in the "comic-book community" attended the broadcast as members of the studio audience, and tried to engage Wertham during the audience participation portion of the program. Naturally, it went nowhere, but afterward, I got up my nerve to approach Wertham.

I wanted to confront him, maybe rage at him for almost destroying something that mattered a great deal to me, but once I was face to face with the monster himself, I realized the creature of my nightmares was just a tired old man who wanted to do right by the world, but was blinded by his own nightmares and preconceptions. All things considered, pretty ironic, wouldn't you say?

Like costumed heroes? Confidentially, we in the comic-mag business refer to them as "long underwear characters"! And, as you know, they're a dime a dozen! But, we think you may find our Spider-Man just a bit...different! (*Amazing Fantasy* No. 15)

WITH STAN LEE'S signature huckster styling, so began the saga of Spider-Man, back in the summer of 1962. Spider-Man was "different," indeed, but to truly understand how (and why) first requires a bit of history....

In early 1962 America, the scariest thing on the spinning "Hey Kids Comics!" rack was *Millie the Model*. This is because, in 1962, while you could *write* a horror comic, and you could *draw* one, you certainly couldn't *publish* it. The Comics Code Authority and millions of nervous mothers made sure of that.

Established in 1954, the Comics Code Authority was an industry response to the ongoing Senate Subcommittee on Juvenile Delinquency, convened to investigate the effect of sex and violence in mass media on the youth of America. No coincidence, this was also the year that Fredric Wertham published *Seduction of the Innocent*, a psychological investigation into the effects of comics on children. Something of a boogeyman for the comics industry, German-born Wertham first caught the public eye as an expert witness in the 1935 trial of notorious serial murderer and cannibal Alfred Fish. His primary interests lay, however, in the effects of an individual's environment on his psychological state, and in 1941 Wertham published *Dark Legend*, the novelized case history of a seventeen-year-old murderer. Here, Wertham argued that an unhealthy fascination with movies, radio plays, and comic books drew the otherwise healthy teenager into an unnatural fantasy world, leading to aberrant behavior and eventually the murder of his mother (Wertham 1941). Published four years later, *Seduction of the Innocent* presented a more generalized account of the effect that exposure to comics might have on children. While the psychological aspects of Wertham's account have since garnered suspicion and ridicule, much of the evidence he presents is overwhelming. The text brims with images and descriptions of grotesque horror, most of it a revelation to readers, who had never given more than a passing glance at what their children were buying off the newsstand. Granted, Wertham also claims that Wonder Woman turns little girls into bullish lesbians and Batman and Robin transform boys into flaming homosexuals, but this only fueled the fears of nervous Americans (Wertham 1954).

Wertham was called to testify in the Senate Subcommittee, which he did gleefully. Restating evidence from his book, and exposing even more of America to repeated comic-book imagery of ocular injury, rape, and decapitated housewives, Wertham's testimony went largely unchallenged by the subcommittee. Wertham's most damning argument was that the comics industry promoted race hatred, stating "I think Hitler was a beginner compared to the comic-book industry." Citing story evidence of racial slurs and lynching, Wertham argued that children would naturally imitate what they read in the comics. Defending the comics industry was William C. Gaines, owner of EC Comics, the leading publisher of romance, crime, war, and, most importantly, horror comics. While Gaines maintained that he only published what he thought was "in good taste," Senator Estes Kefauver challenged Gaines with EC comic-book covers depicting women being strangled by crowbars and decapitated by axes. Although the infamous exchange between Kefauver and Gaines was halted, the effect could not be undone. And while, ultimately, the subcommittee did not find that comics were responsible for rampant juvenile delinquency, America had heard the evidence, and the comics industry was nervous, indeed.

Hoping to appease the masses, and fearing outside control, the comics industry sought to establish an independent censorship board to police their publications, and the Comics Magazine Association of America was born. Among other things, the comics code developed by the CMAA targeted the horror genre, outlawing publications with the words "horror" or "terror" in their titles; eliminating all scenes of gore, bloodshed, depravity, and lust; restricting stories of evil to those with wholesome morals; and prohibiting any depiction of vampires, werewolves, cannibals, and the living dead. Although few today pay any attention to (or even know the implications of) the "Comics Code Authority" stamp on the front cover of comic books, parents in the '50s and '60s were all too aware of what it stood for. In the aftermath of the senate hearings, Gaines's EC Comics was all but eliminated, and the horror genre in comics quickly became a thing of the past. Parents were appeased, but the children of the '50s had not lost their appetite for horror.

While horror comics were being handed their walking papers by the CCA, horror *movies* were having a banner year. The highest-grossing film of 1954 was *Them!*, the story of atomically mutated giant ants terrorizing the Southwest. And America was not alone— 1954 also marked the Japanese release of one of the masterpieces in the atomic horror genre, *Godzilla: King of the Monsters.* Japan, of course, had reason to be afraid: Hiroshima and Nagasaki had been decimated by Little Boy and Fat Man in August of 1945. And, although America and her allies had won the war against the Axis Powers, just as life was returning to normal, the Soviet Union gained access to nuclear weapons technology, and the world turned upside-down once again. The Red Scare loomed over America. Throughout the 1950s, Bert the Turtle taught schoolchildren that curling up under their desks would save their necks, should the U.S.S.R. decide to drop a bomb on the playground outside. But children aren't stupid; while they were learning to "duck and cover," their parents were digging up their backyards and building fallout shelters. For the first time, children understood horror—the horror that, until now, only soldiers had known. And this horror found an outlet in Hollywood: the terrors of atomic holocaust and nuclear mutation fueled the imagination of filmmakers and filmgoers alike. Creatures unleashed from the ocean depths and irradiated giants rampaged across the silver screen throughout the '50s and early '60s, but the hands of comic-book publishers were tied. Although teens and preteens flocked to the movies to gorge themselves on popcorn and nuclear terror, even if comic-book publishers could circumvent the stranglehold of the CCA, parents were now extremely wary about what their children were reading. Kids were hungry for horror, and the comic-book industry was missing the boat. The stage was set for Spider-Man.

Spider-Man was introduced in *Amazing Fantasy* No. 15 in August of 1962. Proudly displaying the CCA seal, *Amazing Fantasy* was a dying mystery anthology—an unusual venue to try out a new character, especially one as strange as Spider-Man, but this was the series's last issue, and no one expected Spider-Man to be a success. The story of Spider-Man begins when Peter Parker, a teenage everyman, is bitten on the hand by a radioactively mutated spider. Children brought up in the '50s, of course, were already intimately familiar with this particular plot device of the horror genre; science was as much a danger as it was a boon, and radioactivity was its redheaded stepchild.

Already, radioactivity had produced the Fantastic Four and the Incredible Hulk, mirroring the atomic horrors of the cinema. But with Spider-Man, creators Stan Lee and Steve Ditko did the '50s horror movies one better, combining the horrors of radioactivity with the horrors of adolescence. In the event that you've sugarcoated your memory of puberty, or simply forgotten what it's like, for most teenagers every morning promises new horrors. An adolescent's body is an out-of-control thing—changing shapes, sprouting hair, and forever breaking out in pimples. The mirror is rarely the teenager's friend: just when he's most concerned about looking his best, the teenager is cursed to look his absolute worst. Add glasses, a sweater-vest, and a two-dollar haircut, and you've got Peter Parker. Tormented by jocks and shunned by girls, Peter is on the low rung of the already unenviable ladder of adolescence. So, naturally, it can only get worse. Having been bitten by a spider, Peter finds he's turning into one.

In a sense, it's nice to know Peter isn't alone: the theme of transformations (particularly into bugs) is hardly a new one in literature. Traditionally, however, it doesn't go well. In Franz Kafka's famous short story "The Metamorphosis," Gregor Samsa wakes one morning to find he has turned into a "monstrous insect." Gregor's family, incapable of understanding his insect speech, shuns him, and Gregor's life becomes one of imposed solitude. Eventually, his father, in an attempt to chase him away, throws an apple core at him, and impales him in the back. The apple core rots and Gregor's wound becomes infected. Gregor dies, and the cleaning lady sweeps him up and dumps him in the trash. This is a tale of psychological horror—of finding oneself transformed, and being ostracized by the world: the nightmare of adolescence, magnified. Before being bitten by the radioactive spider, Peter is already an outcast, alienated by both his peers and the scientists he admires. The transformation he undergoes only further sets him apart from those around him—who among them can possibly understand the transformation Peter is experiencing?

The classical myths, too, are filled with transformations. Mortals, having angered the gods, are transformed into crows and cows and owls, seemingly without end. In one such story, Arachne, a weaver, claims her skill outshines even that of Athena, the goddess of weaving. Arachne unwittingly enters a contest with Athena, who is angered by the subject of Arachne's tapestry, and strikes her on the head. Arachne, ashamed, runs off and attempts to hang herself. Athena takes pity, transforming Arachne into a spider, and her rope into a cobweb. The story of Arachne is, of course, where we derive the name of the biological class of spiders, *Arachnida*, and the fear of spiders, *arachnophobia*.

Predatory, cannibalistic, and...well...creepy, spiders were an unusual choice for a superhero motif. Although there are certainly exceptions to the rule, historically, superheroes embodied admirable qualities, and themes were chosen to reflect these. Spiders, on the other hand, are more typically objects of disgust and fear. Topping the list of phobias, arachnophobia reportedly affects half of women and one in ten men, many more than are struck with the fear of heights, flying, or even death. It has even been suggested by psychologists that a fear of spiders is an evolutionary trait in humans, selected in the days when our ancestors slept out in the open or in caves.

In and of itself, the spider theme was not an entirely new one for costumed heroes, however. In the golden age of pulp heroes, following in the footsteps of The Shadow, Popular Publications introduced The Spider in 1933. Wealthy socialite-about-town by day, Richard Wentworth stalked the underworld by night in a cape and theatrical fangs. Later, in 1940, The Tarantula, another spider-themed detective, this time in garish purple and yellow tights, was created for DC Comics. With a web gun to snag villains and suction cups that allowed him to scale buildings, the character of The Tarantula was even called "Spider Man" by a news broadcast in his opening story. But The Tarantula failed to capture the imagination of readers. Comic-book readers had seen gimmicks come and go. But where The Tarantula sometimes *acted* like a spider, two decades later Peter Parker was *becoming* one.

Certainly, one major difference between Spider-Man and the atomic horror films of the '50s is that Spider-Man is not, by all outward appearances, a monster. Giant ants terrorizing the desert are monsters. Dinosaurs rampaging across Tokyo are monsters. A teenage boy in colorful lycra tights is not a monster; he's fashion-challenged. Peter Parker might have been transforming into a spider, but you wouldn't have known it by looking at him. Having been bitten by the radioactive spider, Peter doesn't grow new limbs or mandibles, he doesn't develop a forehead full of eyeballs, his abdomen doesn't balloon to bulbous proportions. He simply gains the powers of a spider, and learns to sew spandex. Deforming Peter as a result of his spiderbite was out of the question. First, the Comics Code required that "special precautions to avoid references to physical afflictions or deformities" be taken. And second, Lee wanted his readers to be able to relate to Peter. Giving him spider abilities was already stretching the bounds of relatability; deforming him would have been going too far. That said, the fact that Peter Parker had not turned into a monster did not place him outside the horror genre; quite the opposite, what he *had* become entrenched him in the genre all the more securely.

In *Purity and Danger*, essentially a study of comparative religion, anthropologist Mary Douglas theorizes that something is perceived as "impure" when that thing crosses certain categories firmly entrenched in a culture's beliefs. Thus, she notes, the East African Nuer people regarded deformities at birth, seemingly both human and animal, as baby hippos mistakenly born to humans. Regarded as dangerous to the people, the "baby hippos" were "returned" to the river (Douglas 39). Similarly, Douglas argues, in parts of West Africa, if a cock crowed at night, rather than at dawn (when it was "supposed" to), it was regarded as an abomination, and put to death (*ibid*). In north Congo (now Zaire), she claims, the Lele people avoid flying squirrels because they are unable to classify them as animals or as birds. (Douglas 168) Now, should you think this a peculiarity of "primitive" African peoples, consider the laws of Leviticus, third book of the Bible. The laws of Leviticus outlaw sowing one's fields with two kinds of seed, wearing clothing woven of two kinds of material, or mating two kinds of animal. Each of these (and many more besides) is regarded as an impure act—an abomination. Today, of course, many still feel the same way about interracial relationships.

In his seminal paper, "The Nature of Horror," philosopher Noël Carroll argues that our reactions of disgust and fear to the elements of horror may be based on a similar principle. Zombies, vampires, and mummies combine the categories of the living and the dead, while werewolves, the lizard men, and the Creature from the Black Lagoon blend the characteristics of humans and other animals. Haunted houses, possessed cars, and robots, meanwhile, are non-human things with human-like attributes, and the monster that savages an Arctic expedition in the 1951 film, *The Thing*, is an enormous, bloodsucking carrot. At times, the monsters of horror are categorically "incomplete"—ghosts lack bodies, the Blob lacks form, and zombies might be missing any number of bits. Inversely, Dr. Jekyll and Mr. Hyde combine two men into one, and Frankenstein's monster many more besides.

Peter Parker may not look like a monster. But, then, neither did Dr. Jekyll or the Body Snatchers—and that's precisely what made them so creepy. He does, however, mix the categories of man and spider. As the song goes, he "does whatever a spider can"—and what spiders can do, men aren't supposed to. Shortly after being bitten by the radioactive arachnid, Peter instinctively leaps from the street to avoid a car, clinging to the wall of a building, several stories up. Spotting him scaling the wall, a child declares, "Mommy! Look at the man walking up the side of a building!" The mother replies without looking: "That's the last horror movie I take *you* to, young man!" (*Amazing Fantasy* No. 15). Clearly, she doesn't need to see horror to recognize it; she knows it by its trappings. And so should we. There is a scene in the exceptional horror film *The Exorcist III* in which a patient in a mental ward is briefly seen skittering across the ceiling. The audience does not react to this scene with awe; it reacts with fear and revulsion—and not merely from surprise. Although the patient appears human enough, she does what humans aren't *supposed* to do. She does what spiders do—she does what Spider-Man does.

Once Peter puts on his costume, the line between man and spider becomes all the more blurred. Unlike other costumed crime-fighters of his day, Spider-Man's mask eliminates all trace of humanity from his face, replacing it instead with two huge, inhuman unblinking eyes. More than this, the characteristics of his body become more spider-like: inhumanly flexible, Spider-Man's limbs twist and bend in bizarre ways; he clings flatly to walls, and nimbly creeps along wires and webs. He doesn't walk like a man—for the most part, he doesn't walk at all.

Changing Peter outwardly, physically, into a spider would have been more in line with the horror films of the '50s, but then Spider-Man would almost certainly have been quashed by the CCA. By making him *act* like a spider, Lee and Ditko not only created a CCA-friendly character, but one much more fundamentally creepy than a mere giant spider would have been. In Spider-Man, Stan Lee and Steve Ditko gave readers all the elements of horror—nuclear fear, alienation, metamorphosis, and category mistakes—but wrapped them in a colorful unitard. Spider-Man was something the comic-reading public had never seen before—the archetypal horror character, presented as an archetypal superhero character—a mixed message that captured the attention and imagination of readers, and snuck under the radar of the CCA.

Perhaps readers didn't consciously pick up on all of the elements of horror inherent in Spider-Man—indeed, perhaps Stan Lee wasn't aware of them when he wrote the eleven-page story that introduced the character. Fear is a strange thing—we try to avoid it in our daily lives, yet seek it out in the fictions of the cinema, novels, and comic books. Perhaps no coincidence, between the publication of *Amazing Fantasy* No. 15 and Spider-Man's second appearance, seven months later in *Amazing Spider-Man* No. 1, America came closer than it ever had before to the holocaust that it had feared for more than a decade. For thirteen days in October of 1962, the Cuban Missile Crisis put America on the brink of nuclear war, and the comic-book-reading kids, teens, and twenty-somethings felt the threat of annihilation as much as the adults. No longer was impending nuclear war some far-off hypothetical scenario—it was sitting off the coast of Florida. And Spider-Man did what the giant bug-and-slug movies of the '50s did— it gave readers catharsis, a means of venting their fears. And the sales on *Spider-Man* soared.

Catharsis is a form of emotional cleansing, brought about by an indirect exposure to one's fears and anxieties. Catharsis is not a matter of *soothing* fears, but of *engaging* them so that we can look them in the eye and walk away unscathed. Readers experienced through Spider-Man what they feared experiencing themselves. The barrier between fiction and reality kept these horrors at a safe distance— close enough to see, but not close enough to touch. Peter Parker was someone readers could relate to—but wouldn't want to be. He gained fantastic powers, yes, but the price was *being* Peter Parker: going through what he goes through, and becoming what he becomes. Through the window between his world and ours, we witnessed our fears given flesh. We were awed, astonished, and horrified—and we came back for more, because it wasn't *us* that it was happening to.

Spider-Man remains a wildly popular franchise. In 2000, despite several previous and failed attempts to reimagine the character of Spider-Man, Marvel launched *Ultimate Spider-Man*, a modernized re-telling of the story of Spider-Man from the ground up, the first of Marvel's heroes to be retooled for what would become a sweeping dark mirror of the Marvel Universe. Writer Brian Michael Bendis was given the task of placing Spider-Man in the modern day, and was given the freedom to reimagine the hero as he saw fit. In the end, Bendis made few major changes to Spider-Man's origins. What he did change was the spider. Today, the Red Scare isn't what it was. The Cold War has passed, and science has moved in other directions. Today, we have stem-cell research, the genome project, and eugenics—so, naturally, Bendis's spider wasn't radioactive; it was genetically altered. Just as the Spider-Man of 1962 mirrored the fears of its readers, so too did the Spider-Man of 2000. And when the blockbuster *Spider-Man* movie was released in 2002, it used Bendis's idea. Even more, it expanded upon Peter's Kafkaesque metamorphosis, having him wake up (like Gregor Samsa) transformed into something he wasn't the night before. And so, in the movies, just like in the comics, Spider-Man continued to blend horror and hero—and audiences loved it. In his opening blurb to the character's first story, Stan Lee promised we'd find Spider-Man "just a bit...different." And different he was. The elements of horror pop up in the strangest places. And, every once in a great while, horror wears long underwear.

DARREN HUDSON HICK is a Ph.D. student in the philosophy department at the University of Maryland, where he also earned his M.A. He earned his B.A. at Trent University in Peterborough, Ontario, and his M.Phil at the University of Wales, Lampeter. He is the former managing editor of *The Comics Journal*. He lives on a diet of coffee and cigarettes, and wears a size 7¾ hat. More on Darren, his research, and his work can be found at www.typetoken.com.

References

Douglas, Mary. *Purity and Danger: An Analysis of Concepts of Pollution and Taboo*. London: Routledge & K. Paul, 1966.

Franz Kafka, "The Metamorphosis," *The Complete Stories*. New York: Schocken Books, 1971. 89–139.

Lee, Stan (w) and Steve Ditko (i). "Spider-Man!" *Amazing Fantasy* No. 15. Marvel Comics: Aug. 1962.

Noël Carroll, "The Nature of Horror," *The Journal of Aesthetics and Art Criticism*, 46 (1) (1987): 51–59.

Wertham, Fredric. *Dark Legend*. New York: Duell Sloan, 1941.

Wertham, Fredric. *Seduction of the Innocent*. Toronto: Clarke, Irwin & Company, Ltd., 1954.

LAWRENCE WATT-EVANS

Peter Parker's Penance

One of the reasons storytellers tell stories (probably the main reason) is in an attempt to understand why we do the things we do, why we are the people we are. Through the characters we create (or inherit) and the stories we choose to tell, we explore our own demons in a continuing, life-long effort to make sense of the world. Spider-Man is one of only two characters in comics (Batman being the other) whose inner life is more interesting to most writers than his actual adventures. Lawrence Watt-Evans offers a compelling theory as to why so many of us who've written him find that to be true.

CONSIDER TWO BOYS.

The first is a lad not yet in his teens who sees his beloved parents gunned down in the street by a petty crook, and who is helpless to do anything to save them.

The second is a teenager whose beloved uncle is gunned down by a petty crook, and who realizes that he could have prevented this by stopping that same man earlier.

By lucky chance, both boys have exceptional abilities. Both swear to fight crime, so that other innocents will not suffer as they have. Both youths train themselves, both equip themselves with a miniaturized high-tech arsenal, both put on lurid costumes, and both go out on the streets, taking the fight to the foe.

Except the first boy becomes a grim avenger, a creature of the night, a humorless, relentless, obsessed crimefighter, so focused on his unending war against evil that even his best friends sometimes doubt his sanity.

And the second becomes your happy-go-lucky, fun-loving, wise-cracking, friendly neighborhood Spider-Man, always ready with a smart remark.

How does *that* work?

Logically, shouldn't Spider-Man be just as grim and driven as Batman? Or even worse? After all, he really *is* partly responsible for his uncle's death, where there was nothing young Bruce Wayne could have done to save his parents. Yet there Spidey is, web-swinging happily through the streets and tossing off quips as if he hadn't a care in the world. Isn't that a bit, well, heartless of him? What happened to all that guilt, all that angst over his uncle's death? Is Spider-Man just laughing through his tears?

Y'know, it *really* doesn't look like it. It looks like he's having a fine ol' time out there. Oh, maybe not when he's face to face with Galactus, or having the snot beat out of him by the Hulk, but when he's tackling the sort of street-level thug who killed Uncle Ben he genuinely seems to be enjoying himself. Webbing guns out of their hands, hanging them from lampposts—come on, he's *playing*.

That just doesn't seem *right*, does it?

But wait! What about when he's *not* Spider-Man?

Ah, that's an entirely different picture. Peter Parker is not exactly Mr. Excitement. In fact, he lives a life of worry and turmoil. It does *not* look like he's having fun. He looks miserable. He's got a gorgeous wife, a glamorous job, a satisfying secret life, but he clearly considers himself a loser.

How's that again?

Say, what's going on here?

Let's leave Spidey for now and look at Batman again for a moment, shall we?

Ah, yes, the Batman. When he's not obsessively fighting crime, he's Bruce Wayne, millionaire playboy, majority stockholder in Wayne Enterprises, chairman of the Thomas Wayne Foundation. Envied and admired by most of Gotham City's upper crust, he's got it all—looks, money, fame, respect, power.

And *he doesn't care*. That's the thing—"Bruce Wayne" is a front, a role he trots out now and then just to keep up appearances. It's not who he is; the wealth and glamour is just a disguise, a tool. His *real* identity is Batman, the avenger, the dark warrior, the humorless obsessive. Wayne Enterprises exists to supply him with the money and equipment he needs to continue his relentless battle against evil. The Wayne Foundation exists to try to cut crime off at the roots by fighting the poverty and injustice that drive people to desperation. His money is just a necessary fuel for his secret life. He has no real family, no love life, no friends as Bruce Wayne; his only friends are people like Alfred, Robin, Oracle, Commissioner Gordon—his companions in Batman's war against crime. Everything he does, everything he is, is targeted at his crusade. It's all he wants, all he lives for. Bruce Wayne or Batman, it's the same guy underneath, and that's Batman.

But for Spider-Man, Peter Parker isn't just a front. Peter Parker is his attempt to have something resembling a normal life. It's who he really is. It's who he was before the radioactive spider sank its fangs into him, and who he still wants to be. The child who was Bruce Wayne is gone, leaving only Batman, but Peter Parker was a little more established, a little more certain of his identity, and he's still Peter Parker, not Spider-Man.

And Peter Parker is generally pretty miserable. He certainly isn't rich or famous or handsome or successful, like Bruce Wayne. . . .

But—why not?

Why does he consider himself a loser, and behave accordingly?

Before that spider bit him, before Uncle Ben was killed, Peter Parker was on track for a pretty good life. Maybe *he* didn't think so, but he was. Really, think about it.

Yes, he was an orphan. Yes, he was a nerd. But so what? That was high school. It wasn't real life. He had a loving home, even if it wasn't with his parents, and he had a brilliant scientific mind. His classmates mocked him, but his teachers didn't—they respected and encouraged him. Science nerds may be looked down on in high school, but ten years later, when the captain of the football team is selling shoes, the nerds are pulling down six-figure salaries from major corporations—or perhaps *running* major corporations, like Steve Jobs or Bill Gates. The jocks look back on high school as their glory days, but the nerds look back on graduation as the beginning of everything important in their lives.

And maybe Peter Parker wasn't exactly a ladies' man in high school, but he did all right. Betty Brant and Liz Allan were fighting over him, for heaven's sake! And later, a hot blonde named Gwen Stacy adored him, and he wound up marrying a *model*. A smart, funny, utterly devoted model. As Mary Jane herself put it—face it, Tiger, you've hit the jackpot. Clearly, Peter Parker had the right pheromones; even when he wasn't trying, he attracted women.

And why not? He's not ugly. He's smart and witty and modest—what's not to like?

Brains, family, friends, charm, health—so why *didn't* Peter Parker wind up rich and happy?

He tells himself that it's because he's just naturally a loser, an unlucky guy, and that the need for Spider-Man interferes with everything else. Uh-huh, sure. Being a superhero is such a thankless chore.

Then why does he look like he's having fun when he's Spider-Man, and like his puppy just died when he's Peter Parker?

I'm not buying his explanation. It just doesn't fit the facts. What *really* went wrong for Peter Parker, and right for Spider-Man?

What went wrong? Well, first, he didn't stick with his plan for a career in science. He became a freelance photographer, and even though it was originally intended to be a stopgap to get him through a financial rough stretch, he *stayed* a freelance photographer. Unless you're Alfred Stieglitz or Ansel Adams, there isn't generally a lot of money in that. His plans for a career in the sciences just sort of faded away—he let a few setbacks completely derail him. His excuse was that he couldn't devote the time to it and still keep up with his responsibilities as Spider-Man.

Oh, come on. Night classes. Part-time work. He's got the brains, he's got the contacts—he could do it if he wanted to. He could still go back to it, even now. People expect scientists to be eccentric. Keeping odd hours is entirely within acceptable tolerances, so long as the work gets done. He *could* do it.

But he doesn't.

Instead he keeps on working for J. Jonah Jameson and the *Daily Bugle*, even though he knows that Jameson's an obnoxious cheapskate, and worse. Oh, he's occasionally made half-hearted efforts to sell his photographs elsewhere, but just as he has with his scientific studies, he gave up far too easily. He's never tried to study photojournalism, never tried to develop multiple markets for his work the way most freelancers do; instead he just keeps on selling Spider-Man pictures to a man who loathes Spider-Man.

This is *clearly* self-hatred at work.

As for his love life, he seemed to deliberately sabotage that for awhile, too. He willfully misunderstood Betty Brant's concerns, refused to take Liz Allan's attention seriously, actively avoided meeting Mary Jane for months. Okay, he got Gwen Stacy killed, and that was a genuine piece of horrible misfortune directly related to being Spider-Man, but if anything he was *less* reluctant with women after that; it certainly wasn't the *start* of his romantic failures.

Really, if you look at what he actually *does*, rather than what he *says*, it's clear that Peter Parker is deliberately sabotaging himself in any number of ways. He *says* it's all because of Spider-Man, but it doesn't really look like it. He's screwing up his own life, and ignoring opportunities to straighten it out.

So why would he ruin his own life?

That's easy. Why does anyone reject happiness? Guilt.

Peter feels he doesn't *deserve* happiness. After all, he let Uncle Ben get murdered, when he could have prevented it. He can't allow Peter Parker to ever have all the things Uncle Ben wanted for him, if Ben isn't there to see it. Ben Parker was encouraging him in his plans to study science, so with Ben gone, science is no longer where he's meant to be. He can't have the research career that his uncle was guiding him into, because that uncle is gone, and it's *all his fault*.

Ben would tease him about girls, and offer him advice, and Ben and May provided his role models of a loving couple, so with Ben gone he can't have that, either. So he screwed up his love life.

Ben never let him worry about money, even when things were tight, so with Ben gone he's constantly obsessing about it, even while he's refusing to find a steady, high-paying job.

Everything Uncle Ben wanted for him, he's unconsciously reject- ed. He's not worthy of it. He's turned his entire life as Peter Parker into a constant penance.

But on the other hand, there's one thing he does that's directly, openly meant to make up for his failure to save his uncle, one step toward making amends, and that's being Spider-Man. Tracking down criminals, defending the weak and helpless, making the streets of New York a little safer—that's what he knows he *should* be doing, so that no other Uncle Bens will die through his failure to act.

And that means that when he's Spider-Man, *the guilt goes away!* Because he's out there doing what he should have done all along. When he's swinging on a webline, that huge burden is lifted from his shoulders. When he punches a mugger it's a *relief*—it's one more bad guy who won't kill anyone's uncle, who won't threaten Aunt May or Mary Jane. He's making it right with Uncle Ben.

Of *course* he feels good when he's Spider-Man! It's the only time he's out from under that crushing weight of guilt. He makes jokes as he fights villains not to disconcert them, but because he is feeling no pain. He feels *good*. How can he be grim when he knows he's doing the right thing?

When he's Spider-Man he's the fun-loving, happy-go-lucky guy that Uncle Ben wanted him to be.

When he's Peter Parker he's the loser who let Uncle Ben die, and who has been suffering for it ever since.

It's the guilt that makes the difference. Bruce Wayne knows it wasn't his fault that Thomas and Martha Wayne were murdered; he's fighting crime not out of guilt, but out of a determination not to see other innocents suffer as he did. It's obsessive altruism. He's turned his whole life into a battle against the external evil that destroyed his happy life.

For Peter Parker, though, it *is* guilt. He let Uncle Ben die, and he's turned his whole life into penance for the personal failure that de- stroyed his happy life—and he's making absolutely sure that he *never gets that happy life back*. It's all neurotic compensation for that one careless moment when he let a criminal go free.

Oh, there are times he slips up and enjoys life even when he's not swinging around New York in his tights. Aunt May and Mary Jane have worked hard to cheer him up, and sometimes it even works for awhile—or at least, he pretends it does, so as not to upset them. But he hasn't continued his education. He hasn't looked for work in the sciences. He hasn't told J. Jonah Jameson to get stuffed, even though he knows perfectly well that Jameson is guilty of attempted murder and other crimes.

(Yes, Jameson has tried to kill Spider-Man, and that's attempted murder. He's let his newspaper be used in various possibly criminal conspiracies. Mr. Jameson, however well-intentioned he may think himself, is not a nice man—and Peter knows it, but continues to work for him.)

Ordinarily, someone as guilt-ridden and self-destructive as Peter might well have wound up dead, in prison, or in therapy by now, or might have simply gotten *over* it. Mourning is all very well; survivor guilt is a powerful thing, but there comes a time when one should move on.

Peter Parker hasn't let himself move on. He hasn't dared serious therapy for fear of revealing his secret identity and endangering those he loves.

Instead, he goes out to play in his tights.

Being Spider-Man has become his escape from guilt, but it's also how he can *keep* feeling guilty, and not move on. It gives him a way out when his life becomes unbearable, a way to avoid breaking under the strain. It gives him something other than himself that he can blame for his failures—he has to be Spider-Man, so he doesn't have time to improve his life. The world *needs* Spider-Man. He can't attend night school or get an online degree because he has to go fight Doctor Octopus or the Kingpin, and there just isn't time to do both.

So he tells himself.

But what it really is, is that he can't let go. Spider-Man is, in a very real sense, all he has left of Uncle Ben. Aunt May has moved on, and Peter *could*—but deep down, he doesn't want to.

Because being Spider-Man is *fun*.

And if he lets go of the guilt, if he admits to himself that his life is a mess and maybe Spider-Man should have a slightly lower priority, if he acknowledges that he's done what he could to make up for letting Uncle Ben die—in short, if he grows up—then he'll be letting Uncle Ben go, and he'll be losing his excuse for spending so much of his time out there reveling in the sheer physical delight of swinging on his web, dodging danger, and punching out thugs.

If he admits that he's being Spider-Man for fun, rather than out of duty, then he can't justify letting it ruin his life. The whole emotional structure he's built up for so long will collapse.

He's not ready to face that. And with the system so wonderfully balanced, so perfectly self-sustaining, he probably never would be— if not for outside forces. Now that he's been convinced to reveal his identity to the world, maybe it will all fall apart—or maybe he'll finally be able to let the guilt go and enjoy *both* sides of his life. It's too soon to tell.

But for years his guilt, and the need to escape it by swinging around New York punching out thugs, have kept Spider-Man in business.

For which all those New Yorkers whose purses might have been snatched, who might have been accosted in dark alleys, who might have been injured or killed in the collateral damage of some super villains' attacks, can be very, very grateful.

LAWRENCE WATT-EVANS is the author of some three dozen novels and more than 100 short stories, mostly in the fields of fantasy, science fiction, and horror. He won the Hugo Award for Short Story in 1988 for "Why I Left Harry's All-Night Hamburgers," served as president of the Horror Writers Association from 1994 to 1996 and treasurer of SFWA from 2003 to 2004, and lives in Maryland. He has one kid in college and one teaching English in China, and shares his home with Chanel, the obligatory writer's cat.

KEITH R. A. DECANDIDO

Superman vs.
the Amazing Spider-Man

In 1976 I had the good fortune to be involved with one of comics' seminal events: the first crossover story between Marvel and DC Comics, which featured the long-anticipated meeting of the Man of Steel and Your Friendly Neighborhood Webslinger. For a lifetime fan of both characters, it was a wish come true. It also taught me a lesson I should have learned much earlier: Be careful what you wish for. Trying to wedge such starkly different personalities as Superman and Spider-Man into one story forced me to confront some of the same issues Keith R. A. DeCandido discusses in his essay. . . .

EVERYONE ALWAYS WANTS to know who'd win in a fight. Could the Hulk beat the Thing?[1] Could Batman beat Superman?[2] Could Superman beat Flash in a foot race?[3] And then you go between universes—can Thor beat Superman?[4] Can Batman beat Captain America?[5] Can Superman beat Spider-Man?[6]

But it's not the fight that interests me, but rather the representation of the respective characters in the pantheon of heroes. After all,

---

[1] Don't know, but Marvel's gotten a *lot* of mileage out of the question, including a recent mini-series.

[2] Yes, if Batman had plenty of time to prepare, at least according to *The Dark Knight Returns*.

[3] Depends; that's been fodder for many a comic book, not to mention cartoon, over the decades.

[4] No, according to *JLA/Avengers*, but heaven help Superman after he cleans Thor's clock.

[5] Neither *Batman/Captain America* nor *JLA/Avengers* gave a definitive answer, but my money's on Cap.

[6] Don't be silly. . . .

the symbol of DC Comics is Superman, and the symbol of Marvel Comics is Spider-Man. Yes, there are arguments to be made for Batman and the X-Men, but ultimately it's Supes and Spidey that are first in line in the mass consciousness for superherodom. It's no coincidence that the first ever team-up comic between Marvel and DC featured these two, back in 1976.[7]

The question of who would win in a fight is of less interest, beyond the chatting-over-a-beer stage, simply because fights are volatile things. There are so many elements that factor into who would win a fight beyond simple raw skill set that it's impossible to predict. Sure, Superman *probably* would win in a fight against Spider-Man, but there are several circumstances under which Spider-Man *could* win the fight. In the aforementioned 1976 team-up comic, Spider-Man was surreptitiously zapped with a red-sun blast by Lex Luthor, enabling him to (temporarily) wipe the floor with Superman. Heck, all things being equal, Superman would make mulch out of Batman, yet Frank Miller wrote a quite convincing defeat of Superman by Batman, in part because all things are *never* equal.[8]

No, what's of more interest—what actually *matters*—is who's the more interesting character.

You can probably guess my answer by virtue of this essay appearing here rather than in 2006's *The Man from Krypton*.[9] But I think it's worth examining precisely why the webhead is so much cooler than the big blue Boy Scout.

We should begin at the beginning, and the reasons *why* the strange visitor from another planet and the teenager who was bitten by a radioactive spider chose to become heroes. In a lot of ways, neither character had a choice. Their adoptive parents were a powerful influence—but the form that influence took is what makes the difference.

When Kal-El landed on Earth, it was in Kansas farm country. He was taken in by two salt-of-the-earth farmers who adopted him as

---

[7] *Superman vs. The Amazing Spider-Man.*

[8] *The Dark Knight Returns.*

[9] Instead, I wrote "Actor and Superactor," which ranked the ten actors who've portrayed Superman on screen. Check it out! You'll be glad you did. . . .

their own son, and taught him good old-fashioned American values. They were decent people and they passed on their goodness and decency to the boy they named Clark Kent. Superman's ethic was very nicely summed up in the 1978 *Superman* film, when Jonathan Kent gave young Clark a speech about how he was given his powers for a reason, and it probably wasn't to score touchdowns.

When Peter Parker was bitten by a radioactive spider and given strange powers, he chose to pursue a career as an entertainer. An orphan, Peter was raised by his aunt and uncle, May and Ben Parker, and Peter needed the money to help them climb above poverty level. When given the opportunity to stop a thief, he passed—even though his powers would have made it easy—thinking that it didn't concern him. That same thief later murdered Uncle Ben. Spider-Man caught the man, but not before realizing how important it was to use his powers for good.

Superman fights for truth, justice, and the American way because that's how he was raised in the heartland. Spider-Man fights for the same things because to do otherwise would sully the memory of his uncle. With all respect to salt-of-the-earth farmers, guilt is more interesting than inherent decency.

Superman never has a reason to give up being a hero. Sure, he hits the occasional speed bump—in the comics, he left Earth for a time due to guilt over killing someone, and in the recent feature film, he had done likewise in search of his home world, and then there was the period when he was dead—but overall, Superman's heroism is never challenged. He rarely has any good reason to stop being Superman, and the reasons he's been given have either been external or felt contrived (or both).

Why should he give it up? The world loves him. He's the world's greatest and most respected superhero. Metropolis is full of monuments to him. The front pages of the *Daily Planet* are full of near-hagiographies of him. The only people who hate him are the bad guys. He has friends and family to support him. Yes, his home planet was destroyed, but that's not a world he even remembers all that well. His parents are still alive and well in Smallville (a change that was made only twenty years ago, but which has taken root), and his eventual marriage to Lois Lane has been a steady and happy one.

Spider-Man, on the other hand, has every reason to stop, and on numerous occasions has, usually because the despair of his life has gotten to be too much.

The harder part would be coming up with a good list of reasons why he *should* remain a superhero. He's not well-respected or well-liked, not even always by his fellow superheroes (though he is now serving in the New Avengers, which probably helps). The front page of the *Daily Bugle* is full of excoriations that list everything he's done wrong, whether real or perceived. He's been accused of numerous crimes, up to and including murder, several times over the years. Many of his dearest friends and family are dead—his parents, his uncle, his best friend Harry Osborn, the first love of his life Gwen Stacy. His aunt has been old and infirm for forty years now, and his eventual marriage to Mary Jane Watson has been rocky and difficult and has included both a (possible) miscarriage and a nasty separation.

One of the most compelling Spider-Man stories ever told was the "Master Planner" storyline, entitled "If This Be My Destiny..." (*Amazing Spider-Man* Nos. 31–33). It was a three-part story from the early days of *Amazing Spider-Man*, when Stan Lee and Steve Ditko were still doing the book. The Master Planner was, in fact, Doctor Octopus, Spider-Man's biggest villain, and he came very close to stopping Spider-Man. In addition to everything else, Aunt May was sick with radiation poisoning thanks to a blood transfusion from Peter, and our hero had the only antidote.

Unfortunately, Octopus had dropped twelve tons of machinery on Spider-Man in an underground cavern, leaving him trapped.

Spider-Man is strong, but he's not *that* strong. Yes, he can bench press more than the most toned guy at your local gym, but in the superhero community he's got nothing on the likes of Thor or the Hulk or the Thing. Twelve tons of machinery on his back should have finished him, leaving him trapped forever.

But Aunt May was in trouble. So Spider-Man gathered every inch, every muscle, and threw it off his back. The sequence where he does it is one of the most famous in comics history, and includes a stellar full-page shot of our hero getting the weight off his back, enabling him to eventually save his aunt's life.

Another of Spider-Man's most memorable tales was the death of Gwen Stacy. The love of Peter Parker's life, Gwen was kidnapped by the Green Goblin, who had learned Spider-Man's secret identity, and taken to the Brooklyn Bridge. At one point, the Goblin tosses Gwen over the side. Spider-Man shoots out a web-line to try to stop her from hitting the water, but her neck snaps with the impact of stopping suddenly in midair. Gwen's death is second only to Uncle Ben's in terms of tragic impact on Peter Parker.

Decades later, these two stories still count among the finest Spider-Man stories ever told, if not the finest comics stories ever told, and the reason why I bring them up in this essay in particular is because they could not have worked with Superman, even a little. Twelve tons of machinery? Superman would shrug to take care of that problem. And if Lex Luthor tossed Lois Lane over the side of the Metro-Narrows Bridge, Superman would fly at supersonic speeds to catch her with no ill effects.

Superman's heroism comes easy. Spider-Man's comes at a price.

Then there's the matter of who they are. The character we follow in *Superman* and *Action Comics* and the rest is Superman, who occasionally disguises himself as Clark Kent. The character we follow in *Amazing Spider-Man* and *Peter Parker: Spider-Man* and the rest is Peter Parker, who occasionally disguises himself as Spider-Man.

This is the difference between the frontline Marvel heroes and the frontline DC heroes: the meaning of the dual identity. Batman is the real person; Bruce Wayne is simply a persona he puts on. Even though Batman wears the mask, Wayne is the true disguise. Wonder Woman is who Diana of Themyscira is. And Superman is who Kal-El of Krypton is. Superman takes it one step further in that it's Clark Kent who actually wears a "mask"—to wit, his glasses. Superman is who he is—he even has a Fortress of Solitude that enables him to get away from it all, and when he does that, he's always Superman and always in costume. Clark Kent is simply the persona he puts on when he wants to interact with the normal folks.

But Spider-Man is the disguise, not Peter Parker. The schlub whom we've followed through high school and college, through freelance *Daily Bugle* photography and high-school science teaching, through dozens of relationships and a sometimes-rocky marriage, is the real person. The guy in tights is the persona *he* puts on. He *is* the normal folk. And this distinction is generally true for all frontline Marvel superheroes. The Fantastic Four don't even *have* secret identities as such; everyone knows who they are. And while technically some of the X-Men have secret IDs, they don't matter much. It's telling how rarely the assorted codenames were used in the three *X-Men* films, and how little difference it made.

Superman comic books star an icon. Spider-Man comics star a person. People tend to make for more compelling characters.

Most of the above arguments lead to the same conclusion, which I think trumps all others on the subject: Peter Parker is a real person with whom the reader can identify. Superman really isn't.

Yes, both of them have cool powers. Yes, both of them have hot wives. But of the two, Spider-Man is the one whose tribulations are easiest to understand. Truly, can anybody claim to understand what Superman goes through?

Clark Kent has a stable family life. He grew up on a farm with wonderful parents, moved to Metropolis, and embarked on a successful career as a journalist. He's on staff at the *Daily Planet*, has a steady income, a good readership, and is considered to be excellent at his job. The closest thing he had to a difficulty was that the woman he loved was more enamored with Superman than of Clark Kent— but was that really a problem? Superman was who he truly was all along. Eventually, they got together and married, and it's been a good union for both of them.

Peter Parker lost his parents at a young age and was raised by his elderly, financially stuggling aunt and uncle—until his uncle was shot and killed. He was a student when he first got his powers, and he has continued to live the life of either a student, a freelancer, or both, selling the occasional photograph to the *Daily Bugle* to pay the bills while attending high school, college, and (on and off) graduate school. Lately, he's also been a high-school science teacher. None of these are equivalent to the well-respected, high-paying position of a front-page reporter at the *Daily Planet*. He constantly wonders where his next paycheck will come from. The first woman he fell in love with was killed, and his life with the second has remained a constant struggle.

True, Peter's wife is a model, and damn good-looking, but it hasn't helped them much. It's worth mentioning here that Mary Jane's professional life is at least as difficult as Peter's, and she has the added stress of being married to a superhero. Many comic fans (and some creators) have stupidly decried Peter being married to Mary Jane because they believe that Spider-Man—the ultimate Hard-Luck Harry of the superhero set—being married to a supermodel violates the whole point of Spider-Man. This wholly ridiculous statement is belied by the actual stories themselves. Mary Jane *isn't* a supermodel by any definition of the term. She's a working model, yes, but if she *were* a supermodel, she'd be regularly traveling all over the world, always working. Mary Jane has *never* been written that way. Her field is, in fact, an even more volatile one than Peter's, since his photographic skills are more likely to increase over the years, whereas Mary Jane's shelf life as a model is limited by age. Mary Jane is as much a freelancer as Peter is—and one without an equivalent to Peter's unique skill, getting Spider-Man on film. She's also tried to pursue an acting career, which isn't exactly a step up in terms of stability. So anyone who makes this complaint is simply ignorant of the realities of the work.

It all boils down to what makes for compelling drama, especially in a serial narrative. Conflict and struggle are often at the heart of what makes fiction work. If those struggles are too easy, the reader loses interest. The biggest difficulty when writing a Superman story is coming up with a way to challenge a character who can change the course of mighty rivers. Kryptonite was a handy device when it was invented by the writers of the Superman radio drama, but it quickly grew into a crutch—with multiple colors of kryptonite that all did different things. The reboot of Superman twenty years ago streamlined kryptonite, but it remains a crutch, not just in the comics, but in the *Smallville* TV show. But Superman is such a powerful character that writers are forced to make up a substance he's allergic to in order to have there be *something* he can't easily overcome.

Spider-Man has no such Achilles heel, but he doesn't need one, because he possesses simple human frailty. Superman can escape to the Fortress of Solitude when it all gets to be too much; Spider-Man has no such refuge, just a series of tiny New York City apartments. Spider-Man isn't the strongest person in the world, or the fastest, or the smartest (though he is of above-average intelligence), and in fact there are dozens of heroes who are stronger, faster, and smarter.

Having said all this, it's not as if Superman is unappealing. If nothing else, he's a hero who gives hope, the living refutation of the notion that power corrupts. Spider-Man's credo is that with great power comes great responsibility, and Superman embodies that concept more than any other superhero you can name.

But while the guy I'd want to save me from the burning building or the natural disaster would almost have to be Superman, Spider-Man's the one I want to read more about. And have dinner with.

KEITH R. A. DeCANDIDO has been a fan of Spider-Man since seeing his live-action adventures on *The Electric Company* as a kid. His first short-story sale and first novel sale were both collaborative Spider-Man tales ("An Evening in the Bronx with Venom" with John Gregory Betancourt in 1994's *The Ultimate Spider-Man* and *Venom's Wrath* with José R. Nieto in 1998), and solo he's also written a Spidey short story ("Arms and the Man" in 1997's *Untold Tales of Spider-Man*) and a Spidey novel (*Down These Mean Streets* in 2005). He's become a regular Smart Pop contributor, having also written essays in *Finding Serenity, The Man from Krypton, Star Wars on Trial, The Unauthorized X-Men,* and *King Kong Is Back!*, with more to come. Find out less at his official Web site at DeCandido.net.

References

Busiek, Kurt (w) and George Pérez (i). *JLA/Avengers*. DC Comics/Marvel Comics: 2003.

Byrne, John (w). *Batman/Captain America*. DC Comics/Marvel Comics: 1996.

Conway, Gerry (w), Ross Andru (p), and Dick Giordano (i). *Superman vs. The Amazing Spider-Man*. DC Comics/Marvel Comics: 1976.

Lee, Stan (w) and Steve Ditko (i). *Amazing Spider-Man* Nos. 31–33. Marvel Comics: 1965.

Miller, Frank (w) and Klaus Janson (i). *The Dark Knight Returns*. DC Comics: 1986.

ROBERT B. TAYLOR

Raimi vs. Bendis
Reimagining Spider-Man

As someone who's walked the film adaptation tightrope myself once or twice, I can confirm it's not an easy balancing act—especially when you have, on the one side, fan expectations, and on the other, the peculiar demands of film as a dramatic form. Film communicates by visual shorthand, and a director has only moments, perhaps only seconds, to communicate complex emotions and ideas while retaining dramatic pace. Comics, too, communicate in shorthand, but the comic-book writer and artist have the advantage of working in a static media rather than a dynamic one. Readers can return to a panel for a second look, giving them more time to absorb all the information and drama it can communicate; a viewer's attention is constantly shifting as the movie progresses, and that puts an entirely different set of demands on the storyteller. All things considered I think Sam Raimi and his collaborators did a fine job adapting our favorite web spinner to that other visual storytelling medium, but as Robert B. Taylor's essay shows, we don't all experience the same story the same way....

IN ISSUE NO. 54 of the comic book *Ultimate Spider-Man*, everyone's favorite teenage superhero slings down from the sky onto a New York street doubling as a set for the movie *Spider-Man*, starring Tobey Maguire and directed by Sam Raimi...or, at least, cartoony comic-book versions of them. Spidey drops down alongside Maguire, who's harnessed to the side of a building, faces Raimi and his fellow filmmakers, and proceeds to tell them off: "You suck! And you suck and you suck. All right, *Evil Dead 2* was cool, but the rest of you suck." A few panels later, he adds: "And your movie is going to tank! You know why? Because you aren't me. You're fake. You can't do this!" And with that he backflips gracefully through the air, landing high up on top of some filmmaking equipment.

Picked-on high-school student/costumed crime fighter Peter Parker might have been a little harsh toward Raimi and crew. In Parker's defense, he was a bit miffed. And not because cameras were rolling during this entire exchange (thus saving Sony $1.2 million in special effects, a producer notes), but because his already-hectic life was subject to big-screen treatment at all and he wasn't able to earn a dime off the project. So there was plenty of pent-up anger involved. At least he wisely credited Raimi for *Evil Dead 2*—apparently a masterpiece in any universe. And certainly he was off base when he predicted the movie's failure, an unlikely scenario if the *Ultimate* universe version of the *Spider-Man* movie was to satisfy the public as the actual film did, to the tune of $403 million domestic.

But there just may have been a sliver of truth in something Parker said, one quick flash of critical insight when none was actually meant. "Because you aren't me," Spidey says, thinking that Hollywood could never fully realize his complex life. "You're fake." When considering Raimi's real-world *Spider-Man* movie and its sequel, Parker, surprisingly, may have a point.

Marvel's *Ultimate Spider-Man* and Sony's *Spider-Man* major motion picture series share a (dare I say it?) almost symbiotic relationship. Each was designed for the same purpose—to reinvent Spider-Man as a character, placing him firmly in a twenty-first-century world, and telling the story of his origin to a generation of youngsters who weren't around for Stan Lee's original run of comics, the various cartoons, and the failed live-action TV series. They both were reboots, though occurring in different media, and debuted only nineteen months apart. *Ultimate Spider-Man's* inaugural issue shipped in October 2000, while the first movie opened in theaters in May 2002.

There are also a few key parallels in the methods used by *Spider-Man* director Raimi and *Ultimate Spider-Man* writer Brian Michael Bendis to retell the beginning of Peter Parker's illustrious career as New York City's most famous superhero. Each gives us the Green

Goblin as Spidey's first "A"-grade nemesis, with Doctor Octopus following shortly thereafter. (Not surprising at all, considering they rank quite high as Spider-Man villains that comic fans concern themselves with and the non-comic-reading public has actually heard of.) And while Parker grew up awfully fast in the original run of comics, moving quickly through high school and college within the first ten years, Raimi and Bendis know the geeky teen who was bit by a spider works better as just that—a high-school loser who has great power suddenly thrust upon him. In this regard, Raimi is somewhat limited by the natural aging of his actors, but he began the first movie in the right place—with Parker getting on a school bus—and seems to have kept his characters as young as is believable. Bendis has no such limitation and is free to have Peter in high school for as long as he wants. Six years later, the *Ultimate* version of Spider-Man still attends high-school classes by day.

For all of these reasons, it's only natural and fun to compare the movies to the revamped Spidey comic. And, hey, let's face it: if you care about the integrity of Spider-Man as a character, if you've proudly taken a firm stand on one side of the organic vs. mechanical web-shooters debate, if you've spent the money to buy this book—you live for this stuff. Although once the comparisons begin, a somewhat shocking conclusion can be drawn. While Raimi's movies certainly aren't bad, it's surprising that they are so universally enjoyed and respected for their honest retelling of the Spider-Man legend, because, quite frankly, Bendis has done a supremely better job in presenting a new and improved version of Spidey's universe that honors the original Lee stories while freshening up the franchise. In short, despite the huge box office, the smashing critical reviews, and all the love from the comic-book community, Raimi dropped the (webbed) ball in several profound ways when he reimagined Spider-Man beginnings. Luckily, Bendis was around to pick it up.

Let us begin by looking at the key event in Peter Parker's life, the tragedy that defines the man he becomes in all incarnations—the death of his father figure and beloved uncle, Ben Parker. In any version of the Spider-Man tale, Ben's loss must be felt deeply by not just Peter and his aunt May, but by the reader/viewer as well. The entire dramatic thrust of Spider-Man's beginnings depends on it. The wall crawler's origin was first told by Stan Lee in a blistering eleven pages in *Amazing Fantasy* No. 15, originally printed in 1962. Even with such a short amount of space, Lee was careful to set up the loving relationship between Peter and Ben using only four frames, two on the second page—which showed Ben waking Peter up for school with a tender stroke of his head ("Gosh, Uncle Ben—you're worse than a room full of alarm clocks!")—and two more on page eight, which defined Ben's nurturing of Peter's scientific ambitions by showing him and May presenting Peter with a new microscope. ("Gosh, that's terrific!" said young Pete, examining the gift. "You're the greatest family any fella ever had!") These four frames successfully established the strength of the Parker family unit. By the end of that issue, Ben Parker was shot dead and young Peter had learned a hard lesson that would drive him for eternity.

Building upon this brisk setup should have been a no-brainer, but instead of expanding the relationship between Peter and Ben in the movie, Raimi actually shrinks it. Movie-version Parker is bitten by the spider before the audience even meets Ben and May, and Ben and Peter barely share a scene after. There's a hint of a tender relationship when Ben reminds Peter about the kitchen that needs painting and Peter playfully responds, "Don't start without me!" But by the time the two actually spend time together on screen, Ben's sternly telling Peter "we need to talk" and the two are in the car, exchanging harsh words. Since no real emotional connection is established, the drama and pathos is all but sucked out of Ben's demise. Later, after graduating, Peter says to May, "I missed him a lot today." Unfortunately, the movie leaves you wondering why. *Spider-Man 2* finally shows the viewer a heart-to-heart talk between Ben and Peter. Too bad it's all in Peter's head and Ben is a figment of his imagination.

It could be that Raimi made the mistake of assuming that *Spider-Man*'s core audience wouldn't need to be shown the full nature of Ben and Peter's relationship because it's already so well established in Spider-Man lore. Hell, the strong bond between the two characters may be so ingrained in Raimi's own imaginative skull that he never realized he didn't fully translate it to the big screen. Unfortunately, glossing over certain key story points—no matter how obvious such things are to those who know and love these characters—only weakens the film series as a stand-alone entity meant to show how fully dimensional well-written comic-book characters can be.

It's ironic then that over in the flat, static pages of *Ultimate Spider-Man*, these characters seem more fully formed thanks to Bendis's approach in introducing them. Uncle Ben was around for the first four issues and was firmly established as a caring, fatherly presence in Peter's life. He was written as a reasonable man, who wouldn't sue Osborn Industries after the fated spider bite because, after all, it was only an accident. And besides, he didn't want to ruin Peter's friendship with classmate Harry Osborn by taking Harry's father's company to court. In issue No. 1, Peter and Ben were together subjected to a wild rant by Aunt May (who insisted Pete had social anxiety disorder) and shared a knowing smile—beautifully illustrated by Mark Bagley—that defined the warm relationship the two shared better than anything shown in the films. Yes, Peter and Ben fought in *USM*, too, but not long after, the two were hugging, a warm reminder of how much they meant to each other. When the taped outline of Ben's body was shown on the floor of the Parker home, the effect was devastating.

So, right from the beginning, Spider-Man's movie presents a somewhat shaky origin story, while the comic succeeded in taking what Stan Lee wrote and expanding it appropriately. Yes, it's easier to flesh out relationships when you have an innumerable amount of comic pages in which to do it, rather than a two-hour movie. But establishing the Peter-Ben dynamic is of absolute importance, and Raimi and his writers failed momentously to do so.

It's certainly not the only time.

There isn't much intelligent conversation to be had in nitpicking the movies to death for some of the questionable but ultimately minor creative choices that were made. The organic web-shooters, the silliness of that plastic Goblin mask—all standard-issue fanboy whining that accompanied the release of the first *Spider-Man* movie. There's especially no time for nitpicks when considering the more important aspects of the Spider-Man universe that were unfortunately skewed in the transition to the big screen.

For example, since Lee first created the character, Spider-Man has been universally known as the smart-aleck superhero—the one who talks back to super villains while he's smacking them down (and gets even wittier when he's on the receiving end of a butt-whupping). With that personality trait being both indisputable and necessary, can anyone explain why the movie version of Peter Parker hardly ever brings the funny? In the first *Spider-Man* film, Parker spouts off exactly four jokes. Only one is chuckle worthy—Spidey telling J. Jonah Jameson, "Hey, kiddo, let mom and dad talk for a minute, will you?" while he battles the Goblin right outside the *Daily Bugle* publisher's office. None of the jokes are directed at the Goblin. In *Spider-Man 2*, the one-liners, which should be Spider-Man's trademark, are even fewer. (Not surprising, since Parker spends most of the movie a lovelorn mess.) The only good one is the bit between Spidey and the VH1 guy in the elevator, concerning the costume getting kind of itchy and riding up in the crotch. Spider-Man doesn't make fun of Doc Ock at all. Never. Not once. At one point, Doc Ock tells Spidey he's getting on his nerves. "I have a knack for that," Parker responds. It's half-hearted, but it's the best there is.

Meanwhile, *Ultimate Spider-Man* is laugh-out-loud hilarious on a monthly basis. In Parker's first fight with the Green Goblin, a brawl that occurred at Peter's school, Spidey made his grand entrance with an announcement of, "Head's up! Big time superhero comin' through!" From there, the webbed wonder slung one-liners almost as often as he threw punches. He asked to see the Goblin's hall pass. He asked the Goblin if he was the new home ec. teacher. After the Goblin started viciously throwing balls of fire generated from his fists, Parker remarked, "Listen, I don't want to tell you your business, but that's kind of a fire hazard."

In *USM*, Spidey is one funny dude—just as the character has been since the '60s. Not only that, Bendis adds another dimension to Spider-Man's signature jokey demeanor courtesy of Peter's inner monologue. "Look at me being the smart-mouth when I'm scared out of my mind," he thought during the fight with the Goblin. "I guess it's either that or I pee in my tights." See? Even when Peter searches his own soul, it's funny.

Another defining character trait that's largely missing from the movies, especially the first one, is Peter's skill as a scientist. He's not a nerd just because other students pick on him. Peter's also a nerd because he's really, really freakin' smart. It's a superpower he has before the spider ever bites him. Yet evidence of Peter's intelligence is largely absent from the first *Spider-Man* movie; it's really only mentioned in passing. Raimi tells us Parker is smart—yet another quick reminder of an important fact we already know about the character from the comics—but he never fully shows us. (Although Peter does seem to be an excellent tailor, considering the kickass Spider-Man costume he whips up on his own.) In the films, there's no surprise microscope from Ben and May. And the one tangible negative effect of introducing the biological web-shooters is that, since Peter doesn't construct his own mechanical shooters, we've lost another example of Parker ingenuity. In *USM*, Bendis wisely doesn't write Peter too smart to be believable. He's just a teenager, after all. But Bendis's story makes it very clear that Peter is a special kid, someone who could achieve great things even without all the webs and wall crawling and spider-sense. In the second frame featuring Peter in issue No. 1, Bendis has Peter go on about the properties of sodium carbonate. At home, Peter had converted his aunt and uncle's basement into a science lab, and the webs Spidey swings on are the end result of an incomplete formula started by Peter's father that Peter was able to finish. The kid knows how to use his noggin. *Spider-Man 2* finally hints that Parker is a budding genius through his interest in Otto Octavius's fusion studies. Maybe in part *three*, we'll actually get to see Peter put his brain to work.

Another, perhaps more minor, misstep the Raimi movies make with Peter is that a large part of the burden of guilt he carries for the death of Ben is absent thanks to a quirk in the story structure. In all versions of the tale, Peter refuses to stop a criminal during a robbery and then later discovers that the robber is the man who killed Ben. In *USM*, Parker didn't interfere with the robber because he figured the crime wasn't any of his business. He was essentially lazy about it, a cocky teenager who was just imbued with superhuman powers and didn't have time for other people's problems. It's easy to see why he would blame himself for Ben's death for the rest of his life. In the *Spider-Man* movie, the robber is ripping off a wrestling promoter who just got done ripping Parker off himself by not paying him the full money that was promised for Spider-Man's bravura in the ring. With the scene staged that way, who can blame Peter for not tripping the crook as he fled? Wouldn't we all do the same thing if the guy who just screwed us was getting his comeuppance? Peter would certainly still feel guilt upon learning the circumstances of his uncle's death, but Raimi's telling of the story removes the edge from Peter's lapse in judgment.

In the movies, Peter's not the only character who gets a free pass for moral improprieties. Consider the filmed versions of Norman Osborn, the Green Goblin, and Otto Octavius, Doctor Octopus. Spidey's eternal tormentors are not supposed to be pleasant men. And yet Raimi and his writers insist on providing excuses for their crimes against humanity. In fact, when looking at the movie versions of Norman and Otto as men, neither of them is all that bad a guy. Osborn only becomes a bomb-hurling killing machine after he floods his system with flawed performance enhancers that his company is manufacturing for the United States military. Norman's personality splits in two, with one half becoming the evil Goblin consciousness. Thus, the Goblin isn't a manifestation of Norman's nasty side; it's an unfortunate side effect. The movie even suggests that Osborn doesn't *remember* the crimes he commits as the Goblin.

Octavius is presented as even more of an innocent sent down a dark path by circumstance. *Spider-Man 2* presents him as a loving husband and warm-hearted scientist who uses four sentient metallic arms, which connect to his nervous system through the spinal cord, for lab work. When an inhibitor chip that protects his higher-brain functions from the influence of the arms breaks, the arms take control of the man, manipulating Octavius to become evil by using his grief over his wife's death and his disappointment over the failure of his life's work against him. Otto even stops talking in terms of "I" and starts using "we" instead—indicating his snake-like co-conspirators. *Spider-Man 2* makes it very clear that Otto is a man done wrong and even allows him closure at the end during his Darth Vader-esque "I will not die a monster" redemption.

There's nothing wrong with Raimi trying to offer some insight into the motivations of Spider-Man's villains. But Raimi fails to provide any interesting emotional reasons for why Norman and Otto act out so violently. He cops out and gives the bad guys cheap alibis instead. "It wasn't me, your honor. The big metal arms are responsible!"

Granted, this take on the villains is similar to Lee's original, simple approach of having lab accidents make these guys mentally unbalanced. But Bendis wisely one-ups Raimi and Lee by presenting Norman and Otto as fully despicable right from the start. In the *USM* universe, lab accidents don't magically turn good people bad. They give already evil men the power to do unlimited damage—a far more interesting method for updating these villains. And they don't come more nefarious than Bendis's version of Osborn, who tried to have Peter murdered *before he even became the Green Goblin*. Bendis's pre-Goblinized Osborn was a complete and total bastard. He was belligerent to Harry and didn't care about the welfare of his employees. He ran Osborn Industries with no regard for the safety of the consumers buying his products and at one point championed the cigarette industry as a perfect example of how to sidestep federal health regulations. Greed and power consumed him.

When Norman discovered that a teenager was bitten by a genetically altered arachnid in his own labs, he first decided to only spy on the boy. Once it looked like the bite might kill Parker, he realized the fallout could destroy his company, so he sent his own personal assassin to eliminate the problem. (It's a good thing Osborn keeps a professional killer on the payroll. In the *USM* universe, he's never sure when he'll have to kill a fifteen-year-old boy just to protect his bank account.) When he does morph into the Green Goblin, an organic transformation that disfigures Norman and gives him the ability to generate those fireballs, you get the feeling you're seeing Osborn's true self without the human mask.

USM also offers a version of Octavius who is largely responsible for his own corrupt legacy. His arms were fused to his body via an accident at the labs of Osborn Industries, where he was employed as a scientist. Of course, he only worked there as an industrial spy, stealing corporate secrets for a competing company which had Otto on their payroll (and a slew of illegal test subjects, including Flint Marko—soon to become the Sandman—in their basement). After the spider bite, Norman had Harry bring Peter back to the lab, where Octavius stabbed a needle into Peter's arm while our hero's back was turned, drawing some blood for analysis. It's a total reversal from Raimi's warm and cuddly version of Octavius, who acts almost fatherly toward Peter. *Ultimate* Doc Ock's rampage began when he discovered that the government decided to leave the arms attached to his body just to see what kind of fun things would happen, and Parker wasn't surprised. Once he realized Octavius needed to be stopped, he quickly sized up his enemy, ending with: "Plus, if memory serves, he wasn't the nicest guy to begin with." No, Pete, he sure wasn't.

In the end, however, the success of any Spider-Man retelling ultimately hinges upon the respect given to Peter Parker himself, while both in and out of the mask. In the Spider-Man movies, Raimi provides the one thing that Bendis never can—those dizzying, spectacular, live-action shots of Spider-Man soaring from web to web above the streets of Manhattan. Seeing Spider-Man in action on the big screen is worth the price of admission every couple of years. But if Raimi wants his version of Peter Parker to completely embody the soul of what Bendis and Lee before him have put on the comic page, he needs to do better in showing not just Spider-Man's feats of daring, but also the other aspects of Peter's character that make him special, even when he's not web-slinging his way through Times Square.

ROBERT B. TAYLOR is a pop-culture writer living in Pittsburgh, Pennsylvania. He's a Marvel Comics boy at heart but will argue passionately that *Batman Begins* is the best superhero film ever made. He contributed the essay, "The Captain May Wear the Tight Pants, But It's the Gals Who Make Serenity Soar," to the Smart Pop anthology, *Finding Serenity: Antiheroes, Lost Shepherds, and Space Hookers in Joss Whedon's Firefly.* His TV column runs weekly in *The Herald,* the newspaper of record for Rock Hill, South Carolina. You can find him online at www.robert-b-taylor.com.

LOU ANDERS

The Tangled Web We Weave

The Spider-Man I knew and loved as a reader in my early teens was a geek (well, not a geek, exactly, because in those days a geek was a sideshow freak who bit the heads off chickens, but you get what I mean). By the time I began writing him, years later, Peter the Geek had become Peter the College Photographer, and the move away from the science-based hero Lou Anders describes below was already pretty far along. At least we still have Reed Richards....

WHEN I WAS a kid, my folks bought me a Spider-Man web shooter. It was a dart gun that strapped on to your wrist, and it fired a suction cup-tipped plastic dart that trailed a few feet of white string. The suction cup didn't stick well, and the string was too short, and I don't think the whole of it lasted very long, but I ran around the house quite happily with it and a red ski mask we'd drawn webs on with a black magic marker. I loved Batman as a kid— I read Batman, I watched Batman, I collected Batman toys—but I always wanted to *be* Spider-Man. I would blow out all the air from my lungs (so I wouldn't float) at the deep end of the pool, and then crawl up and down the wall pretending I was scaling a building in New York. I'd jump in and, as I sank, try and recreate a scene from the 1977 television show *The Amazing Spider-Man*, where Nicholas Hammond was thrown off a building and only managed to catch onto a gargoyle at the last second before he smashed into the ground. I could hold my breath for *minutes* more than anybody else when I was young (Writer's Note: Don't smoke kids, I can't do it anymore!), and the only reason I practiced this was so I wouldn't have to interrupt my imagination with the need to constantly breathe. And I think I knew even back then that Silly String would have made a better web shooter than the dart, but I couldn't figure out a way to strap it to my arm effectively. You can get Silly String-fueled web shooters now, too, and do you think I'm jealous? Damn straight. But I always wondered about those web shooters Peter Parker made, and why Spider-Man's abilities were divided between biological mutations on the one side and scientific inventions on the other. Unlike most superheroes, he seems to have two origins for the price of one.

Spider silk, it turns out, is remarkably interesting stuff. It's not "the strongest fiber in the world" as it's often mistakenly labeled—there are some carbon nanotubes that rightfully claim that distinction—but it is still pretty "amazing" (pun-intended), largely because it can stretch up to forty percent of its length without breaking. It's also lightweight, flexible, and waterproof. All of these qualities, plus the fact that spiders produce their webs at room temperature and under low pressure, means there's always been a great deal of commercial interest in producing more of the stuff. You can't harvest the silk in "industrially useful" quantities like you do that of silk worms because spiders are predators and cannibals; if you collect them in large numbers, the unsociable little beasties will eat each other (watch out, MJ—keep Peter well-fed!). And as for synthesizing the silk artificially, well, MIT's been working on that one for at least half a century, even before the 1962 comic book in which Peter Parker was first bitten by the radioactive little guy.

The difficulty lies in the fact that spider silk has highly repetitive DNA encoding, which makes figuring out just what does what quite a challenge, and only a few varieties of silk have been mapped to date. This hasn't stopped the attempts, though, as artificial spider webbing would have all kinds of applications, from high-strength fibers that could be used in artificial tendons to lightweight bulletproof gear. What gives the silk its remarkable properties is that it is a polymer with two distinct alternating regions, one comprised of small, hard crystallites and the other of soft, elastic material. These two regions operating in conjunction gives webbing both its toughness and its flexibility.

So far, Dr. Paula T. Hammond of MIT's Institute for Soldier Nanotechnologies seems to be in the lead. Her team is working with polyurethane enhanced with nanoscale particles and has succeeded in producing a fiber that's both soft and stretchy. And, interestingly but not surprisingly, Hammond says that everyone's favorite friendly neighborhood wall crawler is actually quite popular at MIT. "Indeed—Spider-Man is among the inspirations for us and many other researchers in the area!" Dr. Hammond says. As to her institute's research, she adds:

> We are still trying to come close to gaining natural silk's properties, and at this point this is still an unsolved problem. We have learned more about the impact of ordering of molecules in these polymers and how it affects mechanical properties, but it is still difficult to reproduce spider silk's nanoscale structure and other properties. It is my expectation that efforts from our and other groups [are] leading us to a better understanding that might end in synthetic systems or biologically inspired synthetic systems.

So while these are the most exciting results to date, let's say that no one there is going to be catching thieves just like flies anytime soon. All of which is to say that the idea that a high-school teenager working in his aunt's attic room can synthesize a substance that the best brains of MIT haven't been able to crack in decades of research is ludicrous. If Peter Parker were *that* smart, he'd have every major university and pharmaceutical corporation calling. He'd be the Bill Gates of biotech. Heck, forget Gates, he'd have a company to rival Tony Stark's. Talk about "with great power comes great responsibility." A kid that smart and he just uses it to make web-shooters? Where's the responsibility there? He should be out building new limbs for amputees and bullet-proof clothing for our cops and soldiers. He doesn't even have bullet-proof clothing for himself!

On the other hand, in 2000 a Canadian biotech company called Nexia did succeed in producing spider silk protein via genetically modified goats. The goats were given spider genes and their resulting milk contained the necessary proteins. While Nexia has yet to be able to spin this into a usable fiber—replicating the process conducted by spiders' sophisticated spinnerets may prove just as difficult as acquiring the silk proteins in the first place—Nexia did prove that a genetically modified organism could produce the necessary proteins.

Which suggests that the organically generated webs of the recent films and the ability to spin, which were bestowed upon Peter Parker when he was bitten by a *genetically modified* spider, make a good deal more sense. Hey, by now we all know that radiation doesn't give you superpowers—it gives you cancer. But genetic engineering is a wide-open frontier we can still get worked up about. So as controversial as this switch from Parker-constructed to organic web shooters was when it was first announced, it really does make a whole lot more sense and doesn't stretch credibility with a modern audience as much as the original explanations. (I'm not saying it doesn't stretch credibility *at all*—only that it doesn't do so *as much*. I know what we're working with here.)

Still, even though the switch to organic shooters is a logical and necessary alteration in the Spider-Man mythos, we do diminish an important aspect of the character. In the original comics, Peter Parker designed not only the actual spider silk, but a variety of applications into his web shooters. The wrist-mounted devices, fired by a double tap from his middle and ring fingers, passed in its default setting through a special mesh that gave the substance its web design. It could be made to fire a web (for netting bad guys), a line (for swinging, natch), or (rarely) globs of undifferentiated adhesive. The webbing could be an insulator or a conductor depending on the mixture. The shooter could even be modified to fire other substances. Ironically, Peter never learned to drive—why would he need to?—and wrecked his Spider-mobile on its first joy ride. But beyond this, he was a veritable Mac-Gyver. Peter also built electronic spider-tracers, for tracking bad guys, and a utility belt which projected an image of his mask called a "Spider Signal." He's quite an inventive boy. But in the films, we're not even sure how he managed to design his own costume. (I tried making a variety of superhero masks when I was a teenager, too, and believe me, none of mine turned out nearly that good).

What we've really lost here, in the recent translation to the big screen, is the aspect of Spider-Man as a budding scientist and inventor. Oh, he's still—in Tobey Maguire's words—"something of a scientist" himself, but that's a lip service being paid to a dangling notion that has lost its full narrative justification. Now Peter is a teenager with *an interest* in science. He is not the maverick scientist that he was envisioned as in 1962. This is an outcome of a single character point decision—and not one I personally oppose—but it also seems indicative of a wider trend, one that ties into the way that the sciences have come to be perceived in contemporary America. To understand this, let's look back at how things used to be.

Spider-Man's co-creator Stan Lee has said in interviews that he deliberately gave all of his superheroes white-collar professional jobs in their "normal lives." Growing up as he did as a child of the Depression, Stan gave his creations the occupations that were seen as respectable, enviable, and stable in his day. Thus Daredevil's alter-ego Matthew Murdock was a lawyer, Dr. Stephen Strange was a famous surgeon, and Reed Richards, a.k.a. Mr. Fantastic, was a genius scientist.

Peter Parker was a departure from previous superheroes in that instead of having a teenaged sidekick, the teenager *was* the hero. Nonetheless, it was part and parcel of his character that Peter was a scientist-in-training. Not only does this account for his being present at the lab accident which gives him his spider powers in the first place, but it also allows him to create the mechanical web shooters that complete his arsenal of super abilities. And a scientist was something that a fifteen-year-old contemporary of Peter Parker might have wanted to be back in the early '60s.

If one may be forgiven for talking about another cartoon character and a rival superhero franchise, there was a gag on an episode of *The Simpsons* that will help illustrate the next point. In the episode "Marge vs. the Monorail" (Episode 412), when Homer is trapped in the out-of-control train, Marge phones him and they have the following exchange:

MARGE: Homer, there's a man here who thinks he can help you.
HOMER: Batman?!
MARGE: No, he's a scientist.
HOMER: Batman's a scientist.
MARGE: It's not Batman!

Because Batman is a scientist, too, right? The young Bruce Wayne spent his entire life, from the moment of his parents' death until he donned the black cowl, studying chemistry, forensics, and a host of related disciplines to help him utilize his crime-fighting lab. Well, I'm afraid that's gone, too. In the recent *Batman Begins*, which in every other respect sees the Caped Crusader finally done justice on the big screen, this Batman doesn't find his path until an aborted attempt at taking revenge on his parents' killer goes awry. It's great theater and the movie is really top notch, but, there we go again—removing the science from the superhero. Which is why, when Lucius Fox explains how he synthesized an antidote to the Scarecrow's fear toxin and Bruce Wayne asks if he's meant to understand the technobabble, Fox replies "It's a bit technical." The line gives us a good running joke that Wayne later uses on a former Wayne enterprises executive when firing him, but it makes a liar of Homer Simpson. Batman, like Spider-Man, is no longer really a scientist either.

Now, to be fair, the Spider-Man movies really do a commendable job of treating Spider-Man as a parable about the responsible uses of scientific knowledge—with Parker as the advocate of responsible science and the host of "mad" scientists as misguided researchers who put ego ahead of altruism. But the move away from Parker the inventor really is indicative of the way in which the whole role of scientist is increasingly marginalized in today's society. In fact, the notion of the scientist-hero is so far gone from the popular imagination that Alan Moore is able to resurrect it as a pastiche character in the pages of his *Tom Strong* comic book. In the "real world," the lack of interest in science and technology among modern-day teenagers is alarming.

Recent surveys indicate that fewer U.S. students are enrolling in science, technology, engineering, and math programs every year. In the last thirty years, the United States has dropped from number three to number seventeen in global rankings of countries with college students earning science and engineering degrees, while only 5.5 percent of high-school students taking the ACT college entrance exam in 2002 planned to major in engineering, down from 8.6 percent in 1992.[1] Previously, the dearth in American students was made up for by foreign students, but since the events of 9/11, new immigration policies have made it difficult for foreign students to come to the U.S.A.—many of whom have traditionally stayed to work for American companies and become American citizens. As 25 percent of America's scientists and engineers are in their fifties and expected to retire by 2010, we are looking at a crisis that will have serious repercussions for the American economy and for our place as a world innovator.

Spider-Man responsible for our GNP, you say? Surely that's a lot for a comic book to take on—it's just a story, man! True, but we are a media-centric society, and the attitudes displayed in our narratives have measurable effects on the choices of our citizens. If Martha Stewart makes cookies with a tangerine-colored mixer, Kitchen Aid sees a spike in sales of appliances of that color. It's not for nothing that the Milwaukee School of Engineering gave James Doohan an honorary engineering degree. The university awarded him that honor after a spike in applicants citing the *Star Trek Enterprise's* Montgomery Scott as the reason they chose engineering for a degree. Contrast this with today's teenagers, who won't study science, and who think fame through reality television is not just a worthy goal, but a realistically attainable one!

Nor is the lack of interest in science limited to today's youth. As famed science fiction editor Gardner Dozois writes in the introduction to his anthology, *Galileo's Children: Tales of Science vs. Superstition*:

> Even today, the pope interdicts cloning, the president of the United States pushes to make stem-cell research illegal, mention of the theory of evolution is banned from textbooks and explanations of 'creation

---

[1] According to *Research Horizons Magazine*, Spring/Summer 2005.

science' are inserted instead, and politicians of both political parties vote against money for space exploration, or any other kind of research where the instant up-front financial benefit to the bottom line is not immediately evident. The battle of science against superstition is still going on, as is the battle to not have to think only what somebody *else* thinks is okay for you to think. In fact, in a society where more people believe in angels than believe in evolution, that battle may be more critical than ever (15).

And speaking of superstitions... recently, this marginalization of the role of scientist has reached back to the original source material, re-envisioning Spider-Man's origins in the comic book itself. In a controversial but critically acclaimed run of comics penned by *Babylon 5's* J. Michael Straczynski, Peter Parker was told his power had supernatural aspects to it. Peter learned that there was a reason he was "singled out" by the radioactive spider that bit him by a supernatural force—a totem spider spirit associated with an ancient Inca religion—who chose him to be a contemporary embodiment of a shamanistic power specifically because he was an underdog who would know how to fight back if given the chance. As collected in a graphic novel titled *The Book of Ezekiel*, Parker emerged from an ancient South American temple to ask, "I still don't know the truth. I mean, all this... the spider the way I saw it in there, the spider the way I... the way it happened to me.... What's the truth? The magic, or the science?" To which Miguel, descendant of Inca kings, replied, "Tomorrow the sun will come up. You can tell me all the reasons of science that it does come up, the oribital mechanics, all the laws of thermodynamics. All I can say is that it will come up because it is *meant* to come up. I see no contradiction. Do you?" (*Amazing Spider-Man* No. 508).

Well, yes. And so, I think, did a rather famous astronomer named Galileo Galilei. No offense to Straczynski, who is a wonderful writer and an important one in the history of series SF television—I simply cite him as evidence of a growing trend, and one that I think *does* matter. But if it doesn't matter, then hey, let's break out the Ouija boards and all play "Light as a Feather, Stiff as a Board," why don't we? Because recently, in *Spider-Man Disassembled: Changes* (*Spectacular Spider-Man* Nos. 15–20), Spider-Man underwent another genetic mutation that granted him organic web-shooters, so now the film's alteration has been worked into the comic book Spider-Man as well.

So much for Peter the inventor. The world has moved on, and science just isn't sexy anymore. And that's a real problem, because our realities flow from our imaginations, and how we see the world today is how we build it tomorrow. So perhaps Peter should just throw in the towel, quit that job working as Tony Stark's assistant, and think about launching an all-superhero version of *Survivor* or *The Amazing Race*. A shame, but maybe we were all expecting too much from a kid who never even learned to drive a car.

LOU ANDERS is an editor, author, and journalist. He is the editorial director of Prometheus Books's science fiction imprint Pyr (www.pyrsf.com), as well as the anthologies *Outside the Box* (Wildside Press, January 2001), *Live Without a Net* (Roc, July 2003), *Projections* (MonkeyBrain, December 2004), *FutureShocks* (Roc, January 2006), and *Fast Forward* (Pyr, February 2007). He served as the senior editor for *Argosy Magazine's* inaugural issues in 2003–2004. In 2000, he served as the executive editor of Bookface.com, and before that he worked as the Los Angeles liaison for Titan Publishing Group. He is the author of *The Making of Star Trek: First Contact* (Titan Books, 1996) and has published more than 500 articles in such magazines as *Publishers Weekly*, *The Believer*, *Dreamwatch*, *Star Trek Monthly*, *Star Wars Monthly*, *Babylon 5 Magazine*, *Sci Fi Universe*, *Doctor Who Magazine*, and *Manga Max*. His articles and stories have been translated into German, French, Danish, Italian, and Greek and have appeared online at Believermag.com, SFSite.com, RevolutionSF.com, and InfinityPlus.co.uk. Visit him online at www.louanders.com.

References

Becker, T. J. "Wake-Up Call for U.S. Innovation." *Research Horizons Magazine*, Spring/Summer 2005. http://gtresearchnews.gatech.edu/newsrelease/innovation.htm.

Dozois, Gardner (editor). *Galileo's Children: Tales of Science vs. Superstition*. Pyr: August 5, 2005.

Hammond, Paula T. 2006. E-mail correspondence with the author, 11 June.

Straczynski, J. Michael with Fiona Avery (w), John Romita, Jr. (i). *Amazing Spider-Man Vol. 7: The Book of Ezekiel*, collecting *Amazing Spider-Man* Nos. 503–508. Marvel Comics: October 1, 2004.

RICHARD HANLEY

The Perfectibility of Spider-Man

To quote Wikipedia (and I'm one of those people who think it's as useful in its way as the Britannica), the term philosophy is derived from the Greek words philo sophia, or "love of wisdom." Myself, I tend to believe it's more a love of the process of reasoning itself—in other words, a "love of thinking." If that's so, given Peter Parker's ongoing internal dialogue and endless worrying over the right or wrong or meaning of his every deed, then Peter Parker is a philosopher, and I'm certain he'd feel a strong affinity for the philosophical discussion Richard Hanley brings us below....

Issue #1: Suping Things Up

The Civil War series of 2006 raised the issue of whether or not superheroes should have secret identities, with Spider-Man joining Iron Man in favor of compulsory superhero registration. The "war" arose because superheroes came to be regarded (not unreasonably) as weapons of mass destruction, and the people demanded some regulation.

But perhaps there are other ways to make the superhero world a better place. *Civil War*, at least as of this writing, has demonstrated the glaring need for a superhero cleanup detail, and it's typical for a battle between the good and the bad guys (and gals) to leave a swathe of destruction. The good guys of course try to limit collateral damage to life, limb, and property while the baddies generally proceed without such regard, but nevertheless the world frequently ends up being trashed. I'm not saying Spider-Man and his ilk are responsible for cleaning up the mess, but wouldn't it be great if someone super powerful—perhaps The Janitor, or Hoover-Lady, or Rebuildo, or Yportne (think about it)—was?

And while we're at it, how about someone to do the intellectual clean-up work? We could have superheroes to break down persistent prejudice (The Spinster, The Fat Squad), or to promote a social agenda (Universal Health Care Boy, Peace Lady). Or someone devoted to stamping out bad reasoning wherever it is found (Logic-Man, who by day is the mild-mannered academic, Phil O'Sopher).

You get the point. But none of these suggestions would make sense if we didn't conceive of different possibilities for the world being *good* or *bad*, and *better* or *worse*. These are questions of value. *How can we, as individuals and as humankind, make the world a better place? How can we be better individuals? How can humankind be better? How good do we have to be?* The only answers I'll take seriously are ones that assume things can be better than they are—this is not the best of all possible worlds, and we are not the best of all possible people.

Value is a traditional philosophical issue. (In fact, it's practically issue No. 1 in the *Philosophy* series—very collectible.) Unfortunately, when people hear "philosophical" they react very much like J. Jonah Jameson when he hears "Spider-Man": with contempt borne of ignorance. Like Spidey, philosophy often gets a bum rap, especially from the folk who think that any intelligent person with a free afternoon can figure it all out.

What can you expect from me in what follows? As a professional philosopher, I don't want to just crap on about Spider-Man for awhile, the way any halfway intelligent fan might. Philosophy should be informed and relevant, and the best philosophy is adversarial, and makes you uncomfortable—no doubt another reason it is unpopular. In this article I want to give you a taste of the adversarial process, by addressing what other philosophers have written on these topics (yes, philosophers *have* written about Spider-Man!). Published arguments shouldn't just disappear into the ether—they should be addressed. And if it makes anyone uncomfortable, I've done my job.

Issue #2: Worthwhile Investments

Some things matter to us only as instruments to obtain other things that matter. Take money (but not mine, please). Money has instrumental value, and only instrumental value. We tend to take the same view of material possessions, education, employment—indeed, practically everything we value. However, if you ask the ordinary person on the street what they value for its own sake and not as a mere instrument, the most common answer is *happiness* (understood as pleasure, or the absence of pain and suffering). This is a pretty good answer. But there are powerful reasons for thinking that happiness isn't the only thing that matters for its own sake, and that it's not even the most important thing. (For instance, if you imagine a Matrix-like existence that is designed to promote happiness and eliminate suffering, but where you are deceived and cut off from the real world, you probably think you're better off relatively unhappy outside the Matrix.)

Another answer philosophers have given is that it is good for its own sake for you to do what it is in your (human) nature to do. Aristotle thinks this is the life of rational contemplation, others think it is becoming one with God, others think it is whatever path we freely choose for ourselves, and so on. (This account seems to require an optimistic view of human nature, according to which it presumably is in the relevant sense *against* our nature to rape, pillage, murder, and otherwise inflict great harm.)

These two answers are enough to go on with. We can even connect them, if we like, but with caution. Philosophers like Plato, Aristotle, and Kierkegaard think that humans can only be truly "happy" doing what it is in their nature to do, but by "happy" they mean something different from being in a pleasant subjective state.

We can ask about an individual person like Peter Parker, assuming he survives the spider bite; is he happier being Spider-Man, or not? And we can ask what it is in Spider-Man's nature to do. Likewise, we can ask what is better for humankind as a whole, in the sense of promoting happiness, and we can try to figure out what might count as being in the nature of humankind to pursue.

Issue #3: With Great Power Comes...What?

Figuring out what is good and bad for us is one part of the task of determining what to do with our lives. The other part is figuring out what our obligations are. Should we do the most good we can? This is the opinion of the utilitarians, who claim that the only right actions are those which maximize the overall good (happiness, according to most utilitarians). Actions are evaluated entirely according to their consequences.

Does Spider-Man act according to the dictates of utilitarianism? Not according to Charles Taliaferro and Craig Lindahl-Urben, apparently reasoning without a net:

> A [Marvel] superhero acts from the belief that damage to a single person, especially an innocent, cannot be tolerated. Superheroes do not engage in utilitarian thinking by which some harm to an innocent person can be outweighed by creating greater goods for the majority. When presented with a choice between saving an innocent individual and saving a group of people, the typical superhero is incapable of making the choice.... It is what the hero does next that raises him or her to superhero status—he or she saves both the individual and the group. The superhero is always focused on the intrinsic value of the individual person.... The superhero view of life is not at all utilitarian (Morris and Morris 62–74).

To this I say: *Where is Logic-Man when we need him?* Since it clearly is possible to save both the individual and the group, and this result presumably is the best available, the superhero action described is indeed compatible with utilitarianism! Of course, a limited being like Spider-Man is bound to run into situations where he really can't save someone, as in *Amazing Spider-Man* No. 121, where Gwen Stacy died. And since he can't save everyone, there will be situations where he has to choose to let someone die. Not being comic-psychic, I can't say what exactly Spider-Man would always do, so I'll consider instead what Spider-Man *should* do.

Should Spider-Man act in utilitarian fashion? Practically every philosopher who has written on the subject says No.[1] I have not the space for a full defense of utilitarianism, so let me just assert that, like Spider-Man and philosophy, utilitarianism has gotten a bum rap. It has weaknesses, but these are not nearly so bad as its critics claim, and their own favored alternative tends on balance to be no better off, at least where conformity to common sense intuition is concerned.

Part of the problem here is that some "common sense" pronouncements are taken too seriously. Folks love to say high-minded things like "damage to an innocent person cannot be tolerated," but give them some relevant examples (warfare, for example) and they readily abandon these knee-jerk sound bites as obviously false, and endorse a more nuanced view. Consider again the death of Gwen Stacy. It seems that it was Spider-Man who really killed her in the attempt to save her. But although he undoubtedly would feel terrible knowing this, is he really to blame? Most of us would say no, the Green Goblin is, but why, exactly? No mere sound bite gives an adequate explanation.

And what came next is even more difficult to explain. In his rage, Spidey attacked the Green Goblin, beating him almost to death. He stopped just short, and the Goblin took the opportunity to try to impale him with the glider. Thanks to his spider-sense, Spidey leapt away just in time, and the Goblin was killed instead. Was Spidey wrong to get out of the way, to "duck harm" as the philosophers Christopher Boorse and Roy Sorenson have put it? Again, most of us say no. But suppose the Goblin had instead been standing next to Spider-Man, and not in the path of the glider at all. Would it have been okay for Spider-Man to grab the Goblin and use him as a "shield," thereby saving himself? It is very uncomfortable to say yes. (Especially when we change the case so that the person killed is entirely innocent. Most people say it's okay to "duck" and seriously wrong to "shield.") As Boorse and Sorenson point out, there seems no morally principled way to draw a distinction between the two cases. So we should take seriously the possibility that our common sense and moral thinking are just plain wrong about some things.

---

[1] For a nice summary of the standard reasons for rejecting utilitarianism, see Christopher Robichaud, "With Great Power Comes Great Responsibility: On the Moral Duties of the Super-Powerful and the Super-Heroic," in Morris and Morris (177–193).

I prefer to forget about utilitarianism for the nonce, and look instead for principles any reasonable morality can endorse. Peter Singer has proposed what I shall call the Principle of Beneficence (POB) and paraphrase here:

> If you can prevent something bad from happening, without sacrificing anything of comparable moral significance, then you are obligated to do so.

This is not strictly utilitarian, since what is of moral significance might include rights, or personal autonomy, or personal relationships, or virtue, and so on. In other words, the POB is a schema, and you have to plug in a theory of moral significance.

The POB has been criticized mainly for obliterating the distinction between obligatory actions (wrong and blameworthy not to perform, and not praiseworthy to perform), and *supererogatory* actions (good and praiseworthy to perform, but not wrong or blameworthy not to perform—actions, as we say, *above and beyond the call of duty*). But this criticism is overblown. All the standard cases of supererogation are cases of self-sacrifice, and many such actions are *not* required by the POB. For instance, suppose you find yourself in a situation where no matter what you do, exactly one person will die. You act so that it is *you* who dies, and the defender of the POB can call this supererogation. They just mean something slightly different by it. (Maybe they should call it super*hero*gation!)

Nevertheless I think the POB is mistaken as it stands, because it does not seem to take reasonable ignorance into account. You may be able to prevent something bad, but not know this, either because you don't know it is happening, or else because you don't know your full abilities. In such cases, it seems you are off the moral hook, as long as your ignorance is not *willful*. So I propose a friendly amendment:

> If *you know* you can prevent something bad from happening, without sacrificing anything of comparable moral significance, then you are obligated to do so.[2]

---

[2] Probably there are plausible weaker principles, involving reasonable belief rather than knowledge. I'll just assume that knowledge is to be had in the relevant circumstances.

Spider-Man 2 picks up particularly on the theme. Peter Parker decides that, on balance, he is better off not being a superhero, especially one who gets undeserved bad press. He can't hold down a job, pay the rent, pay attention to his friends, study enough, and so on. Moreover, he worries that his more personal relationships will endanger those he cares about by making them targets for his enemies.

What does the (amended) POB demand of a superhero like Spider-Man? Given that you know that someone really needs your help, it's all about how powerful you are. The more powerful you are, the more the POB demands. So it's just plain *wrong* that Superman should have an ordinary job as a reporter—better for Clark Kent to be a recluse like Bruce Wayne, and use his time more productively.

But Superman doesn't have to worry about mundane things like putting food on the table or sleeping. The less powerful Spider-Man does—though surely he could get a better job, working from home (webmaster?!)—and can justifiably spend less time saving people. Spider-Man cannot let himself get too run down (and get, for instance, a duodenal ulcer), because this would reduce the overall level of good he does. But can he just walk away from the beating of a man in an alley, as he does in *Spider-Man 2*? Not according to the POB.

Helping that man is the sort of obligation that you and I have, and we're not super. But how far do non-super obligations extend? The aforementioned Singer has made himself very unpopular by using the POB to argue for a significant obligation to help the absolutely poor of the world, those in a state of privation so severe that their health is under constant threat from starvation and disease. The absolutely poor have what James Rachels calls the *other* weight problem. (An American—or Australian, or European, and so on—who has a "weight problem" is of course typically someone who has *too much* nutrition.)

Think about it. If the extra resources that go into making an American overweight were redirected to the absolutely poor, it might save the lives of whole villages! And it's not just fat people, and not just food. American houses are very large, yet contain small families, with a glut of practically everything: cars, televisions, toys. We are lucky,

lucky, lucky! (And don't pretend for a moment that we *deserve* this over-abundance—we just happen to have been born in the right place at the right time.)

Isn't buying one more TV for a household that already has three a lot like ignoring the man being beaten? Indeed, isn't it in some respects worse, since we place ourselves at no risk at all in donating the money to charity instead?

While you ponder that, consider Spidey again. Just as we can't pretend that the world isn't full of terrible suffering while we scarf down the calories in front of our high-definition electronics, Spider-Man has to employ his considerable resources in monitoring his surroundings for opportunities to help. Most of the time he does. But might he not then have an obligation to move to another country, where he could be even more help?

(This seems a no-brainer in the case of Superman. Is Metropolis really where he ought to spend most of his time? Shouldn't he instead be shuttling between e.g. the Sudan and somewhere equally horrific? And if there were a Super-Duper Man, his obligations would be more extensive still. Which might make you wonder, what's Extra-Super-Duper *God* doing while all this suffering is going on?)

It's a serious question whether or not Spider-Man has time for personal relationships. That depends, as we noted earlier, upon what he needs to keep himself in super shape. If he would go nuts without a girlfriend, okay. But in *Spider-Man 2*, indulging himself with Mary Jane seems instead to reduce his superpowers. Not okay.

Now add some more fuel to the fire Singer has tried to light under us. Philosopher Peter Unger gives an argument (without clearly endorsing it) that even Singer doesn't go far enough. Common sense morality allows begging, borrowing, or stealing in certain circumstances to provide help when someone desperately needs it. Put another way, when common sense applies, the POB doesn't count such things as property rights as fundamentally overriding. So if you could hack into the financial resources of a Scrooge, you arguably ought to use your abilities to redirect some of his resources toward the absolutely poor. And if Spidey has to be a Robin Hood, and break the law to help those in need, so be it.

Issue #4: Must We Be Moral Saints?

You might now be ready, like Singer's critics, to conclude that all this just shows the POB is mistaken. But then you have to put up or shut up, and show why sometimes you have obligations to help, and other times you don't. (I don't think anyone has yet shown this, by the way.)

One worthwhile attempt at undermining Singer and Unger-style arguments rests on observations made by Susan Wolf. Moral "saints" are strange and tedious creatures who wouldn't make very good friends, and we needn't aspire to be like them. Other kinds of excellence seem worthwhile, too—such as fine musicianship, or perfecting one's backhand.

I don't think this works as an objection to Singer and Unger. First, the argument for an obligation to sacrifice a good deal to help the absolutely poor does not in practice require that we give up all other pursuits. Second, the sorts of excess Singer targets do not typically fall under the category of the pursuit of excellence—more like the pursuit of corpulence, and mediocrity. Third, pursuit of certain sorts of excellence is perhaps best left to those with the relevant talent, who can then provide (morally significant) satisfaction to the rest of us

After all, if these other pursuits really are so very valuable, then that value can be included in the judgment of moral significance. This in turn raises a very uncomfortable issue. Suppose Spider-Man is faced with the choice between saving a person, and saving an excellent artwork. Now I expect common sense, off the top of its head, to confidently pronounce that of course you save the person, because human artifacts are replaceable, and humans aren't. I'm not so sure—this sounds to me like another knee-jerk sound bite. To investigate your own intuitions, you need to consider a range of cases. Start with a very valuable artifact, like the Mona Lisa, or the Statue of Liberty, and with, say, a guilty murderer. Are there any circumstances in which you would sacrifice the person for the thing? If so, vary the example, and introduce an innocent volunteer. Then an innocent bystander, and so on. When I run through these cases, I find I believe that some artifacts can be less replaceable than some persons, even innocent ones.

When we put the Wolf approach alongside the Singer and Unger arguments (assuming that we indeed can prevent a lot of suffering cheaply), here's the uncomfortable conclusion: much of what we in the developed world do is morally unimportant, and we do it at the expense of the lives of the absolutely poor. Taken to an extreme, this might imply that we ought to sacrifice the lives of some of those who are not pulling their considerable weight, to support the poor who need help to develop their worthwhile talents! (This conclusion is somewhat tempered by reasonable doubt, of course. Since persons are so valuable, they should not be sacrificed lightly.)

Spider-Man perhaps ought to be alert to such possibilities. And if that makes him a moral saint, I don't think it would be tedious to be around him!

Issue #5: Why Be Good?

Some writers have investigated superhero motivation. If you're so powerful, why not just join the villains, take over the world, and reap the benefits? Stephen Layman focuses on Spider-Man's motivation, and argues that if to be moral is to be reasonable, then something like the Christian supposition of the possibility of a good life after death is required to provide the incentive (Morris and Morris, 194–206). Layman's suggestion is that it must be a possible pay off, in the long run, for you to have overriding reasons to be moral.

I grant that this approach makes the motivation issue easier in one sense—it simply reduces moral motivation to *prudence*, and nobody is surprised that you have reason to do what is in your own best interest. But I have to say that this seems an infantile approach to moral psychology, and sidesteps the main issue—namely that moral motivation is puzzling precisely because morality and prudence come apart.

I suspect Layman is not considering all the kinds of reason one can have. If someone who can scan my thoughts sincerely threatens to shoot me if I don't believe that 2 + 2 = 5, I grant I have prudential reason for believing that 2 + 2 = 5. But does prudence override math here, so that on balance, I have *more reason* to believe that 2 + 2 = 5 than that 2 + 2 = 4? I would say it is the other way around—the example only shows that it can be in your best interest to be irrational. In my view, moral truths are like truths of mathematics—they couldn't possibly be false—and I have no less reason to believe them and act on them. So I like Spider-Man's answer in *Spider-Man* the movie, when the Green Goblin asks him why he "bothers" to help people: "Because it is right."

Notice also that on Layman's view, atheists apparently have no long-run prudential reason to be moral, and hence, apparently, no overriding reason to be moral. Spider-Man gives no indication of being traditionally religious, so are we to conclude that he really has no overriding reason to do the right thing? If so, then I'm a masked menace's uncle, and you can stick that in your *Daily Bugle*.

Issue #6: Being All That You Can Be

Given that Spidey can and does have motivation to be moral, and given that something like the POB is correct, we must consider whether or not Spider-Man should remain as he is. For one implication of the POB is that one might be obligated to transform, if one is able to transform into something with greater abilities. Suppose that Peter Parker had the choice of whether or not to become Spider-Man (as he did in *Amazing Spider-Man* No. 500). Did he have an obligation to expose himself to the spider bite?

Of course, this is an unusual situation. Here is a "true" story I heard recently: a boy put a spider in a microwave oven to irradiate it, then got it to bite him, and died forthwith. (Mothers, don't let your sons read comic books!) When I heard this apocryphal tale, I was suffering the effects of a probable spider bite. First, I developed a painful swelling behind my ear. No sooner had the swelling gone down than I caught a mild cold, and then a fairly serious bacteriological infection. Thanks to antibiotics, I seem fully recovered.

Now maybe I wasn't bitten by a spider at all. Or, if I *was* bitten by a spider, maybe it was just a coincidence that I caught a cold and an infection soon afterward. Maybe, but then again, maybe not. The point is that our entire, and entirely rational, attitude toward a spider bite is negative. A spider bite is not the sort of thing that bestows benefits on the bitee. If I claimed to be better—never mind super—at sports or math or logic on account of my spider bite, you would rightly think I was in fact worse, at logic at least.

To put it more carefully, a spider bite could only be a benefit the way accidentally breaking your leg could be—if being laid up is really what you need, and you wouldn't have taken a rest otherwise. Your *leg* is not better for being broken, and the benefits could have been had (and more cheaply) some other way.

The odd thing about Peter Parker's spider bite is that it is a mixed blessing—it undoubtedly bestows benefits as well as harms. And by benefits, I don't mean of the broken leg sort. Arguably, Peter is better off for the bite, and such benefits were not to be had in other ways.

Even if Peter was not better off for the bite, the POB rules he should have chosen it, if he knew that the result would be that he would thereby gain the ability to prevent great evils, with no equivalent cost.

Do we humans have analogous obligations to transform ourselves? This depends, obviously, on what kinds of transformation are possible for us. Begin with physical transformations, like Peter's. We have had prosthetics for a while now, and these are generally designed to compensate for a particular loss. We can also imagine cases where we can actually improve on nature through prosthetics.

Some object to such improvement. It is well-known that some deaf parents oppose cochlear implants for their deaf children. There can be good reasons for this. The implants might not work very well. And even if they work well, the deaf subculture is such that an implanted child might have difficulty fitting in. But the objection that deafness is not actually a disability is simply wrong-headed. Other things being equal, *of course* one is better off hearing than not, and it is an insult to the deaf who have achieved great things in spite of this disability to suppose otherwise.

If we focus on physical *improvement* rather than correction, and delve further into science fiction, we may be able to bring that improvement about through genetic engineering. Again, there can be good objections to this—primarily that the costs aren't worth the benefits. But most who object to genetic manipulation seem to think that it's clearly wrong, no matter how beneficial it might prove. This is a view for which no good argument has ever been presented.

There is really no substantial difference between manipulating our genome to produce better people and manipulating our environment to produce better people. Isn't that the point of education, after all? Wouldn't it be great if we could do some of the work *outside* the classroom? As long as we factor in reasonable caution in the face of the unknown, there are considerable opportunities, and the POB seems to imply that we should avail ourselves of them. Of course, it might not follow that everyone has to transform. It may be that only a few enhanced individuals would be enough to do the job. These individuals would be our superheroes.

Issue #7: Sticking Around, or Survival

If an irradiated spider were to bite me, I wouldn't expect to gain superpowers. I wouldn't expect to gain anything at all. I'd expect to be, like the apocryphal boy, *dead*. Nobody dies when Peter Parker is bitten, but does *Peter* really survive the spider bite?

After all, what sorts of transformations can human beings survive? That depends very much on what kind of thing a human being is, and opinions vary. Let's distinguish three common enough opinions: first, that human beings are organisms; second, that human beings are not organisms; and third, an incoherent mishmash of the first two. The last is depressingly common. For instance, there are many conservatives about abortion who declare that you were once an embryo, and yet also claim that you can survive the permanent destruction of your body. Either you are your body, or you are not. If you are your body, you cannot survive without it. And if you are not your body, then you weren't your body when it was an embryo. (I'm sure no such conservative wants to take the only coherent road here: that an embryo is not identical with, and somehow survives the permanent destruction of, the body it transforms into!)

Whether or not you are the organism that is your body, you can survive some pretty radical transformations in that body: growing, developing, losing a limb, and so on. But could you transform into a house, or a tree, or an insect, or an arthropod, and *survive*? I think it is very doubtful that Peter Parker could survive the transformation into a spider. (I suppose some believers in reincarnation might disagree.) It's not even clear whether or not such a transformation is possible—perhaps the only way for something to be a *spider* is (roughly) to come from other spiders. But we can set this aside. We can imagine something enough like a spider, beginning with the eight-limbed thing that Peter transforms into temporarily in *Amazing Spider-Man* No. 100.

Maybe Peter can't transform into a *spider*, but could he transform into something that isn't *human*, and yet survive? In other words, is Peter essentially human, and is the thing he transforms into—Spider-Man—human? If the answers are yes and no respectively, then Peter does not survive.

Forget about individual humans for a moment, and focus these questions instead on *humankind*. What sorts of transformations can humankind undergo, and survive? Presumably, adopting one political system rather than another is no threat to survival (although, depending on the system, it may shorten our future). But could, for instance, large-scale genetic engineering produce so great a transformation that we would not in fact survive it?

In both the individual and kind cases, it is tempting to think that the survival question is just a question of identity. Is Spider-Man one and the same individual as Peter Parker? Would whatever emerges from a large-scale genetic engineering transformation not *be* humankind? But some philosophers (most notably, Derek Parfit) have adopted the view that identity need not be what matters for survival. Roughly, the idea is that what matters in, say, *your* survival is that there be a future person sufficiently like you in relevant respects (whatever these relevant respects might be, and philosophers have different ideas on this), whether or not it happens to *be* you. I'll mostly ignore this view, and proceed on the assumption that identity is what matters for survival.

My preferred answer to what preserves the identity of a person over time is *psychological continuity*. Consider your ordinary survival. You have lots of mental states today, those states are a lot like the mental states you had yesterday, and they exist today *because* of the existence of those mental states of yesterday. Add the states of the day before yesterday, which the states of today and yesterday substantially depend upon, and so on. That is psychological continuity.

It is a consequence of this view that you can survive considerable change, including manipulation of your genetic makeup, as long as psychological continuity is preserved. It is a further consequence that Peter Parker definitely survived the transformation into Spider-Man.

So is Peter necessarily human? Yes, and no. *Human* is an ambiguous term. Sometimes it means *genetically* human, and it is by no means clear that Spider-Man is genetically human. (Superman is definitely not.) But we also use *human* in what philosophers call the *moral* sense—this is the sense we use when talking of universal human rights. Believing in universal human rights does not commit one to the view that all genetically human individuals have them, nor to the view that genetically non-human individuals don't. So even if Peter, or Aunt May or Mary Jane for that matter, are not necessarily genetically human, I think they necessarily are morally human.

Similar considerations apply to humankind. I think we can survive some pretty substantial transformation. We may no longer all be genetically human (some writers call the next stage that of the *transhuman*), but as long as there is sufficient continuity (mediated by mental states) with previous generations, we will remain morally human.

Issue #8: Reasons to Be Cheerful?

If I am right, then to the extent that we can improve ourselves, it not only is a good idea, but may be obligatory, at least for enough of us. But how likely is substantial future improvement of humanity?

There is no overall empirical reason to expect it. Progress has of course occurred, but by any objective measure it has been fitful. Perhaps recent history is more encouraging, as science in particular has gone from a fledgling pursuit to a dominant agent for change. And if I was going to put my money on anything, it would be science.

Other agents for change are either dubious or non-existent. Marx thought that the march of history would necessarily lead to the overthrow of capitalism. Well, maybe it will eventually, but not by the mechanism he postulated. Then there's religion. Practically every religion holds out the promise of a better life for the religious. But if the religious do have better lives, I suspect it's only because they persecute the non-religious. Education is all well and good, but curriculum remains too attached to the politics of the day, so I don't see us radically transforming ourselves that way, either. Finally, although the political conservatives I know tend to put their faith in the invisible hand of the market, I cannot myself invest much in it. I grant that an unregulated market can do some very good things, but even if an unregulated market is overall desirable (and I'm not convinced it is), the chances of the rich and powerful giving up their advantage and permitting true market forces to operate seems remote.

Nope—for me, it's science or nothing. And I don't mean *evolution*. Not because I doubt evolutionary theory (I regard the current widespread opposition to it is an intellectual scandal of the highest order, one which has no effect at all on the relevant science), but rather because evolution is not a mechanism for *progress* (it's more like an unregulated market in species persistence). I mean instead the accumulation of scientific knowledge and the potential applications to technology (if you like, the market for ideas). The problem remains one of priority. Even those who aren't actively opposed to science still place little importance on funding it, hamstring it with arbitrary demands and restrictions, or insist on applications that are not obviously beneficial.

Science is like a superhero. And we the people, recognizing that science has the potential for mass destruction, rightly insist on its regulation. But all appearances are that in the U.S., we've recently put this regulation in the hands of the manifestly unqualified. So unlike Spider-Man in *Civil War*, perhaps we should opt for relatively untrammeled superheroes, and relatively untrammeled science.

And for relatively untrammeled comics. From 1954, comics content was heavily restricted by the requirement of the Comics Code Authority seal of approval. The *Amazing Spider-Man* Nos. 96–98 story arc famously flouted the Authority by depicting Harry Osborn's drug addiction. With great power comes great responsibility, and I'm inclined to think, on balance, that Marvel comics wielded its power more responsibly than the CCA.

And on balance I remain, rather stubbornly, an optimist. And I think this is why I continue to like superhero comics so much. Despite the common theme of misguided scientists like Doc Ock, the typical superhero world is one ruled by the secular concern of making *this* world a better place, using the tools of science and a basic human capacity for goodness. (Spider-Man could not do what he does without his scientific abilities.)

That's the kind of world I want to live in. Faced with real dangers, who're you gonna call? You can keep your priests and astrologers and your Freudian psychoanalysts and your celebrities. I want someone who can actually manipulate the world to our good advantage, and for that, scientific knowledge is the key.

> RICHARD HANLEY is a professor of philosophy at the University of Delaware. He is the author of *Is Data Human? The Metaphysics of Star Trek*, and several articles, including pieces in *Star Wars and Philosophy* and *Superheroes and Philosophy*.

References

Christopher Boorse and Roy Sorenson, "Ducking Harm," *Journal of Philosophy* 85 (1988): 115–34.

Morris, Tom and Matt Morris, eds. *Superheroes and Philosophy*. Chicago and LaSalle: Open Court, 2005.

Further Reading

Parfit, Derek. *Reasons and Persons*. Oxford University Press, 1986.

Passmore, John. *The Perfectibility of Man*. Gerald Duckworth & Company, 1972.

James Rachels, "Vegetarianism and 'the Other Weight Problem'", in Aiken and Follette, *World Hunger and Moral Obligations.* Prentice-Hall, 1977.

Singer, Peter. *Practical Ethics*, Second Edition. Cambridge University Press, 1993.

Unger, Peter. *Living High and Letting Die: Our Illusion of Innocence.* Oxford University Press, 1996.

Susan Wolf, "Moral Saints," *Journal of Philosophy* 79 (1982): 419–439.

MATTHEW PUSTZ

Spider-Man:
Class Straddler as Superhero

Working-class superheroes of the world, unite! You have nothing to lose but your chains. . . .

SPIDER-MAN WAS ONE of my favorite superheroes as a teenager. I'm sure that part of the reason I identified with him was because he was a lonely, alienated guy who didn't have the best luck when it came to relationships. Looking back at it now, though, the more important reason for my identification was his financial situation. Because he has to worry about helping to pay for Aunt May's frequent hospital stays, as well as everyday expenses like rent and tuition, Peter is forced to work at the *Daily Bugle* when he'd rather be focusing on his college classes or fighting crime as Spider-Man. This was a situation I could understand, unlike that of Batman and other heroes, who apparently had no occupation beyond being independently wealthy. Spider-Man knew what it meant to struggle financially, to want to move up in the world, and to feel obligations to the family and friends that might be left behind. As the child of a middle-class family with working-class roots, this appealed to me, and Spider-Man became one of my favorites because of his social class.

Although I wouldn't have thought about it when I read the stories twenty-five years ago, Spider-Man is clearly working class. Peter Parker isn't rich, but he has a job. Unfortunately, being a freelance photojournalist is not the most secure occupation. Presumably, Peter didn't get any benefits or health insurance from the *Daily Bugle*, and if he didn't get any pictures for that day's paper, he didn't get paid, simple as that. But this wasn't Peter's career. It was just a job, something that he could do to pay the bills, something that he did for the money. As I got older, I had to do the same thing that Peter did—working crummy jobs for a paycheck—something that children of privilege generally don't have to do. His "job" as Spider-Man had a day-to-day quality to it as well. Like someone working primarily to pay the bills, Spider-Man's fight against criminals was about doing the job; capturing the Lizard, for example, and then moving on to the next job, like figuring out who kidnapped J. Jonah Jameson. In the comics, he was referred to as "your friendly neighborhood Spider-Man," conjuring the image of other local people providing a service to the community: the neighborhood plumber or volunteer fireman.

Ultimately, then, Spider-Man is an everyday guy, created to be "the average man in the street," according to Stan Lee (*Origins of Marvel Comics* 135). Spider-Man is a hero of the working class, but his class identity is actually complicated. Peter Parker doesn't fit in with his peers at school; he's smart enough to be able to move up and escape his neighborhood. In this way, Peter is an example of the people Alfred Lubrano calls "straddlers" in his book *Limbo: Blue-Collar Roots, White-Collar Dreams*. He describes them as men and women who were "born to blue-collar families and then...moved into the strange new territory of the middle class. They are the first in their families to have graduated from college. As such, they straddle two worlds, many of them not feeling at home in either, living in a strange kind of American limbo" (2). Like many straddlers, Peter Parker's desire to move up in class so that he can use his special skills (both natural and supernatural) is tempered by the strong sense of responsibility and obligation that keeps him grounded in that environment. In fact, it is his status as class straddler that has made Spider-Man into the compelling hero that he is.

Class is a dicey topic in the United States. Many people want to deny its very presence because it violates American myths about equality and opportunity. If class exists as a meaningful category, then that means there is economic inequality in the United States, creating a situation where some people have advantages over others because of their family background. Class suggests that success and failure are not simply matters decided by hard work, as concepts like the American dream and the American work ethic would have people believe. It is also hard to talk about class in the United States because Americans are not really sure what exactly it is, or how many there are. In a country like Great Britain, where class is wrapped around tradition and institutions, it is more identifiable. But in America, people are not really sure if it is about income level, wealth, occupation, education, upbringing, or culture.

Whatever it is, class is a real force in American life. Lubrano argues, "Who your parents are has as much or more to do with where you'll end up in life than any other single factor" (4). For most people, class determines not only whether or not they go onto higher education, but also what college they attend. It can help decide who we spend time with, where we live, what career we choose, and even who we marry. And although money is certainly important, class goes deeper than simply how much a person is paid or how much is in her savings account. Rather, it is a culture that Americans are unwittingly born into, producing shared values and instructions about how to behave. Lubrano writes that class "is script, map, and guide. It tells us how to talk, how to dress, how to hold ourselves, how to eat, and how to socialize" (5). Class is about having the cultural capital to know how to act at a fancy restaurant or in a corporate business meeting. At the same time, though, it's invisible and inexact. While it might be about culture and upbringing, Americans are still able to change their appearance to make it look like they're part of a higher class. They use clothes, cars, jewelry, and more to create a costume to try to mask their true identity. As Lubrano explains, "Any blue-collar kid who works in a bakery can take a trip to the Gap and buy clothes that would make him indistinguishable from a sophomore at Bryn Mawr" (4).

Mobility also complicates discussions about class in America. More than in many other countries, people in the United States are still able to move from one class to another. Among these are Lubrano's estimated thirteen million straddlers who have moved from working-class backgrounds into upper- and middle-class jobs (229). Lubrano explains that, since straddlers are born in the working class (a category that basically corresponds to middle- to lower-middle-class people working at blue-collar jobs), they demonstrate the values of that class throughout their lives: forthrightness, loyalty to family, friends, and even neighborhood, respect for parents, and "an understanding and appreciation of what it takes to get somewhere in a hard world where no one gives you a break" (17–18). Early in their lives, though, straddlers feel different from others in their class. It might be a desire to learn for the sake of learning, or an unwillingness to work at a physically demanding or repetitive job for their entire adult lives. There is always something pushing straddlers to leave.

This is the situation in which a young Peter Parker finds himself. In his origin story in *Amazing Fantasy* No. 15, we saw that Peter and his surrogate parents Uncle Ben and Aunt May were happy, but they couldn't have been wealthy. We didn't see Ben or May working, so we had to assume that they were retired and living on a fixed income. Economically, that is almost automatically going to put them into the working class. When the pair gave Peter a microscope as a gift, Aunt May explained that it was the one Peter "always wanted," suggesting that they had to save for a substantial time before being able to afford such a present (*Amazing Fantasy* No. 15).

Despite the affection that he had for his aunt and uncle, Peter found himself alienated at school where his values, interests, and goals didn't seem to mesh with those of the other teenagers from his neighborhood. In Spider-Man's origin story, Peter's interest in science was demonstrated early on. When a group of popular students lingered after school to make plans for the weekend, Peter approached them to ask if any of them would be interested in joining him at "a great new exhibit at the science hall tonight." They quickly rejected his offer, laughing in his face and calling him a "bookworm" (*Amazing Fantasy* No. 15). Like many straddlers, Peter wanted to fit in, but there was something different about him that made this impossible. He just couldn't force himself to give up his academic interests.

Straddlers often find themselves more interested in school, current events, the arts, and science than their peers; this is one of the things that sets them apart from the other young working-class people they know. These interests often lead to college and careers that are far afield from traditional working-class jobs. For Peter, this interest in science led him to the ultimate characteristic that separates him from his peers: his spider powers. At this "great new exhibit," Peter was bitten by a spider that had been exposed to radioactive rays. Soon after, he discovered the change it had wrought, as he felt that his "entire body is charged with some sort of fantastic energy!" (*Amazing Fantasy* No. 15). It would be this energy that would prompt Peter to put on a mask—to hide his original (class) identity—to become Spider-Man.

Once straddlers recognize the difference between themselves and their peers, they quickly develop goals to fulfill the promise that they see in themselves. But these goals are often complicated by family responsibilities and perceived obligations to the old neighborhood and the working-class values found there. Spider-Man was no different in his desire to "move up," to somehow get out of his working class neighborhood, but like other straddlers his efforts were complicated by class. After testing his powers in the wrestling ring, Peter's initial plan was to make money as Spider-Man through television appearances. His responsibility was to himself only: "from now on I just look out for number one—that means—me!" he announced to a security guard in the television studio where he was working (*Amazing Fantasy* No. 15). When his uncle Ben was murdered, Peter finally realized that he did have real obligations to others, especially to his own family, namely Aunt May.

These obligations—especially their financial aspects—became important plot points in the earliest issues of Spider-Man's regular series. In the first issue, Peter actually offered to drop out of high school to help his aunt pay the rent on their house. She refused, though, because she didn't want him to give up his dream to become a scientist someday (*Amazing Spider-Man* No. 1). In the second story in that initial issue, Peter came up with what he thought was the perfect plan to help his aunt financially: he would join the

Fantastic Four and earn a salary that way. After a brief battle, Spider-Man made his proposal. "Let's get down to business," he explained. "How much does the job pay? I figure I'm worth your top salary!" Unfortunately, the Invisible Girl explained, the Fantastic Four was a non-profit organization. Mr. Fantastic added, "We pay no salaries or bonuses! Any profit we make goes into scientific research!" (*Amazing Spider-Man* No. 1). In the second issue, though, Peter came up with a plan that would work, and one that would become a central part of the Spider-Man mythos. During a battle between Spider-Man and the Vulture, Peter set up a miniature camera to take pictures that he could sell to J. Jonah Jameson. The plan worked, and Jameson paid Peter a tidy sum for the photographs of Spider-Man. Of course, Peter immediately brought the money to a happy Aunt May, telling her that he "paid the rent for a full year and tomorrow I'm buying you the newest kitchen appliances you ever drooled over" (*Amazing Spider-Man* No. 2).

Peter's idea to join the Fantastic Four reflects the straddler desire to move up in the world. If we think of the group as a corporation (albeit a non-profit one), it is easy to see parallels between Spider-Man's proposal and the fact that many straddlers find themselves working for large companies. Many of them feel like they don't quite fit in there either, and some become so alienated by the upper-middle class atmosphere that they eventually leave. It's easy to imagine a scenario where Spider-Man would be accepted into the Fantastic Four only to leave a few years later when their values and culture didn't mesh with his.[1] Peter's other money-making ventures were typical of working class efforts to make money in any way possible in order to help support their family. As Alfred Lubrano explains, the attitude of members of the working class toward jobs is that they are all about money. In their eyes, the purpose of a job is not to have fun, overcome a challenge, or be happy. The point of a job is to make money. "What gives you comfort besides your family?" Lubrano's father once asked him. "Money, only money" (107).

---

[1] In fact, that very thing may be taking place as this is written, with the Avengers, in the Civil War series.

For many straddlers, the most important separation between themselves and people from their working class upbringing is college. But for many straddlers, higher education is a struggle, and the same is certainly true for Peter Parker. And the biggest reason for this is that straddlers (including Peter) often have to pay for college themselves. Although we find out that he was awarded a scholarship to Empire State University during his high-school graduation ceremony (*Amazing Spider-Man* No. 28), it was clear over the course of the next 157 issues (from 1965 to 1978, when he finally graduated from college) that this scholarship did not last. As with most college students, expenses like rent, books, and food created a huge financial drain for Peter, and he was forced to continue working for the *Daily Bugle* to pay for them. Peter realized this early on, announcing shortly after the first day of school that "maybe I ought to forget about college! Even though my scholarship pays the tuition, I still can't afford it! If I could get a full-time job—bring in some real money—that's what we need!" (*Amazing Spider-Man* No. 31). His adventures as Spider-Man—essentially his second job—also caused Peter to be a distracted student who missed classes and was frequently unable to complete his assignments.

Still, Peter was dedicated to the idea of going to college and getting his degree (in part because he didn't want to disappoint Aunt May), but he also had some feelings of ambivalence about it. This came out in the many battles that Spider-Man fought against research scientists—the goal that presumably Peter was going to college to achieve. If we interpret his battles against villains like the Lizard (secretly scientist Curt Connors) and Doctor Octopus psychologically, we can make the argument that Peter was fighting against his own aspirations. Dr. Connors, in particular, was a role model and friend for Spider-Man, but his efforts to solve his disability through science result in his transformation into the evil Lizard. Peter also got into trouble when he relied on his science too much. The most famous example of this took place when Peter, realizing that he could never marry his beloved Gwen Stacy if he remained Spider-Man, developed a serum to take away his powers. The serum backfired and resulted in Peter growing four extra arms (*Amazing Spider-Man* No. 100). Through much of the mid-1970s, Spider-Man's primary villain, the evil genius who essentially manipulated his life for years, was a character called the Jackal. In his final appearances in issues No. 148 and No. 149, it was shockingly revealed that the Jackal was actually Peter's long-time teacher, Professor Warren. Given this, we can see that Peter had some issues with both his long-term goals as well as the people who were supposed to be helping him achieve them. This is not unlike straddlers who know they need a college education to bring themselves out of their working-class environments, but don't enjoy the rhetoric and snobbishness they find there.

College is not where those difficulties end, though. Successful straddlers who find themselves in corporate boardrooms and in government service often find themselves surrounded by members of the upper classes. Lubrano suggests that this brings about conflicts at the office because of miscommunication, clashing personal styles, or divergent values about work. For Spider-Man, his conflicts with members of the upper class came in the form of battles with super villains. The most prominent among these was undoubtedly the Green Goblin, the secret identity of Norman Osborn, a rich industrialist who was able to provide everything for his son Harry, one of Peter Parker's close friends, except quality time together. From the beginning, the Green Goblin was a thorn in Spider-Man's side. But once he discovered the hero's true identity, the Goblin was driven even further insane and became increasingly vicious. In the end, the upper class Green Goblin killed Gwen Stacy, the young, upper class woman Peter had been in love with. It's almost as if the Goblin was an exaggerated version of Osborn, an exaggerated version of the upper-class executive who wanted to deny Peter the goals that he had manifested through his Spider-Man identity. Maybe it seemed to the Green Goblin that Spider-Man had risen above his (Peter's) proper station in life. Maybe the Goblin was offended that Spider-Man was unwilling to demonstrate upper-class values like a desire for individual achievement and a focus on gaining personal power (traditional hallmarks of villains), and hence does not really belong in the realm of people with power.

Whatever it was, the reaction that Peter got from the Green Goblin was similar to (although more dramatic and dangerous than) the reaction that many straddlers get from members of the upper class. According to Lubrano, it is common for straddlers to get more than their share of resentment from co-workers and others who see people rising up from their working-class origins as invaders who don't really have the correct cultural tools to fit into this more privileged group. This attitude might even help to explain the reasons behind *Daily Bugle* publisher J. Jonah Jameson's perpetual anger at Spider-Man. Perhaps Jameson sees himself as a crusading journalist, working to help the people of New York City out of a sense of paternalistic duty. To have a Johnny-come-lately like Spider-Man infringe on his turf, and to do it in a way that lacks the decorum of the upper class, would be particularly infuriating to Jameson. In some ways, it might be akin to the disgust that some members of "old money" upper-class families feel toward the *nouveau riche*.

Straddlers find themselves frequently not getting along with members of the upper classes, but they also have to cope with anger and resentment from parents and other family members who remain in the working class. Alfred Lubrano writes about being called a "traitor" by people from his old neighborhood, in part because he criticized their racism but also because he left the community and the working-class world found there (111). Peter Parker didn't have to deal with anger from his family, but he did have to cope with Aunt May's irrational fear of Spider-Man. Her feelings blinded her so much that she was even able to take in the "polite" Doctor Octopus as a boarder. She didn't see that he was a criminal, simply because he told her that "he was just trying to stop that horrible Spider-Man!" (*Amazing Spider-Man* No. 54). It's almost as if Aunt May had transferred her fears of being abandoned by the upwardly mobile Peter to Spider-Man, the symbol of the difference that was allowing him to move out of his working-class environment. The anger that many straddlers feel from family members is very similar; working-class parents want their children to be successful, but not so much that they abandon the values and people with whom they were raised.

Spider-Man's complicated class status was established early on in the series and continued as these story elements became part of the character's mythos. When it came time to make a big-budget Hollywood film version of Spider-Man, his position as a straddler was re-introduced for both newcomers and those who wanted to see the classic version of the character. The Sam Raimi version of Spider-Man includes struggles with money and jobs. In *Spider-Man 2*, Aunt May can't keep up with her house payments and Peter continues to work as a photographer for the *Daily Bugle* and briefly as a pizza delivery boy. His college classes suffer from his paid employment as well as his obligations as Spider-Man. The class conflicts that he experiences in the comic book appear on the screen through the villains: the Green Goblin/Norman Osborn, owner of a huge corporation and an even more impressive apartment building somewhere in Manhattan; Harry Osborn, Peter's friend but sworn enemy of Spider-Man; and the apparently quite rich Dr. Otto Octavius who, in a fit of pride, thinks that he alone can control the power of nuclear fusion.

In some ways, the movies have even emphasized the class elements in Spider-Man more than the comics, especially through the character of Mary Jane. In the first movie, we discover that she lives next door to the Parkers in a clearly working-class neighborhood in New York. Like Peter, she is a straddler, with plans to use her special abilities—acting—to get out of that environment and move up in the world. It takes time—in the first movie, Mary Jane is working as a waitress—but she is eventually successful, landing a starring role on Broadway in the second film. She is even engaged to be married to J. Jonah Jameson's son John, a former astronaut. But after coming to understand Peter's obligations as Spider-Man, Mary Jane leaves the elaborate ceremony to find Peter in his dingy apartment. Clearly, like a good straddler, she still wants to move up—she hasn't given up her career and she accepts Peter's upward mobility as Spider-Man—but she's also not ready to completely abandon her working-class background to become part of the upper-class world of J. Jonah Jameson and his son.

Through hundreds of issues of comics and two films, Spider-Man has been established as a hero whose class is a central part of his character. The most important demonstration of this can be found in the ultimate lesson of his adventures. At the end of his first story in

Amazing Fantasy No. 15, Peter Parker learned that "with great power there must also come—great responsibility." For Spider-Man, this sense of responsibility is about obligation. It's about giving back to his neighborhood and especially to the people that got him to that point, namely Uncle Ben and Aunt May. In *Amazing Spider-Man* No. 33, the hero was trapped beneath a mountain of debris, with a serum that could save the life of Aunt May just out of his reach. At first, Spider-Man thought his situation was hopeless. But then he reminded himself of his responsibility to them, of the responsibility that he neglected when his uncle was killed. "The two people in all the world who've been kindest to me! I can't fail again! It can't happen a second time! I won't let it—I won't! No matter what the odds—no matter what the cost—I'll get that serum to Aunt May!" Driven by his sense of obligation and responsibility, Spider-Man did the impossible: lifting the debris, he escaped with the serum, eventually saving Aunt May from a certain death. This is the epitome of Spider-Man's working-class background. He may be a straddler. He may want to push himself out of the working class. But his sense of responsibility keeps pulling him back. Straddlers share this sense of obligation, which is why many of them go out of their way to hire fellow working-class people. Many straddlers also frequently go back to their old neighborhoods and try to teach working-class values to their own children.

We can compare this to the attitudes demonstrated by many members of the upper classes. Lubrano suggests they "can grow up with what sociologists describe as a sense of entitlement that will carry them through their lives" (9). In other words, he argues, many members of the upper classes develop a sense of ownership and belonging, a sense that the world somehow owes them a good job and a comfortable life, because that's all they've ever known. In our world, this sense of entitlement might be seen as a personality problem, but in the comic-book world of Spider-Man, entitlement is what motivates villains like the Green Goblin and Dr. Octopus. They believe that the world owes them something; they believe that their power, wealth, or genius means that they deserve special treatment, that the laws and rules of society don't apply to them. It is the job of Spider-

Man, and perhaps every superhero, to show these villains the error of their ways—that their superiority does not entitle them to anything. And Spider-Man knows this better than anyone. It was his brief feeling of entitlement that cost his uncle Ben his life. In learning about responsibility, Spider-Man came to understand that power is an accident, an act of luck, and hence should not be used for personal gain but rather for the benefit of others. And it was Peter Parker's working-class background that allowed him to learn this lesson so well. Struggle, says Alfred Lubrano, "is central to blue-collar life and the chief architect of character" (18). It teaches members of the working class that sometimes they will need help, so they better help others whenever they get the chance to do it. Spider-Man may have the power to move up in the world, to become a straddler who leaves the working class for higher levels on the social hierarchy, but the lesson that he learned growing up—that with great power comes great responsibility—is what makes him a working-class hero.

Ultimately, it is the mask—the Spider-Man identity—that allows Peter to achieve the goal of the straddler: to be part of both the upwardly mobile world and its working-class counterpart. The straddler is one person made into two: one at work or in school, another in the old neighborhood or with family. And Peter Parker is also one person made into two, only his division is more dramatic and more visual than that of other straddlers. The goal of wearing a mask and having a secret identity, as well as the hope of straddlers generally, is to have the worlds of these two people remain separate. As much as Peter would like this to continue, the boundaries are often violated, creating what might be the most important tension in the Spider-Man stories. For straddlers, then, the lesson of Spider-Man is that these two worlds will collide, no matter how much they want them to be secret. What makes the Spider-Man story resonate with readers is this common situation. What makes Spider-Man into a role model, especially for straddlers in his same situation, is his ability to maintain both his upper-class goals and his working-class values in the face of these challenges. And in this way, he is able to create a unified identity for himself that integrates the strengths of both of these worlds.

MATTHEW PUSTZ is the author of *Comic Book Culture: Fanboys and True Believers*, published in 2000 by the University Press of Mississippi. He received his doctorate in American Studies from the University of Iowa, and he has taught there and at Kirkwood Community College in Cedar Rapids, Iowa. He currently lives in the Boston area.

References

Conway, Gerry (w), Ross Andru (p), and Mike Esposito and Dave Hunt (i). *Amazing Spider-Man* No. 148. Marvel Comics: September 1975.

Daniels, Les. *Marvel: Five Fabulous Decades of the World's Greatest Comics*. New York: Harry N. Abrams, Inc., Publishers, 1995.

Fingeroth, Danny. *Superman on the Couch: What Superheroes Really Tell Us About Ourselves and Our Society*. New York and London: Continuum, 2004.

Jones, Gerard and Will Jacobs. *The Comic Book Heroes*. Rocklin, CA: Prima Publishing, 1997.

Lee, Stan. *Origins of Marvel Comics*. New York: Simon and Schuster, 1974.

——(w), and Steve Ditko (a). *Amazing Fantasy* No. 15. Atlas Magazines (Marvel Comics): September 1962.

——(w), and Steve Ditko (a). *Amazing Spider-Man* No. 1. Non-Pareil Publishing Corp. (Marvel Comics): March 1963.

——(w), and Steve Ditko (a). *Amazing Spider-Man* No. 2. Non-Pareil Publishing Corp. (Marvel Comics): May 1963.

——(w), and Steve Ditko (a). *Amazing Spider-Man* No. 28. Non-Pareil Publishing Corp. (Marvel Comics): September 1965.

——(w), and Steve Ditko (a). *Amazing Spider-Man* No. 31. Non-Pareil Publishing Corp. (Marvel Comics): December 1965.

——(w), and Steve Ditko (a). *Amazing Spider-Man* No. 33. Non-Pareil Publishing Corp. (Marvel Comics): February 1966.

——(w), Gil Kane (p), and Frank Giacoia (i). *Amazing Spider-Man* No. 100. Magazine Management Co. (Marvel Comics): September 1971.

——(w), John Romita (p), and Mickey Demeo (i). *Amazing Spider-Man* No. 40. Non-Pareil Publishing Corp. (Marvel Comics): September 1966.

——(w), John Romita (p), and Mickey Demeo (i). *Amazing Spider-Man* No. 54. Non-Pareil Publishing Corp. (Marvel Comics): November 1967.

Lubrano, Alfred. *Limbo: Blue-Collar Roots, White-Collar Dreams*. Hoboken, NJ: John Wiley & Sons, Inc., 2004.

Pustz, Matthew J. *Comic Book Culture: Fanboys and True Believers*. Jackson, MS: University Press of Mississippi, 1999.

Sims, Joe. "Spiderman: Proletarian Hero?" *Political Affairs Magazine* 8 May 2005. http://www.politicalaffairs.net/article/articlereview/181/1/32/.

Wright, Bradford W. *Comic Book Nation: The Transformation of Youth Culture in America*. Baltimore and London: The Johns Hopkins University Press, 2001.

MICHAEL A. BURSTEIN

The Friendly Neighborhood of Peter Parker

Elsewhere I've mentioned how I identified with Peter Parker as a reader before I ever came to write about him, and it wasn't just because his internal life resembled mine. Like Peter, I grew up in Queens, in the early 1960s, and much of the implied world that surrounded him in those early comics felt very familiar to me—eerily so, in some cases. While it's true Peter Parker is in many ways an Everyman that anyone who's passed through the agonies of adolescence can identify with, as Michael A. Burstein points out, those of us who grew up near him have a special sense of what made him the hero he was destined to become....

EVERY COMIC-BOOK SUPERHERO has a home base. It's necessary; a hero has to live somewhere. Even though superheroes often deal with major disasters around the world, they still have to concentrate most of their heroics in one location. And often, the choice of a hero's hometown defines much of what the hero does.

In the DC Comics universe, superheroes tend to live in fictional cities such as Metropolis or Gotham. Editors at DC often refer to Metropolis as being New York City in the daytime and to Gotham as New York City at night. There's a major advantage to using a fictional setting as a character's home base; a writer can kill off the mayor or have a super battle result in citywide destruction without worrying about what the repercussions would be like in the real world.

But when Stan Lee began co-creating superheroes for Marvel Comics in the 1960s, he decided that their heroes wouldn't live in fictional cities. Instead, he located most of the heroes in and around the real city of New York. This not only allowed the heroes to team up, but also encouraged reader identification. A comic-book fan walking past the Empire State Building, for example, might get a thrill from remembering that a major battle took place near there between the Fantastic Four and Doctor Doom just the month before!

If your heroes are living in New York City, the obvious place to locate them is the borough of Manhattan. The tall buildings and teeming streets create the perfect tableau for super-powered battles. And the ideal base for a super-powered team could be a huge office tower, which is where Stan Lee placed the Fantastic Four. But when it came time to create Spider-Man, Lee and co-creator Steve Ditko chose to do something different.

Spider-Man wasn't supposed to be a perfect adult hero, but a hero that the teenage comic-book readers could relate to more easily. As Lee has noted repeatedly in interviews, just because you get bitten by a radioactive spider and develop superpowers doesn't mean that you stop being a teenager with a teenager's typical problems. So Lee and Ditko made Peter Parker a picked-on adolescent, and despite his powers Peter remained a picked-on adolescent.

And, being a typical teenager, Peter didn't have the resources to fund any sort of secret lair or hero headquarters. He didn't have a Fortress of Solitude or a Spider-Cave. What he had was an upstairs bedroom in the house of his aunt May and uncle Ben, a house that stood in the heart of the middle-class neighborhood of Forest Hills, Queens.

Although today Peter Parker's home neighborhood is considered a well-established part of the mythos, it actually wasn't identified until *Amazing Spider-Man* No. 7 (December 1962). On page four, panel five shows the Parkers' home, a modest two-story house set apart from the one next door. Peter waits until his spider-sense tells him that the streets are clear, because, as he thinks, "I can't ever take the chance of someone seeing me leave the house in daylight!" In the next panel, a boy named Bobby shouts to his parents that he sees Spider-Man swinging across the rooftops, although Spider-Man is not actually shown in the panel. The boy's parents, busy talking to a neighbor, dismiss the notion. As his mother says, "What would Spider-Man be doing here, in a quiet residential neighborhood in Forest Hills?"

I was that boy. I grew up in Forest Hills, Queens in the 1970s and 1980s, and from the age of five I was an avid reader of comic books. I admit that I was more of a DC Comics fan than a Marvel Comics fan, but Spider-Man always held a special place of pride in my heart. After all, for those of us growing up in Forest Hills, Spider-Man was one of us. In fact, my schoolyard friends and I used to joke about seeing Spider-Man swinging from the rooftops on our way home from school.

But, sad to say, a fictional setting, even one based on reality, always diverges from the real world. Even from the start, Peter Parker's Forest Hills differed from my own in many respects. Although Peter's Forest Hills was supposed to be middle-class like the real one, it often seemed more working-class. He didn't patronize the familiar stores of the neighborhood, or even attend a high school with the correct name! The Forest Hills of Marvel Comics may have enjoyed a certain level of verisimilitude, but not accuracy.

The reasons for the differences are fairly obvious. Although a lot of books and Web sites claim that Stan Lee grew up in Forest Hills, it just isn't so. According to Lee's own autobiography, *Excelsior!: The Amazing Life of Stan Lee* by Stan Lee and George Mair, Lee grew up on the upper west side of Manhattan and attended high school in the Bronx. Also, as I noted before, it seems evident that Lee and Ditko didn't make the decision that Peter lived in Forest Hills until a few issues of *Amazing Spider-Man* had already been published. It's understandable that their version of Forest Hills would have already diverged from the real one.

But as I was growing up, I would often look up at the rooftops of the commercial buildings of my neighborhood, imagining a web-slinger coming home after a hard day's work of fighting bad guys, and I would ask myself: what would Peter's life, and Spider-Man's life, have been like if he had grown up in the real Forest Hills?

———

In order to answer that question, we must first consider which Peter Parker we're talking about. Although Spider-Man was introduced in the 1960s, there have been other versions of the character since then. For example, the Spider-Man of the Ultimate Marvel line of comics differs from the Spider-Man of the movies, and both differ from the Spider-Man of the original flagship comic book *Amazing Spider-Man*.

And, oddly enough, so does the original Spider-Man differ from the Spider-Man of today.

Theoretically, we can draw a continuous line from the Spider-Man who first appeared in *Amazing Spider-Man* in the 1960s to the Spider-Man who appears in that exact same comic book today. But consider the implications of equating the Spider-Man of 1962 with the Spider-Man of 2007. A Peter Parker who graduated from high school in 1965 would have been born around 1947, and would be sixty years old today. And yet in the current comic book, Peter is clearly meant to be in his late twenties or early thirties. So how do we deal with this issue?

Comic-book companies have dealt with this issue of the age of a character in a variety of ways; in fact, one of the reasons the editors at DC Comics created their parallel universes was so they could create new, younger versions of their old Golden Age characters. The Ultimate Marvel line mentioned before is another example of dealing with this issue of character age. It was launched in the year 2000 with a brand-new, fifteen-year-old version of Peter Parker, who is clearly not the same Peter Parker that has existed since the 1960s. As long as the two characters are clearly different versions of the same person, living in different fictional universes, there's no need to reconcile them.

But how do you reconcile the one, "true" Spider-Man of the 1960s with the one of the year 2007, given how old that ought to make him today? Well, the simplest thing to do is to ignore the problem. Batman is eternally twenty-nine, Superman thirty-four. Comic-book characters age slowly, and we just deal with it.

For purposes of this essay, I plan to look first at Peter's life as it would have been in the Forest Hills of the 1960s, to explore the neighborhood as it would have been for Peter during the time Spider-Man was originally being written. But in the spirit of comic-book time-warping, I'm also going to include a few of the features that the neighborhood of the 1970s would have offered a teenage Peter Parker. Because, to be honest, that's the Forest Hills that I remember the best.

So for now, let us step away from Peter Parker for a bit and examine the neighborhood of Forest Hills. Forest Hills is located in the central part of Queens, one of the four outer boroughs that, along with Manhattan, were consolidated into the city of New York in 1898. Prior to that, the neighborhoods of Queens were a collection of small villages and farms. Forest Hills existed for many years in this state, known under the name Whitepot. Major development of the neighborhood didn't start until the early years of the twentieth century.

The developers originally envisioned the neighborhood as a place where working-class folk could live side-by-side with the middle-class and the well-to-do. Ironically, the development of housing in Forest Hills became so expensive that this dream quickly faded away. In fact, one particular section of Forest Hills, known as Forest Hills Gardens or just the Gardens, is one of the oldest planned communities in the country. Although the community is not closed off to traffic, the residents of the Gardens, who live mostly in Tudor-style homes, jointly own the streets, and so are the only ones allowed to park there. They also pay for a private security force to keep the Gardens safe.

For people who didn't live in Forest Hills, the neighborhood was for a long time associated with tennis, due to the fact that the U.S. Open was played there. But for the residents of the neighborhood, the tournament was barely on the radar. In fact, most residents, who identifed themselves as being solidly middle-class, would shake their heads at the thought that their neighborhood was a swanky place. The housing is a mix of brick apartment buildings and a scattering of private houses. The population, both then and now, is mostly made up of Jewish and Catholic families, who see the neighborhood as being a good place to raise children while still providing easy access to Manhattan.

Today, as in the 1960s, Forest Hills is a major nexus. Subways and buses converge at many places in the neighborhood, but particularly at a street known to any native as 71st-Continental Avenue (please note: *not* 71st *and* Continental, as the one avenue shares the two names). Not only is there a major subway station there, but only a block away from the subway commuters can board the Long Island Rail Road at Station Square, making the trip to Manhattan in less than fifteen minutes. Throughout the 1960s, and even to this day, that avenue and the streets nearby served as a major shopping area for the neighborhood, with stores and restaurants and movie theaters catering to all tastes and ages.

In short, the Forest Hills of the 1960s was a friendly neighborhood of its own, reminiscent of a traditional small American town. It was a place where parents felt safe sending their children to school on foot, a place where, in the afternoon, kids hung out in the playground or the soda shop, took in a movie, or browsed at a bookstore. It was a place that fostered traditional American values.

And now that we've set the stage, let's bring on Forest Hills resident Peter Parker, a typical teenager of the 1960s.

Let's start with his birthplace. In the life-changing issue No. 533 (August 2006) of *Amazing Spider-Man*, which took place during Marvel's *Civil War*, Peter Parker revealed his secret identity to the world. Shortly thereafter, a news program reported details they had dug up about Peter's life. One of these was that Peter "was born in Forest Hills, New York, to Richard and Mary Fitzpatrick Parker."

Forest Hills currently has two hospitals, Parkway Hospital and Forest Hills Hospital. But in the 1960s, Mary Parker would have been most likely to go to Kew Gardens Hospital, as it had a well-known maternity ward. That hospital, which no longer exists, was located on the corner of Queens Boulevard and Union Turnpike, two major thoroughfares that meet at the border of Forest Hills and Kew Gardens. So even though that hospital was technically considered to be in the adjoining neighborhood, it was literally on the border. It's not much of an error to claim that a person born in that hospital was born in Forest Hills.

We don't know where Peter lived when his parents were still alive, but we do know what his home was like once he started living with his uncle and aunt. As I noted before, throughout the early issues of *Amazing Spider-Man*, Peter's house was portrayed as a modest two-story home with an attic. But this was not always consistent. Sometimes Peter's home appeared as a row house, very similar to the houses all up and down the block. The truth is that overly modest houses aren't very predominant in Forest Hills. This version of Peter's home looks more like it belongs in Jackson Heights or Astoria, which at the time had more of the flavor of working-class neighborhoods. Still, there are streets in the real Forest Hills that look close enough to Spider-Man's street that residents of the neighborhood wouldn't have to suspend their disbelief when picking up an issue of the comic book.

But then writer David Michelinie came along and blew away that fragile grasp on the real Forest Hills. In *Amazing Spider-Man* No. 317 (July 1989), he gave Peter Parker's family a specific address. On page four, panel two, we see a change of address form filled out by Peter that gives his address as 20 Ingram Street. (A portion of this form showing the street name but not the full house number had appeared in the previous issue.) As it turns out, a real-life Parker family has been living at that address since 1974. It is possible that Michelinie, needing an address for Peter Parker, checked a Forest Hills phone book, found a Parker family listed, and as an in-joke used that address. But in doing so, he made a mistake.

The real Parker house is a rather large stone Edwardian-style house built in 1916 and situated in Forest Hills Gardens. As I noted before, the Gardens is an expensive subsection of the neighborhood where the residents actually own the streets and pay for their own private security force. From the outside, the real-life Parker house is much more impressive than the drawings of Peter's house found in the comic books. From the inside...well, I could only guess, because the Parkers living there do not want to be bothered by Spider-Man fans (so please leave them alone!). But suffice it to say that a house like that would not be owned or even rented by someone in the dire financial straits that Aunt May and Peter often found them-

THE REAL PARKER HOUSE

selves in. If Peter had grown up in the real Forest Hills, he undoubtedly would have lived in some other part of the neighborhood. In fact, it's more likely that he would have lived in an apartment building rather than a private home.

We turn now to Peter's education. According to the comic book, Peter attended Midtown High. In fact, Midtown High is given as Peter's school on the very first page of his very first appearance anywhere, in *Amazing Fantasy* No. 15 (August 1962). While Midtown High is a nice, generic name for a high school, there is no high school called Midtown High in Queens. There isn't even one by that name in midtown Manhattan. And given the fact that Peter was taken in by his aunt and uncle at a younger age, his Forest Hills education would not have started with high school.

Peter would have started at P.S. 101, School in the Garden, the elementary school located at 2 Russell Place inside Forest Hills Gardens. At the time, grades were generally divided into classes of about thirty students each, and there Peter would have been exposed to the same classmates who would have tormented him for years. This is because after graduating from P.S. 101, Peter and his classmates would have gone as a group to Russell Sage Junior High School. Now, here's where things get interesting. Starting in ninth grade, Peter probably would have gone on to Forest Hills High School, located at 67-01 110th Street—except for one minor detail. It's generally accepted that Peter is a scientific genius. In the 1960s, there were three examination high schools that gifted boys could attend—Bronx Science, Brooklyn Tech, and Stuyvesant. (For those who wonder about the omission of Hunter College High School, remember that Hunter was an all-girls school until the 1970s.) Surely these schools would have analogs in the Marvel universe. If Peter was really as bright as the comic-book stories claim, why didn't Uncle Ben and Aunt May send him to one of those schools? After all, they are free to attend, and all provide a quality education for a gifted science student.

The answer would probably lie in the commute. Even though these schools offered good opportunities for students, not every parent was willing to let their child take the subway and/or public bus to school every day. If Peter had decided to attend Bronx Science, he would have had close to a two-hour commute every day, through some possibly dangerous neighborhoods. Uncle Ben and Aunt May would have surely considered Peter too fragile to send him off to one of those schools—especially considering the excellent reputation that Forest Hills High School had and continues to have in science.

As evidence, one can point to Forest Hills High School's performance in the Westinghouse Science Talent Search, which in 1998 was renamed the Intel Science Talent Search. Every year since 1941, high-school students have competed in the Science Talent Search by doing original research and writing scientific papers that are easily the equivalent of graduate-level work. Many finalists have gone on to become prize-winning scientists in their later years. And over the course of the twentieth century, quite a few schools have pushed their students to excel in the competition. Forest Hills High School is one of those schools. It ranks third in the country in total number of finalists over the history of the competition. In the 1960s, Forest Hills High School had the following number of finalists per year: two in 1964, one in 1965, one in 1966, three in 1968, and one in 1969. That may not seem like a lot, until you realize that there are only forty finalists each year from high schools all across the country. The statistic becomes even more impressive when you add the fact that competitors from Forest Hills came in second in both 1966 and 1968. A real-world Peter Parker would have had no problem pursuing his scientific aspirations at a place like Forest Hills High School. In fact, he might very well have come in first in 1965, the year that he graduated.

We've looked at Peter's home and school. Even though he was considered a wallflower by his peers, he still had friends of a sort, and he might have hung out with them like any typical teenager. So where would teenagers in Forest Hills have hung out?

In the middle of *Amazing Spider-Man* No. 14 (July 1963), Peter's high-school friends gather in the neighborhood soda shop. In the real Forest Hills, only one place would fit that description—Eddie's Sweet Shop, at 105-29 Metropolitan Avenue. Eddie's is owned by Joe Citrano, and has been since 1968. But the store itself has been a staple of the neighborhood since the 1920s, with its dark wood interior, an array of soda fountains and a menu centered on their homemade ice cream. I used to frequent Eddie's as a kid myself, and it was like stepping back in time to an earlier, simpler era in America's history. In the early 1960s, when Peter and his friends would have gone there, the place was named Witt's, for the owner at the time. According to Vito Citrano, the son of the current owner, high-school kids would have stopped by for an ice cream or a soda, but they probably wouldn't have hung out the way Peter's friends do in the comic. However, it was and still is a place for people to take their dates, and there is no doubt that if either Flash Thompson or Peter Parker wanted to ask Liz Allan out, a movie (perhaps at the Midway or Cinemart) followed by a trip to Witt's would have been just the ticket.

It's also possible that Peter might have gone there with Uncle Ben or Aunt May. In fact, given Peter's outcast status, it seems even more likely that he would have done things with his uncle and aunt. In Queens, that might have meant going to Forest Park, browsing

EDDIE'S SWEET SHOP

the Barnes & Noble and Waldenbooks bookstores, or visiting the Queens Zoo and the New York Hall of Science in Flushing Meadows Corona Park.

He could also have gone to major league baseball games.

The New York Metropolitans, better known as the Mets, began playing baseball in 1962. For seven years, the Mets were perennial underdogs who didn't manage to win a World Series until 1969. Is there any doubt that Peter would have identified with them throughout his teenage years?

Well, one doubt. The Mets played at the Polo Grounds, located on 155th Street in Manhattan, until 1964, when they moved to the newly built Shea Stadium in Flushing, Queens. By the time the Mets were established at Shea, Peter was already in college. So Peter couldn't have attended Mets games in Flushing as a teenager.

But as we noted early on, time becomes fluid when discussing comic-book characters. A writer in the early 1960s would never have sent

Peter to Shea Stadium to see a Mets game, but a writer in the decades that followed wouldn't think twice about it. In fact, Paul Jenkins did just that in *Peter Parker: Spider-Man* Vol. 2 No. 33 (September 2001). The charming story "Maybe Next Year" takes the reader back in time to when Uncle Ben took Peter to game after losing game, until finally they saw the Mets win. Anyone growing up in Queens starting in the late 1960s who cared about baseball invariably would become a Mets fan, so the story (if you'll pardon the expression) hits home. (Of course, having Peter describe the subway trip as starting with the G train at Northern Boulevard makes no sense if they lived in Forest Hills. That subway stop is in Jackson Heights, roughly two or three neighborhoods away. They'd most likely have taken the E or F train from Continental Avenue, and then switched for the 7 train at 74th Street and Roosevelt Avenue.)

As for the Zoo and the Hall of Science, they, too, suffer from a time-warp problem. The Zoo opened as the Flushing Meadows Zoo in 1968, and the Hall of Science opened in 1964, as part of the World's Fair. If we assume that Peter grew up in Forest Hills in the 1950s and 1960s, then neither of them would have yet existed when he was a kid. In fact, the Hall of Science would have opened as Peter entered his senior year of high school, a little late for it to have any effect on him. But if we warp time a little bit, as comic-book writers must, we can easily assume that the two institutions were a vital part of his development.

Of course, even when he was a teenager Peter didn't always stay in Forest Hills. Very early in his superhero career, he ventured into Manhattan to sell photos of himself as Spider-Man to the *Daily Bugle*, a tabloid newspaper. At the time, there were many tabloids in New York City, the two most prominent being the *Daily News* and the *New York Post*. The *Daily Bugle* was probably modeled after these two papers, although it should be noted that its typographic style more often resembles that of the *Post*.

Even the *Bugle* didn't exist at first. In *Amazing Spider-Man* No. 2 (May 1963), Peter brings photos to J. Jonah Jameson, but he is presented as the owner and editor of something called *NOW* magazine.

For the sake of argument, however, let's assume that a real-world Peter brought photos of Spider-Man to the *News* or the *Post*. What would have happened? Chances are he would have managed to sell them, and maybe even gotten himself listed as a freelancer. But it's just as likely that the editor would have become highly suspicious of how this kid was getting all these photos. Indeed, a few times Peter had to explain that he was getting all these pictures because he had managed to cut a deal with the real Spider-Man. Technically, that's a violation of journalistic ethics, but probably not enough of one to have put the kibosh on the photos, even had the editor known.

On a more somber note, there is one event that would have had major impact on Peter Parker's young life. Interestingly enough, it didn't take place in Forest Hills, but rather in Kew Gardens, the previously mentioned neighborhood next door. Early in the morning of March 13, 1964, a twenty-eight-year-old woman named Kitty Genovese was returning home from her job as a bar manager in Hollis to her apartment in Kew Gardens. She parked her car in the train station parking lot and was walking back to her place when she was attacked by a man named Winston Moseley. Moseley was driven off by shouts from some of the neighbors, but over a half-hour period he returned twice and finally murdered her. Despite her shouts, and the fact that her struggles woke people in the neighborhood, no one called the police until it was too late.

At first, the murder was just another story buried away in the news, but A. M. Rosenthal, who at the time was the *New York Times* Metropolitan editor, assigned reporter Marty Gansberg to investigate deeper. The article Gansberg wrote, "Thirty-Eight Who Saw Murder Didn't Call the Police," appeared in the March 27, 1964 *New York Times* and triggered a national discussion.

The thrust of the article is contained within the misleading title. Gansberg presented Genovese's neighbors as a group of "respectable, law-abiding citizens" whose apathy and desire not to get involved contributed to her murder. While it is true that some of Genovese's neighbors ignored her screams throughout her half-hour ordeal, the fact is that when Genovese first screamed, lights went on in a near-

WHERE KITTY GENOVESE DIED

by building and a man shouted to Moseley to leave Genovese alone. When Moseley ran away, apparently most of the neighbors believed that was the end of it.

Many years later, others analyzed both the attacks and the sociology of the neighborhood, and presented reasons other than apathy behind the seemingly callous behavior of Genovese's neighbors. But at the time Gansberg's article was published, people took it at face value that thirty-eight New Yorkers had witnessed a murder from their safe apartments and done nothing to intervene. Peter was still in the early stages of his career as Spider-Man in 1964, and still feeling his way as a hero. His own apathy had contributed to the death of his uncle Ben, leading Peter to the oft-cited belief that with great power there must also come great responsibility. One can easily imagine Peter reacting to the shocking news of this notorious murder, one that took place practically in his own backyard, by rededicating himself to his heroics.[1]

Only a few years after Marvel Comics introduced Peter Parker to fans as the hero who lived in Forest Hills, it was time for him to move. The story goes that early on, Stan Lee asked the fans if Spider-Man should grow up or remain a teenager forever. The fans responded that they wanted to see Peter grow, which makes sense if they wanted to continue to identify with him. So in *Amazing Spider-Man* No. 28 (September 1965), Peter Parker finally graduated from Midtown High. Despite his family's dire financial straits, Peter was able to attend college, because Empire State University, otherwise known as ESU, gave him a full-tuition science scholarship.

ESU, of course, is another fictional school that exists solely in the Marvel universe. Given its Greenwich Village location, ESU is most likely a stand-in for New York University. NYU is an excellent school, but if we're assuming that Peter is a stellar science student, there is a university he was more likely to want to attend. That, of course, is New York City's only Ivy League school, Columbia University. Still, it's unlikely that Columbia would have come up with the scholarship money that Peter and his aunt May depended upon for his education. NYU, on the other hand, would have appreciated Peter's value

---

[1] In fact, one writer did imagine that the murder of Kitty Genovese would lead someone to don a costume. In issue No. 6 of the seminal Alan Moore and Dave Gibbons series *Watchmen*, the vigilante Rorschach claims to have been inspired by Genovese's murder.

as a scientist, and it's most likely that he would have ended up there. Regardless, he would have bid farewell to Forest Hills.

But we can't leave Forest Hills behind without answering the most important question of all: where would Peter have bought his comic books?

In the 1960s, comic-book specialty stores like Mike's Comics or Little Nemo's, both of which were staples of Forest Hills for many years, did not yet exist. For decades, kids wanting comics had to buy them at candy stores, which also stocked newspapers, magazines, sodas, and other sundries. Peter probably would have gone to one of the two candy stores on Queens Boulevard, which stood opposite each other at the top of the entrances to the 75th Avenue subway station.

And of course, once Little Nemo's opened in the 1970s, its location right near the corner of Ascan Avenue and Austin Street would have made it the prime place for Peter to buy his books. I know that for a fact, because Peter runs right through that intersection in the first Spider-Man film.

So, in the end, what would have been the fate of a real-world Peter Parker? He would have attended P.S. 101, Russell Sage Junior High School, and then probably ended up at Forest Hills High School. He would have taken in movies at the Midway Theater, bought books at Barnes & Noble and Waldenbooks, and hung out at Eddie's Sweet Shop. He would have gone to Shea Stadium, the Queens Zoo, and the New York Hall of Science, where he would have developed his love of science. He would have won the Westinghouse Science Talent Search and earned a scholarship to New York University. He would have been picked on by his peers, but he would have found solace in science fiction and comic books.

And, like every other child of Forest Hills, he would remember his middle-class roots fondly and find himself drawn to return, over and over again.

MICHAEL A. BURSTEIN, winner of the 1997 Campbell Award for Best New Writer, has earned ten Hugo nominations and two Nebula nominations for his short fiction. Burstein grew up in Forest Hills, Queens, but now lives with his wife Nomi in Brookline, Massachusetts, where he is an elected town meeting member and library trustee. He has two degrees in physics and attended the Clarion Workshop. He taught science for many years and he currently edits science textbooks. More information on Burstein and his work, as well a link to his blog, can be found on his Web page, http://www.mabfan.com.

References

Bates, Rick, Director of Development & Corporate Relations, Science Service. E-mail interview, 13 June 2006.

Citrano, Vito, son of the owner of Eddie's Sweet Shop. Phone interview, 9 June 2006. http://nyzoosandaquarium.com/czabout#qz.

De May, J. "Kitty Genovese." *A Picture History of Kew Gardens, NY.* http://www.oldkewgardens.com/ss-nytimes-3.html.

Frey, Stephen, principal of Forest Hills High School. Phone interview, 9 June 2006.

Jenkins, Paul (w), Mark Buckingham (p), and Wayne Faucher (i). "Maybe Next Year." *Peter Parker: Spider-Man* Vol. 2 No. 33. Marvel Comics: September 2001.

Kistler, Alan, comic-book historian. E-mail interview, 19 June 2006 & 23 June 2006.

Lee, Stan and George Mair. *Excelsior!: The Amazing Life of Stan Lee.* Fireside, 2002.

Lee, Stan (w), Steve Ditko (p), and Steve Ditko (i). " Duel to the Death With the Vulture!" *The Amazing Spider-Man* No. 2. Marvel Comics: May 1963.

Lee, Stan (w), Steve Ditko (p), and Steve Ditko (i). "The Grotesque Adventure of the Green Goblin." *The Amazing Spider-Man* No. 14. Marvel Comics: July 1964.

Lee, Stan (w), Steve Ditko (p), and Steve Ditko (i). "The Menace of the Molten Man!" *The Amazing Spider-Man* No. 28. Marvel Comics: September 1965.

Lee, Stan (w), Steve Ditko (p), and Steve Ditko (i). " The Return of the Vulture." *The Amazing Spider-Man* No. 7. Marvel Comics: December 1963.

Lee, Stan (w), Steve Ditko (p), and Steve Ditko (i). "Spider-Man!" *Amazing Fantasy* No. 15. Marvel Comics: August 1962.

Michelinie, David (w), Todd MacFarlane (p), and Todd MacFarlane (i). "The Sand and the Fury!" *The Amazing Spider-Man* No. 317. Marvel Comics: July 1989.

Moore, Alan (w), Dave Gibbons (p), and Dave Gibbons (i). "The Abyss Gazes Also." *Watchmen* No. 6. DC Comics: February 1987.

Rosenthal, A.M. *Thirty-Eight Witnesses: The Kitty Genovese Case.* University of California Press, 1964, 1999.

Shack, Richard. "Is Spider-Man Real? Spinning a Web of a Tale About Queens' Hometown Superhero." *Queens Tribune,* 9 August 2001. (archived at http://www.queenstribune.com/archives/featurearchive/feature2001/0809/feature_story.html).

Straczynski, J. Michael (w), Ron Garney (p), and Bill Reinhold (i). "The Night the War Came Home." *The Amazing Spider-Man* No. 533. Marvel Comics: August 2006.

About Forest Hills. http://www.queensnewyork.com/forest/hills.html.

"About the City Zoos." *New York Zoos and Aquarium.*

Forest Hills, Queens: Information from Answers.com. http://www.answers.com/topic/forest-hills-queens.

"New York Hall of Science." *Wikipedia, the free encyclopedia.* http://en.wikipedia.org/wiki/New_York_Hall_of_Science.

JOSEPH McCABE

Spinning a Web of Shame

Among other things, shame is about keeping secrets—especially keeping secret our hidden belief of who we really are, inside. In that sense, Spider-Man is by definition a creature born of shame, his true self a secret from those he loves and those he fears. Of course there's more to it than that—there always is—as Joseph McCabe makes very clear. . . .

JUST THE OTHER day I was trawling the aisles of a local beach town boutique (the tacky kind that specializes in the sort of gifts one is apt to consider—or at least *admit* to considering—when on vacation). There, between the rubber vomit and the inflatable girlfriends, I spied a row of refrigerator magnets. One in particular caught my eye.

"I Don't Do Guilt," it boasted.

Though this particular credo wasn't as witty as its surrounding brethren, it got me thinking. For I do "do guilt," and very well, thank you. I used to think my prowess stemmed from my Catholic upbringing, in which I faced not only the omnipresent burden of Adam and Eve's original sin, but the constant scrutiny of God and all of my dead relatives with Him in heaven. But I've met many recovering Catholics over the years (none of us are *ex*-Catholics, mind you—as they say, the Church, like the mob, never really lets anyone go), and most have not shared my hyper-awareness of sin. No, it's not a lingering Catholic thing. For better or for worse, I'm just very comfortable with guilt. I do "do" it. Often. Which accounts, in part, for my fascination with Spider-Man.

Spidey, as everyone knows, was born of guilt. Sure, science served as the catalyst, conceiving him, if you will. Guilt, however, was the midwife, marking him in delivery and forever distinguishing him from all other superheroes. As everyone knows, Peter Parker, upon first gaining his spider powers, used them to make money. But faced with the knowledge his uncle Ben was murdered by a criminal he failed to apprehend when given the chance, Parker vowed to use his powers responsibly. From that day forth, Spider-Man was defined by guilt. It's made for a terrific character, one a good deal more interesting than most other superheroes. For guilt is a complex emotion, more sophisticated than, say, anger, which defines the Batman (whose origin story is the only serious rival to Spider-Man's in terms of human gravitas).

But is there a difference between the guilt experienced by Peter Parker in the comics and what is felt by the hero of the blockbuster Spider-Man films? I believe so. And I believe this difference proves that the films' Parker is a more emotionally damaged character than the comic books'. For the comics' Parker—particularly the character penned by Stan Lee in the first ten years or so of his comic-book appearances (to which I'll limit the scope of this essay)—is a creature of guilt, pure and simple, while the films' Parker experiences not only guilt, but also an emotion that appears similar yet is actually different: toxic shame.

A fair number of psychologists have tried to explain the difference between guilt and shame, but perhaps the clearest distinction is given by Fossum and Mason in their book *Facing Shame: Families in Recovery*: "While guilt is a painful feeling of regret and responsibility for one's actions, shame is a painful feeling about one's self as a person" (5).

Author John Bradshaw elaborates on this distinction in his *Healing the Shame That Binds You*. Bradshaw writes that guilt is an emotion that results from behaving in a manner contrary to our beliefs and values. And so normal, healthy guilt results from a belief that one has acted against their principles, and helps prevent such behavior from recurring. It's the bedrock of one's conscience. Shame, however, tends to cut more deeply. Bradshaw further distinguishes between healthy shame—the kind most everyone experiences at some point in their lives—and "toxic" shame.

Healthy shame informs us of our limitations. It gives our lives boundaries and form. And these boundaries "offer safety and allow a more efficient use of energy." They see that we "don't waste ourselves on goals we cannot reach or on things we cannot change" (4). Bradshaw cites, as an example, the case of famous pro football quarterback Joe Namath. After retiring from the NFL, Namath worked for a while as a sportscaster, but wasn't very successful in this role. In an interview, Namath spoke of his disappointment over his failure to be used by the TV network that had hired him. Bradshaw describes this awareness and admission of limitations as an expression of healthy shame.

Toxic shame, however, not only indicates one's limitations; it is, according to Bradshaw, "the all-pervasive sense that one is flawed and defective as a human being. . . . It is like internal bleeding" (10). Toxic shame, as its name suggests, is like a poison. And like a poisonous snake it rears its head to bite the Peter Parker we see in the movies.

Since I've already broached the subject of religion, let's begin our examination of the movie Parker's shame by considering the character's religious affiliation, since some religions are based upon guilt or shame.

Psychologist Michael Lewis points out (to this recovering Catholic's surprise) in his *Shame: The Exposed Self* that "while it is possible to make claims in either direction, my own belief is that Judaism and mainstream Protestantism are more guilt-oriented, while Catholicism and fundamentalist Christian religions are more shame-oriented. I base this distinction on several factors including the role of forgiveness, belief in heaven (and hell), and the nature of action in this world" (206).

So does Peter Parker belong to an organized religion, and if so, which?

The first decade of Spider-Man stories pretty much avoided the subject altogether. Spider-Man co-creator Stan Lee, however, is Jewish, and set Parker's home in the Forest Hills section of Queens (which, in the early '60s, had a sizable Jewish community). Factor in the presence of Aunt May—who, in the early comics, exhibited many of the traits one associates with the stereotypical Jewish mother—and a case could be made that the Peter Parker of the '60s was Jewish. A vote for guilt-orientation in the comics' Parker.

The movies' Parker also appears to hail from Forest Hills, but the Forest Hills of the current millennium, which is more diverse, both ethnically and religiously, than its '60s counterpart. Aunt May no longer fits the Jewish stereotype. In fact, she's overtly Christian in the first film, saying the Lord's Prayer before going to bed. Sharp-eyed viewers might spot a holy water stoup by the front door of her home in *Spider-Man 2*, a sure sign she's Catholic. And since we're told her nephew has always been an obedient lad, following the examples set by his aunt and uncle, it's a safe bet that if May is Catholic, then so is Peter Parker. Of course, not all Catholics experience *toxic* shame, but if we agree they are more prone to shame than others, then we must admit they possess the sort of soil in which to grow its toxic variety.

There are indicators other than religion that provide clues to the movie Parker's shame orientation.

Just consider the type of person Peter Parker was before his fateful accident. In his first appearance (in *Amazing Fantasy* No. 15, "Spider-Man!") Parker was described by a girl on the splash page as "…Midtown High's only professional wallflower!" Yet on the very next page we saw him approaching another girl. "Sally," he said, "I, eh, was wondering if you're busy tonight…?" She rebuked him in favor of "dreamboat" Flash Thompson, but Parker had already proven that, while he may have been a wallflower, he didn't let shyness *completely* prevent him from approaching people, including the opposite sex.

Now consider the Peter Parker of the first *Spider-Man* film. He claims he's lived next door to Mary Jane Watson his entire life. MJ is someone he's loved since "before he liked girls." But it's implied that the first time he speaks to her is on a class trip—*in their final year of high school*. Based on this evidence, it's safe to assume that the Parker of the films is not simply a wallflower or more comfortable on his own than in the company of his peers. Instead, he's experienced debilitating, soul-crushing shyness since he was a child. And evidence suggests extreme shyness is more indicative of shame than guilt.

For example, in Charles Darwin's *The Expression of the Emotions in Man and Animals* the author makes no distinction between shyness and shame. Both involve the same body language—blushing, eyes looking down, etc. But Darwin does distinguish shyness and shame from guilt. As Lewis puts it in *Shame: The Exposed Self*, "Darwin considers guilt more like regret over some 'fault committed'" (23). Although this certainly describes Parker's feelings upon realizing he could have prevented his uncle's murder, keep in mind that, at this early point in the first *Spider-Man* film, Parker has committed no transgression (at least none we're aware of). According to Bradshaw, "Our shyness is our healthy shame in the presence of a stranger," but "shyness can become a serious problem, when it is rooted in toxic shame" (7). Since MJ has lived next door to Parker for his entire life, it's safe to say she's not a stranger. And the kind of shyness Parker displays at the start of that first film is indeed problematic, and telling. For, according to Bradshaw, another symptom of toxic shame is a "tormenting self-consciousness," a "paralyzing internal monitoring [that] causes withdrawal, passivity, and inaction" (13).

It's also worth considering the duration of the movie Parker's shyness, and what this may imply. We know it's lasted since "before he liked girls." Thus we can assume he began experiencing this shyness at a very early age. What then is its source?

According to Bradshaw, "toxic shame is primarily fostered in significant relationships" (25). Families are quite often at the root, particularly parents. And toxic shame can be triggered by abuse or abandonment.

In the comics, Peter Parker *was*, in one sense, abandoned by his parents, though not in a shame-inducing way. Peter's father, Richard

Parker, was a government agent, who left him in the care of Richard's older brother Ben when he and his wife Mary traveled overseas on an undercover assignment. It was during this assignment that Peter's parents were murdered by the criminal mastermind the Red Skull. So Peter came to be raised by his aunt and uncle. Years later, after becoming Spider-Man, Peter discovered—in *Amazing Spider-Man Annual* No. 5—some newspaper clippings his aunt had hidden away, which described his parents as traitors to their country: the secret of their dual identities had died with them. A great deal of emphasis was placed on shame in that annual ("We'll never tell him—about his parents!" said Uncle Ben in a flashback sequence. "We'll let the shame and the sorrow lie—buried with them!"), and on Peter's eventually successful attempt to clear his parents' names. But since Peter was only briefly shamed by the experience (and after he'd reached maturity), his psyche sustained no permanent damage.

The Spider-Man films, however, have not yet given us their version of the Parkers' history. True, it may be identical to that of the comics, but it *could* differ. What if the movies' Peter was deliberately forsaken by his parents? Or perhaps, even worse, abused by them? It's not unusual for children to be taken from dysfunctional or abusive homes and placed in the custody of their relatives. (Even children in big-budget Hollywood films—witness young Luke Skywalker at the end of *Revenge of the Sith*, saved from the clutches of his father Darth Vader and given to *his* aunt and uncle.) Could Peter Parker have developed toxic shame from his parents through physical, sexual, or emotional abuse? In the movies, the possibility is there. In the first *Spider-Man* film, when asked by Norman Osborn about his parents, Peter quickly responds, "I live with my aunt and uncle," sidestepping the issue altogether.

Though they haven't told us anything of his parents, the Spider-Man films do emphasize Parker's relationships, most of them shame-based, with various parental figures. Such behavioral models, according to Bradshaw, can worsen an individual's toxic shame.

Let's start with the movies' Norman Osborn (a.k.a. the Green Goblin). As in the comics, Osborn is portrayed as a workaholic scientist/

industrialist. He has trouble relating to—or even understanding—his son Harry. There's something about him that's emotionally closed off. But he takes a shine to Peter Parker, and sees in him some of his own incentive and intellect. (On the *Spider-Man* DVD's audio commentary track, director Sam Raimi remarks, "In some way [Osborn] had to be a surrogate father to Pete." This dynamic was largely unexplored in the '60s Spider-Man comics, and it serves as further proof of the films' psychological depth.) In both comics and film, Osborn, like Parker, suffers a harrowing lab accident, and finds himself with enhanced, superhuman abilities. He also finds his psyche split in two—between the benevolent Norman and the wicked Goblin. While we might directly attribute this split to his accident, it's possible that Osborn suffered some level of shame beforehand, which damaged his relationship with his son. And as his accident amplified his physical abilities, so too could it have amplified his psychological condition.

But the Osborn of the first *Spider-Man* movie is also distinguished from the comics' Osborn by his dying words to Parker—"Don't tell, Harry," he says. (In the comics, Osborn died silently.) Are his last thoughts of sparing his son the sins of his father, or of simply saving face? Whatever the case, they're words of shame. And Parker, who continually wrestles with his own shame (and so can relate to Osborn), honors them.

Spider-Man 2 presents another shame-based paternal figure for Parker, and another foe for Spider-Man—Dr. Otto Octavius (a.k.a. Doctor Octopus). Like Osborn, Octavius is admired by Peter Parker for his scientific discoveries, and is transformed by a lab accident. But Octavius is given a deeper sense of shame. His wife is killed by the same accident that gives him his powers, and the grief Octavius experiences over her death, and the destruction he's caused, ultimately prompts him to sacrifice his life to save New York. His personal shame may run deeper than Osborn's, but it's less damaging to Peter Parker. (Recall Osborn's last acts were a) to try and kill Spider-Man, and, failing that, b) bequeath his shame, and the responsibility of keeping it from Harry, to Parker.) Still, Octavius's remorse at taking innocent lives distinguishes him from his comic-book counterpart, who's initially given no depth whatsoever.

Finally, we mustn't neglect the shame of Parker's greatest parental figures—Aunt May and Uncle Ben.

Ben Parker's appearances in both the Spider-Man films and comics are brief. He's present in merely five panels of *Amazing Fantasy* No. 15 before his off-panel death, and so we know little of his background. In the first *Spider-Man* movie, however, the screen time he's afforded, though slight, is telling—he's been recently laid off, and he's troubled that he's unable to provide for his family. Moreover, this might have happened before, and often! ("This isn't the first time we've hit hard times," says May, "and it won't be the last.") Ben may not experience toxic shame, but he is presented, like so many of the men in Peter Parker's life in the Spider-Man movies, as, initially, a figure of shame. In the '60s comics, these same men—excepting perhaps Norman Osborn (who shares the movie Osborn's poor relationship with his son)—cannot be considered shame-based paternal figures, if only because they're not given the psychological depth necessary to contain the emotion.

And what of Aunt May? In *Spider-Man 2*, after Ben is murdered, she believes herself responsible, since it was she who sent him out that night to find Peter and give him a ride home from the library. "It wasn't fair that he had gone like that," she says to Peter. "He was a peaceful man, and it was all my doing." She's even ashamed when Peter tells her she can't afford to give him money (mirroring Ben's shame from the first film, when he was unable to support her and Peter).

With so many shame-based figures in his life, is it any wonder the movies' Spider-Man experiences toxic levels of the emotion?

Of course, the most important figure of shame for the movies' Peter Parker is the person who grows closest to him—Mary Jane Watson, who experiences her own toxic shame.

The Mary Jane of the '60s comic books was arguably the most well-adjusted character in Marvel Comics. Intended to complement the neurotic figure of Peter Parker, her diamond-bright disposition shined through the dark void of his world. Her backstory would only be developed decades later, when her personality was explained as masking a troubled childhood. Her father, we were told, was a failed writer, who blamed his wife and daughters for his failure; and both verbally and physically abused them. In the Spider-Man movies, however, we're immediately made aware of MJ's dysfunctional home life, when we hear her abusive father yelling at her. It helps explain MJ's attraction to the wounded Parker, and it contributes to the attraction he feels toward her. Remember that abuse often leads to toxic shame. And so, like Spider-Man, MJ is a product of her debilitating experiences.

Applying, once again, Bradshaw's reasoning, MJ like so many shamed children, is shamed whenever she is needy because her needs clash with those of her father. She grows up and becomes an adult, but beneath the mask of adult behavior, there is a neglected, insatiable child with a "hole in [her] soul" (26). MJ attempts to "repair" this hole by putting herself with a number of different boyfriends—Flash Thompson, Harry Osborn, John Jameson. One could argue that each is a kind of father figure, possessing physical strength, wealth, and prestige (respectively). But the only man who can truly help MJ is Peter Parker. Fans can argue the merits of organic versus mechanical web shooters as much as they want, but the films and comics diverge at a more intriguing point: In the classic '60s comics, Parker adored MJ because she was not like him—in the films, he's drawn to her because she is.

Toxic shame is perpetuated by those shame-based individuals who seek out and marry their own kind. "Each looks to and expects the other to take care of and parent the child within him or her. Each is incomplete and insatiable" (*Healing the Shame That Binds You* 39). It's yet another piece of evidence that the movies' Parker lives a life filled not just with the guilt experienced by his '60s comic-book counterpart, but with toxic shame as well. Fortunately for Parker (and those of us who seek resolution in narrative fictions), toxic shame can be overcome. (So can guilt, but the selflessness Parker displays as Spider-Man helps him deal with that emotion.) Though Parker and MJ's mutual attraction is *initially* unhealthy—indicating a somewhat desperate neediness—the two are given the time to mature and grow as individuals before coming together in *Spider-Man 2*.

No matter what fate has in store for the webbed wonder in *Spider-Man 3*, he's more than capable of handling it. Why? Because he's already confronted his worst enemy, the most fearsome opponent he'll ever face: his own toxic shame.

Spider-Man 2 is a film that's all about confronting one's shame. Almost all the characters try to do it. Sometimes they fail—as in the case of Harry Osborn, when he finds he cannot silence the voice of his father crying out for vengeance against Spider-Man inside his head ("You're weak," says Norman Osborn. "You'll always be weak, until you take control!"). Sometimes—as in the bittersweet case of Otto Octavius—they rise to an extraordinary occasion.

Mary Jane Watson also confronts her toxic shame. She decides she won't run from the demons of her past and marry for the sake of convenience or escape; and she refuses to let present circumstances dictate her future. Instead, she chooses to stand by Parker at the film's end, and to remain at his side to confront whatever dangers await.

But it's Parker who makes the biggest decision. At the beginning of *Spider-Man 2* he's made a life of isolation for himself, because of his toxic shame. No matter what he does, he believes his actions will only make his life worse. He obsesses over his one great sin, and punishes himself by rejecting all forms of companionship. He no longer shares an apartment with Harry Osborn, but lives alone. When opportunities for friendship arise, he rejects them out of hand. His landlord's daughter, for example, fancies him; but he's uninterested. He creates what Bradshaw refers to as "shame spirals"—in which toxic-shame sufferers obsess over their perceived failures and limitations, which only sends them crashing into depression.

Eventually, Parker's toxic shame grows to unmanageable levels. One could argue that this is the reason he loses his spider powers—because his belief in himself is at a critical low, and he's entered depression. But the loss of these powers also presents Parker with an opportunity. He's given a break from his role as Spider-Man. And he takes the time to realize that not everything in his life is terrible. He *can* do well in school. He *can* be attractive to women. It's during this time that he begins confronting his toxic shame head on.

He tells his aunt he's responsible for his uncle's death.

It's the single most courageous act we've seen him perform. It's an epiphany for the character, and it's the emotional climax of the film. (It's also the reason at least one critic commented that with *Spider-Man 2* the superhero film finally "grows up.") By confessing his sin, Parker starts taking action against his depression and rejecting unhappiness.

This is also the final bit of proof that the movies' Parker suffers from toxic shame. In the comics—at least the first ten years' worth—Parker did *not* tell his aunt he was to blame. Why? Simple—he felt guilt, not shame. And he could handle his guilt as Spider-Man. But in the movies, Parker's awareness of his sin drags him deeper into the waters of toxic shame in which he already struggled to stay afloat . . . and he can only be saved from drowning by confronting his personal problems *as* Peter Parker. The consequences of his shame, paradoxically, are what allow him to defeat it.

The writers of *Spider-Man 3* have my sympathy. It's difficult to imagine a genuine emotional challenge for Peter Parker that comes close to rivaling his own toxic shame. Fear perhaps? Psychologists often remark how the two things that keep human beings locked in place, paralyzed and unable to grow, are the shame of our past and the fear of our future. So then, toward the future?

I'll go along for the ride. After all, I do fear, too.

JOSEPH McCABE is the author of the Bram Stoker and International Horror Guild Award-nominated *Hanging Out with the Dream King: Conversations with Neil Gaiman and His Collaborators*. His writing has appeared in such publications as *SFX*, *Total Film*, *RES*, *Paste*, and *The New York Review of Science Fiction*. He is a contributing editor of *Comic Book Artist*, and has contributed to the Smart Pop anthology *The Man from Krypton: A Closer Look at Superman*. He'd like to thank his mother for introducing him to the concept of guilt, and for making him, when he was eight years old, a truly amazing Spider-Man costume for Halloween.

References

Bradshaw, John. *Healing the Shame that Binds You.* Deerfield Beach: Health Communications, Inc. 1988.

Darwin, Charles. *From So Simple a Beginning: The Four Great Books of Charles Darwin.* Ed. Edward O. Wilson. New York: Norton, 2006.

Fossum, Merle A. and Marilyn J Mason. *Facing Shame: Families in Recovery.* New York: Norton, 1989.

Lee, Stan (w) and Steve Ditko (p, i). "Spider-Man." *Amazing Fantasy* No. 15. Marvel Comics: August 1962.

Lee, Stan (w), Larry Lieber (p) and Micky DeMeo. "The Parents of Peter Parker!" *The Amazing Spider-Man Annual* No. 5. Marvel Comics: November 1968.

Lewis, Michael. *Shame: The Exposed Self.* New York: Free Press, 1992.

Spider-Man. Dir. Sam Raimi. Perf. Tobey Maguire, Kirsten Dunst, Willem Dafoe. Sony, 2002.

Spider-Man 2. Dir: Sam Raimi. Perf. Tobey Maguire, Kirsten Dunst, Alfred Molina. Sony, 2004.

ROBERT GREENBERGER

Spider-Man: Ultimate Loner— Ultimate Partner

If comic-book heroes are a kind of Rorschach test—what we see in them reveals as much about ourselves as it does about the character—then Robert Greenberger's study of our web spinner's varied career as a loner and a joiner tells us a lot about both ourselves and the storytellers he interviews. How do we see Peter Parker? As the eternal outcast, forever outside human society? Or as a desperate, would-be joiner, looking for the acceptance and partnership he'll never find? What do you see when you look into this particular dark mirror?

THE FIRST TIME Peter Parker used his newly acquired powers was to earn money by challenging a professional wrestler in the ring. The teenager with the slight build stepped into the squared circle and easily bested Crusher Hogan. Peter could have had a lucrative career wrestling with his webbed mask gimmick.

But most readers know what happened next: looking out only for himself, he let a thief run by, and that same thief subsequently killed his uncle Ben. Guilt drove Peter to don a colorful costume and become a superhero, so he could prevent other criminals from taking the lives of others' loved ones in his beloved New York City.

The thing that made Spider-Man unique when he debuted was that he was a superhero the reader could relate to: a teenager who felt out of place in the world, like his young teen readers. Peter's parents were long dead, and then one of the two people who raised him was gone. The media, as represented by the *Daily Bugle's* acerbic J. Jonah Jameson, declared him a vigilante and a menace. He had no friends as Peter Parker, and certainly no one would befriend him while he wore that full-face mask. After all, arachnophobia was a common fear, similar to instinctual dislike of reptiles and insects.

As written by Stan Lee and illustrated by Steve Ditko in the 1960s, Spider-Man became one of the freshest characters to grace the four-color pages in years, earning both reader sympathy and empathy, something that couldn't be said of Superman or Archie. With each passing issue, Peter was thwarted at anything approaching success. He couldn't even gain public support while defeating villains such as Doctor Octopus and the Lizard. Not when Jameson kept spinning the news, proclaiming that Spider-Man was in league with the creeps and creatures. Girls such as Liz Allan, whom Peter liked, swooned when Spidey swung by, but as himself Peter was mocked by those same girls in the high-school hallways.

Peter fretted, trying to provide for Aunt May, who was struggling financially and ailing physically. He had gifts, both natural and spider-powered, but they never seemed adequate for making home a safe haven for him and his sole relative.

After awhile, even a superhero needs someone to talk with. Like the wrestlers who eventually wind up partnered with someone for sensational matches, your friendly neighborhood Spider-Man was destined to find himself paired up with other costumed crimefighters through the years.

Just a year earlier, Stan Lee had created the Fantastic Four, a family of adventurers including another sympathetic superhero—the Thing, a man turned to living rock, who hated how his presence instilled fear in the general public.

When Spider-Man graduated to his own title some months later, it made perfect sense to Lee for the two creations to meet. Cleverly, he had down-on-his-luck Parker approach the Fantastic Four about a job, figuring the salary would help Aunt May pay the rent. He was hurt and resentful when he learned they did not draw salaries, and he gave up on the idea of joining a team.

Distancing himself from his super-powered peers was something that Spider-Man did and did well. It was certainly in keeping with his character as Lee and Ditko rapidly developed it. Teen readers identified with the sense of isolation Peter experienced, and it helped set him apart from not only Marvel's Distinguished Competition, but from the other characters Lee was generating for his growing heroic line.

As a result, it wasn't until *Amazing Spider-Man* No. 14, in July 1963, that Spider-Man crossed paths with another "hero." This one was the Incredible Hulk, another loner—but where Peter was filled with guilt, the jade-jawed giant only had rage and anger. The notion of heroes crossing paths only to exchange blows was about as old as superheroes themselves, although it hadn't been seen for quite some time. Marvel had pioneered the concept during the Golden Age when the Sub-Mariner and Human Torch would have epic battles that actually crossed from title to title. But as the 1960s dawned, there were only a handful of superhero comics being published, so the crossover battle of titans had been shelved as a story concept.

Because readers loved to see their favorites mix it up, however, Lee and the other writers and artists were only too happy to oblige. Spidey had to wait a mere two more issues before tangling with another hero, this time Daredevil. In these early meetings, the fights were brief and usually ended with the heroes clearing up the misunderstanding, shaking hands, and going on their merry way. The guest appearances must have boosted sales or interest, because the Fantastic Four's Human Torch returned in the very next issue, as well as in No. 19 and No. 21. By now, their friendly rivalry was well established, and clearly Lee was enjoying himself with the two peers. Even after all these meetings, the Torch remained uncertain about his webbed ally. "Sometimes I think he's really a terrific guy...and other times I wanna knock his block off," he mused at the end of issue No. 21.

In 1964, Spider-Man crossed paths with numerous heroes both in his title and other books. He paid the Fantastic Four a return visit in their first annual and also was a natural choice thematically to be sought by Giant Man and the Wasp in *Tales to Astonish* No. 57. There were numerous cameos in Spidey's first annual, but it wasn't until the following summer that he spent the entire story in the company of Dr. Strange, Marvel's master of the mystic arts. It made sense, given that Steve Ditko drew both tales, but since it was the first time Spider-Man had dealt with something beyond Marvel's pseudo-science, it was also a stretch. Here, for a change, Spider-Man was the everyman, the readers' guide into the world of magical dimensions and supernatural tools. He handled himself well in the topsy-turvy dimensions that were Ditko's forte. Still, Spidey noted toward the end, "The only thing wrong with this evening is . . . when I wake up tomorrow, I won't believe a word of it!" His science and Strange's magic worked side-by-side without friction, an unnatural but successful pairing.

Kurt Busiek, who has written his share of Spider-Man tales, said, "I tend to think that it's his being so utterly out of place in the mystic or bizarre that makes him work with Dr. Strange—he reminds us how weird it is. Maybe the upshot is that wherever he doesn't have commonalities, he's got entertaining contrasts. Sometimes both."

The following year, the annual featured a meeting with the Avengers and his first offer to join a team. Interestingly, the Avengers were divided on whether or not to offer him membership until they contacted Daredevil, who provided a ringing endorsement. They then summoned Spidey to Avengers Mansion, irritating the webslinger, and he arrived only to find them undecided on how best to test him for membership. First, Spider-Man was offended he even needed to be tested and then got into a fight with several members as their personalities clashed. Finally, Spider-Man was sent to locate and bring back the Hulk, their former member and now a rampaging beast. Spidey scoured the city and fought the Hulk, only to let him go when he concluded his opponent needed help, not imprisonment. He returned to Avengers Mansion, saying he couldn't find the incredible one and had decided against membership. The Avengers were stunned by the rejection, allowing some to rethink their position on him. As he left, Captain America, a fine judge of character, began to observe that, while a good ally, Spider-Man lacked the discipline and commitment to be a full-time Avenger. On his way back to Queens, Spidey concluded, "Well, maybe it was just fate's way of saying Spider-Man was cut out to be a loner!"

Similarly, the X-Men suspect Spider-Man's skills mark him as a mutant and, in a humorous bit of business, Beast and Ice Man try to recruit him in 1965's *Uncanny X-Men* No. 27. Though they failed, the theme of the solo outcast versus the team of outcasts would play again and again as they became close allies (most notably in 1972's *Marvel Team-Up* No. 4).

It wasn't until 1972, when comic-book characterization matured further, that more distinct exchanges appeared, and this is where comparing Spider-Man to his tag team partners gets interesting. In an era of rapid expansion, Marvel was adding titles, and one was *Marvel Team-Up*, which paired Spider-Man with other characters throughout the Universe. While obviously an imitation of DC Comics's *The Brave & the Bold,* which teamed Batman with other superheroes every month, *Marvel Team-Up* was a logical step given Spider-Man's expanding popularity.

His first three issues were spent with his sometime pal the Human Torch, easing the transition into the new series, which differed from *The Brave & the Bold* by including issue-to-issue continuity even though the partners may have changed. With each passing issue, Spidey was fighting or fighting alongside the full spectrum of the superhero community. As a result, the writers (Roy Thomas from No. 1, Gerry Conway from Nos. 2–12, Len Wein from Nos. 13–27) got to compare and contrast the webslinger with gods (Thor), things of science (Vision, Iron Man), tyros (The Cat), and others.

Along the way, it became apparent that Spider-Man was adaptable to the situation. For example, in the Cat team-up (No. 8), Spidey took the lead because Cat was new to the costumed crimefighter game, but he was clearly ready to let the God of Thunder take point when the action required they go to Jupiter (No. 7). Those entertaining contrasts Busiek pointed out above started showing up with greater regularity.

As the 1970s progressed, Spider-Man's appearances grew in number, from those two titles to his quarterly *Giant-Size Spider-Man*, and by decade's end his second solo monthly, *Peter Parker, the Spectacular Spider-Man.* None of this lessened his demand as a guest star to boost sales across the line. It was becoming almost *de rigueur* for Spidey to be the first guest star in new titles. Roger Stern, who wrote a celebrated run of *Amazing Spider-Man* and was a staff editor for a time, noted, "While some good stories appeared here and there in *Marvel Team-Up*, I thought the book was Marvel's second-biggest misuse of Spider-Man. (The biggest was *Spidey Super Stories*.)

"To me Spider-Man will always be a loner, and I still miss the days when it was a *big deal* when Spider-Man crossed paths or locked horns with another hero. (*Amazing Spider-Man* No. 16's 'Duel with Daredevil' is still one of my favorite stories.) Spider-Man works best in team-ups when they are rare."

Former editor Glenn Greenberg added, "*Marvel Team-Up* was a fun enough series, and wisely, it never impacted on the 'main' Spider-Man continuity and was never considered essential reading, so it was easy to ignore or dismiss those stories if you wanted to. Spider-Man being a regular member of the Avengers—living in Avengers Tower with Mary Jane and Aunt May and interacting with Captain America, Iron Man, Wolverine, etc. on a regular basis—is far more problematic with respect to the character and how he's been portrayed for most of his publishing history."

Such ubiquity may have been good for sales, but it certainly didn't help his core characterization. Marv Wolfman, a longtime fan turned writer and editor who had his turn chronicling the webslinger's adventures, said, "Actually, I always thought he didn't work in teams. He teamed up with other heroes because it was a way of selling another Spider-Man book, just like *World's Finest* with Superman teaming up with Batman, which also never made sense. For Batman, at least. To me, every time Spidey is accepted by someone else it cuts into the core personality defect that motivates the character."

Even the Cat saw that early on, when she tried to enlist his support. "Why me?" he asked her.

She answered, "Because you're a loner, Spider-Man...an outcast. You know what it means to fight an established order...and you're willing to battle for the things you believe."

Busiek suggests: "I think that the reason he does good team-up (as opposed to team) is that he's a great reactor—he tends to riff off of the other guy's shtick nicely, whatever the other guy's shtick is. But team-ups, however monthly they might be, are presented as unusual occurrences, and Spidey's reactions are good because he's reacting as if the situation isn't normal, isn't something he's used to. Teams, by their nature, are an ongoing, normalized setting, and I never think he fits those well.

"Spidey's not a member of *Force Ten from Navarrone*, he's Bob Hope to everyone else's Bing Crosby (or vice versa). He's made for buddy-movie patter, not ongoing teams. That's why the best recurring hero-foil for him is the Torch; there's no pretense that they're the World's Finest of anything; they're Hope and Cosby in cranky mode, on the *Road to Latveria*."

The notion of Spider-Man as a great reactor may have reached its zenith in an annual that continued a storyline from 1977's *Marvel Two-in-One Annual* No. 2. The story was a large cosmic spectacle that actually began in *Avengers Annual* No. 7 and finished here as Spidey and the Fantastic Four's Thing took center stage in combating the mad would-be god Thanos. Spider-Man was once again the every-man—perhaps the weakest powered member when compared with the Thing, Captain Marvel, and the Avengers—and was feeling very much in over his head, which by 1977, after more than 100 team-ups, was saying something. But he showed us what was really at stake should Thanos have succeeded in possessing the limitless power of the Cosmic Cube and remain unchecked. If Spidey was scared, we were certainly in deep trouble.

This is not to say it's been all downhill from there. His team-ups have continued unabated, stretching from comics to animation, as he led Ice Man and Firestar in NBC's *Spider-Man and his Amazing Friends*. The stories showed teamwork and played off the difficulties of three twenty-somethings protecting their identities and trying to have a real life. He was once again the anchor for the audience's emotional identification, given the regular appearance of Aunt May and the way life tended to dump more on him than anyone else.

His ease at working with others was also seen in novels, notably several from Marvel's uneven run via iBooks. One of those book's authors, Pierce Askegren, offered the following assessment:

Generally, I see Spider-Man as that guy you put up with because of a strong commonality of interest (sports, comics, whatever). In real life, he probably wouldn't be much fun to be around—the defensive banter that readers find so amusing would grate on most ears, he's prone to mood swings, and he's often a sore winner. On the other hand, he's good at what he does and he works really, really hard....

I figure people who have known him/worked with him for a long time would more have an easier time of it; i.e., the FF are quite used to his antics and tolerate them (his special association with Johnny aside).

Others are less sanguine because their views of him vary by situation. (In the Spider-Man/Iron Man team-up book I wrote, Peter Parker and Tony Stark get along a lot better than Spidey and Shellhead, mainly because Peter respects Tony Stark *as* Tony and thus doesn't lip off.)

So, sometimes he's the starter yeast in a pairing, and sometimes, he's not so much a partner as another guy in the same story.

As often as Spider-Man gets into trouble on his own, needing a helping hand, he also seems to stumble into someone else's fight with equal frequency. After all, Manhattan isn't that big a location given the density of the superhuman community.

The iBooks line's predominant editor was Keith R. A. DeCandido, who has also written his own Spidey novel, and he added, "I'd agree that Spider-Man works really well when he has someone to talk to, whether it's the villain of the issue or the person he's teaming up with. But part of the fun is that he's generally such a loner that putting him with other people can be great fun. But what makes it fun is the fact that he doesn't fit in. For one thing, it gives him leave to be a complete smartass because he doesn't have any real connection with them. It works with the team-up of the month, it works with the bad guy, it worked when I wrote him working with NYPD cops in *Down These Mean Streets*, who each treated him differently—some with reverence, some with professional respect, some with complete contempt. And he got to be a smartass with all of them."

Spider-Man may have been most simpatico with the science guys like the Fantastic Four's Reed Richards and Iron Man, but he was put alongside everyone from the juvenile Power Pack to horrific Werewolf by Night. His crossing paths with Dracula didn't satisfy as much as when he encountered Morbius, the living vampire caused by science gone wrong. It may be that the horror elements, unlike the supernatural ones, didn't work with the spider theme, or that the entirely visceral way in which a werewolf inspires fear clashed with the far milder media-induced fear of Spider-Man.

And despite being introduced in the pages of *Amazing Spider-Man*, the Punisher, with his monomaniacal vendetta against organized crime, was also not a comfortable fit. As an opponent to Spider-Man, the Punisher worked fine, providing contrasting rationales for existence. But when they teamed, which happened on several occasions, it was never pleasant. Spider-Man does what he does out of guilt for letting Uncle Ben die and because he has taken to heart the lesson that his powers mean he owes something to his fellow man. The Punisher, a Vietnam vet who saw his family gunned down in a mob crossfire, took up his weapons to exterminate the bad guys. To him there were those who let him do his job and those who stood in his way. Even when he and the web-head were after the same prey, their different methods provided contrasts that more often led to fistfights than to actually airing out those differences. It should be noted that deep down inside Spidey, there's an angry young man who wishes he could put criminals out of their misery with the same dispassionate approach as the Punisher, but it's never something Peter would admit.

On the other hand, Spider-Man works so well with Daredevil because they are both loners seeking justice when the system fails. Daredevil's alter ego, Matt Murdock, is older and shares with Peter the cocky banter in a fight, putting them at ease in each other's presence. But were Murdock to meet Parker, they'd probably have little in common given their different disciplines.

As time has passed slowly in the Marvel Universe, a flexible thing in itself, Peter Parker has had his powers for nearly a decade. In that time, the world he lives in has seen a countless increase in costumed heroes and villains. With that time and experience, Spider-Man has suddenly become an older mentor figure to the young ones who find themselves accidentally gifted with powers beyond imagination. That's seen time and again as he tries to counsel the tortured teens Cloak and Dagger. In fact, there's a clear soft spot in his heart for those younger than himself, who grapple with the difficulty of trying to find their own way to use their powers responsibly.

There has also been an explosion of spider-themed heroines, including the teen Araña. Naturally, the two had to meet, and the impulsive webslinger actually had to rein her in, showing how far he has come and what he has to impart to the newer generation of heroes.

In 2005, the impossible happened. Spider-Man joined the newly reformed Avengers. Captain America actually felt Spider-Man had grown and matured and was ready to work alongside the team. Ever since Spider-Man rejected the Avengers back in *Amazing Spider-Man Annual* No. 3, the possibility of his rejoining them has come up repeatedly, with both writers and readers agreeing that the ultimate loner has no business being on the team. This was exemplified in 1983's *Avengers* No. 236, written by Roger Stern, wherein the webslinger shows up unannounced at the Avengers' mansion, ready to be a member in the team's Trainee Program, something introduced over a year earlier. Just as when he tried to join the Fantastic Four for the salary, money, not altruism, was his motivation in this story. After joining them, unbidden, on an adventure, the Avengers offered Spider-Man a place. However, the United States government, with whom they are chartered, were forced to reject Spider-Man's application given the numerous times he had been in trouble with federal, state, and local law enforcement. In typical hard-luck style, Peter Parker was ready to make the move but external influences intruded.

Fans were agog at the notion of Spider-Man being an Avenger after all this time. To the writer, Brian Michael Bendis, it seemed a great dramatic possibility. He told CBR at the time, "Sure, especially with Spider-Man with people yelling, 'He's not a team guy!' See that makes it most interesting for me as a writer because you have a guy who doesn't think he belongs finding out that maybe he does. Cap will ask him, 'How is this not being a team guy working for you?' It's not like Spidey's life is all that great not on a team, so he'll try being on a team. He'll also be surprised at how much respect he gets from the team—Spidey is the hero who's been through it all and managed to come out intact, something his teammates recognize and admire—to Peter's surprise."

For the loner, the hard-luck case, the guilt-ridden hero, things had certainly turned around. He had married the gorgeous Mary Jane Watson, revealed his identity to Aunt May without causing her a fatal heart attack, and had even moved into the Avengers' current HQ high atop a skyscraper owned by Tony Stark. In fact, given their similar high-tech interests, Stark has become a bit of a father figure to Peter, which played out during 2006's *Civil War* saga.

In the *Civil War* story, which sprawled across the Marvel line, superheroes were required by federal law to register their secret identities and powers with the government. Stark, the former Secretary of Defense, sided with the government and publicly revealed his identity. At a subsequent press conference, so did Spider-Man, which turned his world somewhat upside-down.

One of the immediate repercussions was his decision to give up his attempt to teach science at his old high school. After all, he could not possibly endanger his students. As 2006's *Civil War* continues to play out, so too do these decisions, and Spidey is now at odds with many of the heroes he had fought alongside for so long.

While not entirely a loner, he is once more somewhat isolated, taking him back to his roots, and closer to his core persona.

ROBERT GREENBERGER has spent the majority of his adult life working in the comics field as both an editor and executive at DC Comics and Marvel Comics. His writing credits also include more than a dozen young adult nonfiction books on various topics, a smattering of original fiction, and a lot of Star Trek fiction. He makes his home in Connecticut.

References

Askegren, Pierce. 2006. E-mail correspondence with the author, 9 May.

Busiek, Kurt. 2006. E-mail correspondence with the author, 10 May.

DeCandido, Keith R. A. E-mail correspondence with the author, 9 May.

Greenberg, Glenn. 2006. E-mail correspondence with the author, 10 May.

Singh, Arune. "Disa-Bendis-Sembled: Brian Bendis Talks 'Avengers Disassembled.'" Comic Book Resources. 10 Sep 2004.
http://www.comicbookresources.com/news/newsitem.cgi?id=4176.

Stern, Roger. 2006. E-mail correspondence with the author, 22 May.

Wolfman, Marv. 2006. E-mail correspondence with the author, 10 May.

Spider-Man No More

Moral Responsibility, the Morose Hero, and His Web of Relationships

In Nikos Kazantzakis's novel, The Last Temptation of Christ, *and in Martin Scorcese's film adaptation of it, the final temptation Jesus faces is the dream of a "normal life." Satan offers him the chance to abandon his responsibility to God and man, to live like other men: to have a wife, and children, and most importantly, release from the burden that has been given him to carry. Release from the burden—it's a seductive fantasy, one we can all understand, a motif that's driven much of modern heroic fiction. As Brett Chandler Patterson shows us, it's a theme familiar to those who chronicle the adventures of the wall crawler as well.* . . .

ONE IMAGE I remember most from *Spider-Man 2* is a movie poster. Perhaps it made an impression on you, too. For me the poster encapsulates a number of the central themes of the Spider-Man mythology. Peter Parker, dressed as Spider-Man, his back turned to us, is standing on top of a tall building overlooking the city. We notice that Peter holds his mask in his right hand, and we wonder if he is about to put it on, or if he is about to toss it away. Above the picture is the word "Choice." In the context of the film, the poster has greater weight because we know that the story portrays a moment in which Peter Parker decides to give up being Spider-Man. The film follows the results of this choice and ultimately reveals that Peter cannot so easily abandon his crime-fighting persona. The movie poster and the film are both about what drives the Spider-Man mythology—the heart of which lies in the oft-repeated phrase "with great power there must also come great responsibility." Choice and responsibility go hand in hand, and Peter Parker finds that he is haunted by both. Peter faces insecurities, doubts, temptations, and guilt as he tries to live the best life he can. He is a superhero, but Stan Lee gave us a new twist, for Peter is a morose hero. There are times that he, like anyone of us, wishes to escape the burdens of his responsibilities, and the stories that explore Peter's struggle grab our imagination, as we, too, ponder our own responsibilities and whether we are living up to them.

Most of the best Spider-Man stories, the ones that are memorable and drive the mythology forward, are about choice. But what are these choices? What other options does Peter have other than being the crime-fighting superhero Spider-Man? From Plato's discussion of Gyges's ring of invisibility,[1] through the centuries there has been much discussion about how power corrupts. We could think of a number of ways that "spider powers" could corrupt Peter. Stan Lee tells us that Peter first sought to use his powers to make money; he started with wrestling and then talked with a TV producer who promised him a way to make a "fortune" (*Amazing Fantasy* No. 15).[2] Peter was on his way to becoming a celebrity who used his powers only for his own self-advancement. Not long after his uncle's death, Peter contemplated becoming a thief, since he and his aunt May were in financial troubles, but Peter quickly rejected the idea: "I'm no criminal! I'm not a thief! Besides, if I were ever arrested and imprisoned it would break Aunt May's heart!" (*Amazing Spider-Man* No. 1). This choice is not so easily dismissed, though, in the long

---

[1] In Book II of Plato's *The Republic*, Glaucon relates the story of a humble shepherd named Gyges the Lydian who finds a ring that gives him the power of invisibility. Gyges then uses the ring to seduce the queen and murder the king of Lydia. Power corrupted him. Those familiar with J. R. R. Tolkien's The Lord of the Rings will see echoes of Plato's story in Tolkien's description of the temptation that Sauron's ring of power offers.

[2] There has been further speculation about this possibility in alternate-reality storylines. Peter David has recently developed that further in *Friendly Neighborhood Spider-Man* No. 8. Mark Waid and Tom Peyer in *Spider-Man: House of M* detailed a life where Peter did not lose Uncle Ben, became a celebrity, and married Gwen Stacy.

run, because the calumny of J. Jonah Jameson in the *Daily Bugle* often persuades the public into seeing Spider-Man as a menace, and there have been many points where Peter wondered whether he had caused more harm than good. These are the two dramatic examples of corruption—celebrity and thief—but there is another selfish choice, the passive one, the choice not to use his powers for others. This is the choice that will always haunt Peter, for the origin story was built around Peter's quick-second decision not to stop a thief on the run from a security guard, when it was in his power to do so. He said at the time that he did not have time to watch out for anyone but himself. To his horror, Peter would later discover that that same thief soon after murdered Uncle Ben.

Celebrity, villain, and "cop out" are possible choices, but what about trying to live a normal life, trying to go along only as Peter Parker? Although some readers may see this alternative overlapping with Peter's choice to do nothing, writers from Stan Lee forward have clearly portrayed this choice not so much as a selfish impulse as a part of Peter's yearning for self-fulfillment and his desire to live up to responsibilities to his loved ones, responsibilities that he often has to forfeit to his calling as Spider-Man. The lure of the normal life is the most enticing other choice; it is one with which Peter always lives—and yet new responsibilities brought on by his powers consistently pull him away from this life. This is the option that Stan Lee develops in *Amazing Spider-Man* No. 50, the comic basis for *Spider-Man 2*. We learn here and elsewhere that this final alternative involves two parts—the lure of the normal life and the feelings of guilt that his efforts only end in hurting those he loves. He wants to pursue the "normal" life because he feels that he has made a mess of being Spider-Man; he feels that the normal life of Peter Parker would be an escape from the burdens of being Spider-Man. His loved ones would be better off if he were to stop.

Longing for the Normal Life

But what constitutes a "normal" life for Peter? What does he think he is missing? In *Amazing Spider-Man* No. 18, "The End of Spider-Man," Stan Lee portrays Peter's first meditation on giving up the Spider-Man persona: Peter said he was tired of all the bad breaks: that the public thought he was a coward (since he ran out on the Green Goblin to check on Aunt May); that Aunt May was sick and needed him; that he could not fight villains because something might happen to him and further hurt Aunt May; that he did not have time to spend with his love interest Betty Brant (who was spending time with another boy). He took no serious action at this point, but by issue No. 50, "Spider-Man No More," the doubts had grown to the point that he did abandon the role. Stan Lee raised similar reasons and added more: Peter was worried that people on the street were afraid of Spider-Man; Aunt May was still sick; he was feeling guilty for having moved to an apartment with Harry; he realized that his grades were slipping; he could not find time to spend with his friends, most notably Gwen Stacy and Mary Jane; he had to turn down a job with the Osborn Corporation; and he discovered that J. Jonah Jameson had a reward out for Spider-Man. All of these concerns weighed on Peter. At this point in the story, we find the famous John Romita panel: we are in a street alley, watching Peter Parker walk away in the rain, hanging his head dejectedly; near us in a trashcan the Spider-Man costume carelessly hangs out. Peter says he has given up this foolishness to become a man.

Over the years in the comic books, Peter has frequently returned to thoughts of giving up the superhero gig—because the public accused him of being a thief (*AS* No. 71), because he wanted to marry Gwen Stacy and settle down (*AS* No. 100), because he wanted to spend more time with Mary Jane (*AS* No. 163), because he felt that he was wasting his life trying to live up to an overblown sense of responsibility that had hurt too many people (*AS* No. 275), because his "greatest responsibility" was to his wife Mary Jane and his unborn daughter (*PPSM* Vol. 1, No. 63), because he owed more to his family than to a public that still predominantly believed that he was a menace (*PPSM* Vol. 1, No. 98).[3] The film *Spider-Man 2* drew upon

---

[3] From this point forward, I will be abbreviating *Amazing Spider-Man* as *AS*. *PPSM* is an abbreviation for *Peter Parker, Spider-Man*. I am not using volume numbers for *Amazing Spider-Man* for clarity's sake, although Marvel Comics did re-launch the title in 1999. Marvel hopelessly confused the numbering by introducing a numbering for volume two in 1999, then presenting a dual numbering from issue No. 30/471, until reverting to the original numbering with issue No. 500. References to volumes for *Peter Parker, Spider-Man* help to avoid other confusions. See www.spiderfan.org for more details.

this list, though with some changes along the way: Peter cannot hold down a job as a pizza deliverer, cannot get J. Jonah Jameson to pay him for anything other than Spider-Man photographs (which Jameson uses to sell stories that add to the public distrust of Spider-Man), misses classes on a regular basis, finds that he cannot help his aunt (who has received a notice of foreclosure on her house), discovers that Mary Jane has started to date John Jameson, is in trouble with his landlord, misses Mary Jane's play (he has to stop a crime on his way there), finds his best friend Harry Osborn hates Spider-Man (he blames him for his father's death), and has to take pictures of John Jameson's proposal of marriage to Mary Jane. Each concern builds on the next, and after visiting a doctor, who reminds him that he always has a choice, Peter gives up being Spider-Man. Even in Bendis's *Ultimate Spider-Man*, the teenage Peter decided to give up being Spider-Man after the death of Gwen Stacy, who in this version died at the hands of Carnage, a being Curt Connors created from a sample of Peter's blood. Peter felt the guilt and also lamented his inability to save Gwen (No. 65). He continued in a depression through the next several issues; a nightmare encounter with Dr. Strange and a reunion with Harry Osborn magnified his concerns about Mary Jane to the point that he dumped her because he was afraid that he could not protect her either (Nos. 70–78).

From these lists we can see that Stan Lee gave us a new formula for a hero when he introduced Spider-Man. We had a hero who had worries and reservations and second thoughts—a far more "realistic" hero. Peter desires a "normal" life, which primarily translates into having time to keep up with his studies and to hold down a job so that he can pay his bills and spend some time with his family (especially Aunt May) and friends, particularly his love interests (Betty Brant, Gwen Stacy, Mary Jane Watson, and others). But if this normal life is so appealing, what keeps Peter Parker coming back to being Spider-Man? To understand this, the comic writers keep reminding us of Spider-Man's "origin story," where we learned what pulled him into crime fighting. The origin story in *Amazing Fantasy* No. 15 showed us that Peter was on the way to becoming a TV celebrity, using his powers only for fame and fortune, when the death

of his uncle Ben radically changed the course of his life. The tortu-
ous detail about the death, though, as anyone familiar with the world
of Spider-Man knows, was that the killer turned out to be the thief
that Spider-Man had let escape. He could have stopped the man and
helped the security guard who was giving chase, but he chose not to
get involved—he thought that it was not his concern. Peter did not
naturally choose to use his powers to fight crime; the first criminal
he chased was the one who had killed his uncle. When he made the
connection that his neglect had indirectly led to the death of his uncle, he gradually decided not to continue with the life of a celebrity,
particularly when he learned that he could not cash checks that were
made out to Spider-Man without revealing his identity. The moral
slogan "with great power there must also come great responsibility"
has tragic origins that will always haunt Peter. His response to his
uncle's death transformed him into the hero that we know, the person of whom Uncle Ben and Aunt May would be proud.

Thus, it is the image of responsibility that keeps him coming back.
In "The End of Spider-Man" (*AS* No. 18), he resumed being Spider-
Man after Aunt May talked about never quitting. In "Spider-Man No
More" (*AS* No. 50), after enjoying the normal life for a short time,
he rescued a watchman who was being assaulted. When he was reminded of Uncle Ben and recalled his origin story, how shirking responsibility led to the death of someone he loved, he noted again
that he could never renounce his mission; he could never fail to use
his powers to help others. It was a "mysterious destiny," but he chose
to embrace it. After recovering his costume from Jameson, he resumed being Spider-Man. In *Amazing Spider-Man* No. 100, in a drug-
induced dream sequence (a drug designed to remove his powers so
that he could marry Gwen Stacy), he remembered Uncle Ben's death,
the loss of Betty Brant to Ned Leeds, the death of Captain Stacy, and
feared that he would lose Gwen, too. Fighting through his rogues'
gallery of villains, Spider-Man pursued a voice, which turned out to
be Captain Stacy, who told him that he had tortured himself trying to
be "normal," and that he needed to accept that he was Spider-Man;
his powers were his blessing and his curse. We are not sure what Peter would have decided, but when the formula did not make him

normal, he did not have the opportunity to give up being Spider-Man; instead, he had become even more like the spider.[4] In *Amazing Spider-Man* No. 200, Peter received a second chance to stop a criminal running from a guard (it turned out to be the same guard), and he reflected that he had matured, that he was no longer the same person, that Uncle Ben's death did transform him.[5] In this storyline Peter also had a second encounter with the thief who killed Uncle Ben; after fighting with him, Spider-Man decided that he would not use his powers for revenge—he would not kill him, but turn him over to the authorities (as he did originally)—but the poor man did not believe Spider-Man and died of a heart attack. In *Amazing Spider-Man* No. 275 Peter contemplated giving up being Spider-Man yet again, this time in a conversation with Mary Jane, who by this point had revealed that she knew his secret identity.[6] Here he said that he originally took on the persona of Spider-Man out of a sense of responsibility; Mary Jane asked, if that was so, how he could abandon it. Peter argued that he felt like he might be wasting his life trying to live up to an "overblown" sense of responsibility. Later, when Hobgoblin started a new rampage, Mary Jane told Peter that he needed to do something. Peter questioned whether he should get involved when there were other superheroes, prompting Mary Jane to ask where his sense of responsibility had gone. In the next pages, we saw that Spider-Man had indeed come out to face the Goblin. In issue No. 276, Peter told Mary Jane that he could not live with the thought of the people who would be hurt by Hobgoblin if he had not stepped in—that he had to continue to be Spider-Man, that he could not change who he was. In *Amazing Spider-Man* No. 500, when caught out of time and faced with the possibility of stopping the spider from biting his younger self, Peter chose to let the spider bite him because of the number of people who might otherwise die. In the film *Spider-Man 2*, Aunt May gives Peter a pep talk about heroes and society's need for them. Most of the stories of abandonment, and there are several

---

[4] The supposed antidote had instead given him four extra arms. It took him two issues before he could get rid of them, with the help of Dr. Curt Connors.

[5] See also *Amazing Spider-Man* No. 181 on how the death of Uncle Ben transformed Peter.

[6] Mary Jane revealed that she knew and told her own story in *Amazing Spider-Man* Nos. 257–259.

others,[7] do eventually come back to the image of responsibility, often invoking the origin story to reinforce the point. John Byrne entitled his version of Spider-Man's return, "I Can't... (And I Don't Want To)...But I Must!" (*AS* No. 2/443). How are we to understand the word "must"? Why does Peter feel obligated? What does it mean that Peter lives a life of responsibility?[8]

Does Spider-Man Really Have a Choice?

"Responsibility" is a complicated word. There are numerous contexts for defining it, but two dominant ones connect to our discussion. Responsibility invokes (1) the possibility of choice when we are held *responsible* for our actions, but the word also suggests (2) the lack of choice when we *respond* to forces and conditions that we cannot control but which bear down upon us. The first of these two, the most common definition, claims that we human beings have the capacity, the freedom, to be able to determine our own lives. We shape our lives with our daily choices. The American Dream is built upon this premise—that all people can choose through hard work and determination to advance themselves to positions of privilege and wealth in our society. Anyone who does not take advantage of these opportunities—anyone who rebels against that system and violates the rights of others—should be held accountable; they are liable for criminal or civil prosecution. In this setting, the person who succeeds is the "responsible" person, but the person who turns against others should be held "responsible" for his/her actions. Both of these uses imply that we can choose where our lives go and that societies should praise those who are virtuous and punish those who are vicious. "With great power there *must* also come great responsibility."[9] Uncle Ben and Aunt May often are the two figures who anchor this

---

[7] Including the infamous run in 1996 when Peter Parker relinquished the role of Spider-Man to Ben Reilly because he thought that he was a clone and that Ben was the true Spider-Man.

[8] Some readers may have tired of the consistent use of the word "responsibility," but this is the word that is repeated over and over in the comics. Rarely do you see synonyms like "duty" or "accountability." None of the synonyms seem to hold the same connotations, either; they push too far in one direction or the other.

[9] Italics mine.

perspective in the world of Spider-Man. Peter often describes his life in terms of choice; he believes that he will be held accountable for how he is living—by family, by other heroes, by society, or by God.

The second use of the word "responsibility" ironically suggests that there are numerous parts of our lives, perhaps all parts, that we cannot control, that the most we do in life is respond to all those things that are happening to us. The modern disciplines of sociology and psychology, and certain philosophies that go hand-in-hand with them, have been promoting that human beings are so determined by genetics or social (familial) context that any talk of "choice" merely perpetuates an illusion about human existence. Voices in newspapers, courtrooms, and other venues consistently present arguments about criminals to suggest that their actions were not their fault—that any "responsibility" falls on society or nature rather than on the individual. Several ethicists in the twentieth century and today have emphasized that the model for understanding the moral life should be one of "responsibility," not in the sense of choosing our destiny, but in the sense of responding positively to the forces operating around us. Peter Parker often finds himself talking about fate or God, about how he did not choose to get the powers of a spider; he has been thrown into a situation that he must now make the best of.[10] So the word "responsibility" suggests that we are both determined and destined while also being free to choose whether our lives will align with our sense of morality. This dialectic of choice and destiny in many ways shapes the world of Peter Parker, Spider-Man. Peter does and does not have any choice in the matter; the ambiguity and contradictions are there as they are in our own lives.

Does Spider-Man Have Religion?

Discussions about responsibility hinge not only around whether our lives are open-ended or determined, but also call us to consider whether we act as individuals or as social groups. Ethicists, largely

---

[10] This sentiment is succinctly expressed in the title to *Amazing Spider-Man* No. 31: "If This Be My Destiny...!"

following the example of Aristotle, will remind us that any discussion of responsibility also implies a community: we are responsible *to* someone. These ethicists tell us that before we decide what we are going to do in any given situation that we should first remember who we are, who we want to be, and to whom we belong.[11] Questions of identity precede questions of action. Our moral compass is not something that is innate within us, nor is it something that we develop completely on our own in our experiences of life; instead it is something that draws upon the community (or communities) that is (are) most important to us. Often these communities are religious ones. Communities have a particular language; we cannot talk about the world, understand what we are doing in the world, without using that language. In fact, the very word "responsibility" does not mean the same thing to all people. If we push the question for Peter Parker, we must try to locate the community that defines "responsibility" for him, or assists him in his definition of "responsibility."

A quick search on the World Wide Web reveals that there is some division of opinion over Peter Parker's religious community. There are many who see Peter Parker as Jewish, and there are many others who see him as some unspecified denomination of Protestant Christian.[12] Stan Lee has voiced that he was never explicit about Peter's faith because he wanted to make him a more universally appealing character (Davenport). There are, nonetheless, interesting arguments on both sides. On the side of Peter being Jewish, one can argue that Stan Lee, Spider-Man's creator,[13] was Jewish, just as other notable writers behind Superman, Batman, the Fantastic Four, the X-men, and other popular superheroes have been.[14] In subtle ways Stan Lee's Jewish world-view would have influenced the way he shaped the world of his characters: "To me you can wrap all of Judaism up in one sentence, and that is, 'Do not do unto others. . . .' All I tried to do in my stories was show that there's some innate goodness in the human condition. And there's

---

[11] See H. Richard Niebuhr and Stanley Hauerwas, among others.

[12] Of course, these are not the only two opinions, but they are the dominant two.

[13] He was co-creator with artist Steve Ditko, who read objectivist philosophy (that of Ayn Rand).

[14] Stan Lee joins a long list of comic-book writers and artists who have been Jewish: Jerry Siegel, Joe Shuster, Bob Kane, Will Eisner, Art Spiegelman, Jack Kirby, Joe Simon, Chris Claremont, Peter David, Neil Gaiman, Joe Kubert, Brian Michael Bendis, and others.

always going to be evil. We should always be fighting evil" (Wisha). Building off subtle details, many Jewish readers have noted that Peter's New York neighborhood (Forest Hills in Queens) had a significant Jewish population in the 1960s. Overall, Jews have identified with the basic premise of Peter Parker's life—of being gifted and yet misunderstood and vilified (Oirich). And Jewish writer and creator of *Ultimate Spider-Man*, Brian Michael Bendis has noted, "Spider-Man's line 'with great power comes great responsibility'—that's a morality any rabbi would tell you to live by" (Davenport). The connection to Judaism brings a rich theological/philosophical tradition, one emphasizing that human beings fundamentally are in relationship with one another.[15] One noted Jewish philosopher reminds us that Judaism emphasizes the importance of encounters with others;[16] we come to existence in relationship with others. Relationship, not individuality, is primary. Jewish theology primarily defines "responsibility" in terms of being held accountable by God. The Jewish nation is in covenant with God to be a light to the nations; there is a social quality to the covenant from the beginning. If Peter Parker has indeed been Jewish all these years, perhaps we are to see his understanding of "responsibility" in this context.

There is perhaps a stronger case, though, that Peter is an unspecified Protestant—certainly his aunt May is. Brian Michael Bendis has commented that he would like to see more Jewish main characters, but that if he were to make Peter Parker Jewish it would not fit in with the Spider-Man mythology (Bendis).[17] Many writers over the years have approached the character differently, but recent work by Paul Jenkins and Michael Straczynski, writers who are secularists, and that by Brian Michael Bendis and Peter David, who are Jewish, has been more overt in Peter's prayers to God.[18]

---

[15] See Martin Buber's discussion of relationships in *I and Thou*. Human existence is characterized by encounters with other beings either in "I-It" or "I-Thou" relationships.

[16] See Emmanuel Levinas's *Otherwise Than Being*.

[17] It is interesting to note, though, that despite this comment Bendis has Spider-Man using Yiddish phrases and dating Kitty Pryde, who is a professed Jewish character.

[18] Visit www.adherents.com/lit/comics/comic_book_religion.html. See also *Amazing Spider-Man* No. 46/487, No. 48/489, No. 49/490, and No. 53/494. See Bendis's version in *Ultimate Spider-Man* No. 49 and No. 53. Straczynski has also introduced some totemistic religious references to a spider god in Peter's encounters with Ezekiel and in *Spider-Man: The Other*—the world he is creating is not an explicitly Christian one.

The references are vague; we do not see Peter attending church on a regular basis or even making reference to Jesus. His aunt May is usually given more specific references, especially in Peter David's portrait in *Spider-Man: The Other*, where she argues theology with a villain and notes at the end that she is going to go to church to thank God for Peter's return. Her influence, and that of Uncle Ben, on Peter largely seems to be in moral terms, rather than in explicit church attendance. "With much power there must also come great responsibility" is reminiscent of Jesus' "to whom much is given much will be expected" (Luke 12:48). If Peter Parker has been an unspecified Protestant all these years, his definition of responsibility might then suggest the individualism that is often associated with Protestant Christianity in America—God will hold each of us accountable for the way we live our lives. The lack of specificity of a church community might reflect the generalized Protestant character that American public life has supposedly had in previous generations (particularly the 1950s and 1960s). But, on the other side, there are also Protestant theologians who see the importance of the church community and define "responsibility" in that context; they argue that the church community, guided by the Bible, gives us the language and perspective on the world that allows us to understand our lives and to give them "meaning."[19] Fundamentally, we are beings who live in a community and a history that we did not shape; we respond to what has come before us and in anticipation of what will come after us. Peter Parker finds himself enmeshed in a web of relationships; he responds to forces in the world and often has interpreted them as God working things around him. He draws on specific Christian definitions when he uses the words "sin" and "forgiveness" and "responsibility," whether he is fully conscious of this or not.

Despite some significant differences between Jewish and Christian theology, it is important to note that the two share the understanding that God is in control of the world and that God will hold human beings accountable for their actions. There are images of judgment.

---

[19] Once again, H. Richard Niebuhr and Stanley Hauerwas are important here.

We are given the responsibility to take care of those around us. In both theological contexts, there is also the suggestion that we meet God in our relationships with others—that we bear responsibilities to God, to others, and to ourselves—that we are most truly ourselves when we are giving to others. Since we are not given much more to go on, we will have to acknowledge the ambiguity. We will not resign Peter Parker to secularist atheism, though; there is enough evidence to consider Peter to be someone who believes in God, but the exact context—Jewish or Christian—is debatable. The ambiguity, however, does make him accessible to both groups.

Spider-Man's Not Much of a Loner after All

Even if we cannot be completely specific about a religious context, we do have a strong sense of Peter's interpersonal relationships. Where would Peter's story be without Uncle Ben and Aunt May, without Betty Brant and Ned Leeds, without Captain and Gwen Stacy, without Flash Thompson and Liz Allan, without Harry Osborn and Curt Connors, and countless others? Peter consistently refers to these other people when he is making important decisions in his life. In those crucial issues where he is considering abandoning the whole enterprise of being Spider-Man, or whenever he comes to a crucial crossroads in his life, he remembers certain lives and deaths that continue to shape him—most notably those of Uncle Ben and Gwen Stacy.[20] Jeph Loeb's notable *Spider-Man: Blue* was set up as Peter's spoken memorial to an earlier time when Gwen was still alive; in the last issue we realize that Peter has been speaking it to Gwen as if she were still alive. Paul Jenkins has been a master at presenting wistful retrospective visions of lost loved ones and presumed graveside conversation between Peter and his uncle Ben. One of his earlier stories, "Perchance To Dream," had Peter dreaming of all those who had died during his tenure as Spider-Man, his guilt manifested in a

[20] The death of Uncle Ben came in *Amazing Fantasy* No. 15, and the death of Gwen Stacy in *Amazing Spider-Man* No. 121 (where the webbing he shot to save a falling Gwen ended up killing her). Her father had died in *Amazing Spider-Man* No. 90 (where Peter pledged to the dying man that he would take care of Gwen).

web that confined him (*Webspinners: Tales of Spider-Man* No. 12).[21]
The dream took him from Captain Stacy through the Osborns and
the daughter he and Mary Jane had lost, to Gwen Stacy and Uncle
Ben. The cost of being Spider-Man has been too great, but somehow
if he were to abandon being Spider-Man he would betray and cheap-
en the sacrifices of his loved ones. The losses also affect his current
relationships: he does not want Aunt May to end up like Uncle Ben;
he does not want Mary Jane to end up like Gwen Stacy. Of course,
the comic writers have given us plots where Aunt May (*AS* No. 196
and No. 400) and Mary Jane (*AS* No. 13/454) have also been sacrificed, but these were taken back. There have been mistaken attempts
to give Gwen and Uncle Ben back, too, but clones and time travel
and visions fade, returning us to the deaths that significantly define
Peter's character.

Peter is also shaped by family and friends who are living.[22] Stan
Lee has given us a series of masterful plots where Peter was left having to decide whether he was to pursue a villain or to track down the
medicine that his aunt May needed. We often see Peter seeking ways
to protect Mary Jane from the villain who has kidnapped her. But the
dominant way Peter seeks to be faithful to those who are around him
is through his secret identity, his mask. Numerous stories revolve
around the threat of being unmasked; Peter tells us that he is not so
much worried about himself as he is worried about how costumed
lunatics will start targeting his family and friends once they discover who he is. This was what he worried when Norman Osborn discovered who he was all the way back in *Amazing Spider-Man* No. 39.
Mark Millar's masterful twelve-issue run on *Marvel Knights: Spider-
Man* centered on Peter's fears when a mysterious villain discovered
his identity and kidnapped (and possibly killed) Aunt May. He even
believes that he should keep his identity secret from his loved ones

---

[21] This issue was punctuated by a memorable J. G. Jones cover: Spider-Man is kneeling, his head
lowered, while the faces of a number of prominent characters in pale tones haunt him from behind.

[22] The relationships of concern and encouragement are not the only ones that shape Peter. There
are also those ongoing rivalries with numerous villains—from the Vulture to the Rhino, to the
Kingpin to Kraven the Hunter, to Doctor Octopus, the Green Goblin, the Hobgoblin, the Rose,
Venom, Carnage, and many more. Many times Peter returns to the life of Spider-Man because he
feels that he is responsible for opposing these villains.

because he does not want to burden them with concerns about his safety when he is out fighting crime. But his loved ones have often pushed him to share that burden; they have often known more than Peter thinks. Mary Jane discovered Peter's secret on her own before he got around to telling her (*AS* No. 257),[23] and Aunt May, when she found out, scolded Peter for not saying anything (*AS* No. 479).[24]

The creators at Marvel decided to change this status quo radically in the 2006 series *Civil War*; the change was so radical that news of the events of issue No. 2 made it to the *New York Times* and to other national and international news reports (Gustines). In his fictional world, Peter revealed his identity in a national press conference, in support of a superhero registration act. It seems strange that a character who all these years has tried his best, despite notable failures,[25] to keep his identity secret out of a sense of responsibility for those he loves now feels that it is more responsible to reveal his identity so that the public can hold him and all superheroes accountable. Why would Peter support this act and align himself with Tony Stark? J. Michael Straczynski carefully molded Peter's character over the previous two years to set this up—from Peter's losing his apartment and his childhood home (leaving Aunt May and Mary Jane homeless, too) to moving in with the Avengers (moving from going it alone to working with a team) to "dying" and coming back with new powers and a new costume.[26] In joining the Avengers, Peter fostered a friendship with Tony Stark, who designed Spider-Man's new costume, and it was Tony who eventually pulled Peter into the Civil War. Peter's sense of responsibility to society and trust in Tony

[23] Mary Jane has been a valuable foil to Peter from her appearance in *AS* Nos. 42–43 through her rejecting of his proposals in *AS* No. 183 and No. 291 to her acceptance in No. 292 and their wedding in *AS Annual* No. 21 to her enduring the trials of being the wife of a superhero, particularly in recent years.

[24] Some may say, "What about May telling Peter that she knew in *Amazing Spider-Man* No. 400?" Ah, but that was an actress genetically modified to look like May! And true readers will note that Peter did try to tell Aunt May way back in *AS* No. 54, but she turned out to be unconscious.

[25] In "Unmasked at Last!" (*AS* No. 87), he revealed his identity to his friends and was surprised at the distress that it caused; he later called in a favor and had Hobie Brown impersonate Spider-Man to throw his friends off. Also, Mark Millar in *Marvel Knights: Spider-Man* and Brian Michael Bendis in *Ultimate Spider-Man* have portrayed humorous conversations between Peter and Mary Jane about how many people (including villains) know that Peter is Spider-Man.

[26] *Amazing Spider-Man* Nos. 518–520 and *Spider-Man: The Other*.

led him to support the Registration Act, but because Tony did not reveal his full plan to Peter, Peter had doubts along the way, which he voiced to Mary Jane and Aunt May (*AS* Nos. 532–533). But, before this story is over, it appears that his sense of responsibility to his friends, the heroes who are resisting registration, will bring him around to opposing the draconian tactics used by those in support of registration.

In this story, we are reminded once again that Peter as Spider-Man is fundamentally held accountable to the public. More often than not this "accountability" is a lesson in irony, though, for the public frequently accuses him of crimes he has not committed. We readers are brought into the private world of Peter Parker; we see him as the misunderstood hero. We understand why he is often dejected and morose, though he consistently tries to hide it with humor. He intends good, but the public, largely under the sway of J. Jonah Jameson's rumors, always seems to pervert each situation, portraying him as a "menace" instead of a hero. But despite the dour tone of many of the stories, they also bring a notable amount of hope. Spider-Man does accomplish much; he does save lives; he does defeat villains; he does maintain a positive outlook and a sense of humor; he does make a good life with Aunt May and Mary Jane. And there are times when the public does appreciate him.

Although there are numerous arguments against mixing fantasy and reality, Marvel chose to offer a tribute to 9/11 in their comics. It was a natural choice to select Spider-Man, not only because Spider-Man has been perhaps their most successful character, but also because Spider-Man has most often embodied a sense of social responsibility. In issue No. 36/477 of *Amazing Spider-Man*, J. Michael Straczynski showed Spider-Man coming to the wreck of the Twin Towers to help with the aftermath. Spider-Man was not given much dialogue—we had Staczynski's commentary instead—but Spider-Man's presence was meant to be reassuring. In the midst of the chaos, the values that he represents still hold firm. In times of crisis, we learn anew to appreciate those among us who do live responsibly. In the midst of choices and forces beyond our control, we struggle through our lives individually, but also as part of communities. We live in rebellion against or in support of our relationships with other people, noting whether our lives are ones that would bring pride or shame to those we love. In the midst of our concerns and second thoughts, we are drawn to stories about heroes who rise above these challenges, who can find hope in the midst of overwhelming problems. Spider-Man is one of these; it is no small wonder why he has touched the imaginations of so many of us.

> As a boy BRETT CHANDLER PATTERSON loved comic books and tales of the fantastic, but turned to more "serious" studies in high school, and did not rediscover comics (and Spider-Man) until graduate school, where they were a welcomed escape from all those books without pictures! He has long been drawn toward literature, particularly the works of Dickens, Conrad, Greene, Tolkien, and Lewis, and toward theology, notably the works of Schweitzer, Barth, Bonhoeffer, Tillich, Scott, Kort, (H. Richard) Niebuhr, Cone, Gutierrez, and Hauerwas. His current research identifies science fiction as a field for theological reflection. Originally from the Lowcountry, he is currently assistant professor of theology and ethics at Anderson University in South Carolina.

References

Bendis, Brian Michael. Interview by Stefan Blitz and Saner Lamken. *Comicology* No. 4. http://www.twomorrows.com/comicology/articles/04bendis.html.

Bendis, Brian Michael (w), Mark Bagley (p), and Art Thibert (i). *Ultimate Spider-Man* Nos. 49–53. Marvel Comics: Jan.–Apr. 2004.

Bendis, Brian Michael (w), Mark Bagley (p), and Scott Hana (i). *Ultimate Spider-Man* Nos. 65, 70–78. Marvel Comics: Nov. 2004 and Feb.–Aug. 2005.

Buber, Martin. *I and Thou.* New York: Touchstone, 1996.

Conway, Gerry (w), Gil Kane (p), John Romita, Sr., and Tony Mortellaro (i). *Amazing Spider-Man* No. 121. Marvel Comics: June 1973.

Davenport, Misha. "Jews Are the True Comic Book Heroes." *Chicago Sun-Times Home Page.* 24 September 2003. http://www.suntimes.com/output/books/cst-ftr-comics24.html.

David, Peter (w), Mike Wieringo (p), and Karl Kesel (i). *Friendly Neighborhood Spider-Man* No. 8. Marvel Comics: July 2006.

DeFalco, Tom (w), Ron Frenz (p), and Brett Breeding (i). *Amazing Spider-Man* No. 276. Marvel Comics: May 1986.

DeFalco, Tom (w), Ron Frenz (p), and Josef Rubinstein. *Amazing Spider-Man* Nos. 257–259 and 275. Marvel Comics: Oct.–Dec. 1984 and April 1986.

DeFalco, Tom. *Spider-Man: The Ultimate Guide.* New York: DK Publishing, Inc., 2001.

DeMatteis, J. M. (w), Stan Lee (w), Mark Bagley (p), John Romita, Jr. (p), Tom Grummett (p), Larry Mahlstedt (i), John Romita, Sr. (i), Al Milgrom (i). *Amazing Spider-Man* No. 400. Marvel Comics: Apr. 1995.

Gustines, George. "Spider-Man Unmasked." *The New York Times Home Page.* 15 June 2006. http://query.nytimes.com/gst/fullpage.html?res=950 2E2DB1031F936A25755C0A9609C8B63.

Hauerwas, Stanley. *A Community of Character.* Notre Dame, IN: University of Notre Dame Press, 1981.

Jenkins, Paul (w), J. G. Jones (p), and Jimmy Palmiotti (i). "Perchance to Dream." *Webspinners: Tales of Spider-Man* No. 12. Marvel Comics: Dec. 1999.

Lee, Stan (w) and Gil Kane (p), and Frank Giacoia (i). *Amazing Spider-Man* No. 100. Marvel Comics: Sept. 1971.

Lee, Stan (w) and Gil Kane (p), and John Romita, Sr. (i). *Amazing Spider-Man* No. 90. Marvel Comics: Nov. 1970.

Lee, Stan (w) and John Romita, Sr. (p), and Jim Mooney (i). *Amazing Spider-Man* Nos. 71 and 87. Marvel Comics: Apr. 1969 and Aug. 1970.

Lee, Stan (w) and John Romita, Sr. (p), and Mickey Demeo (i). *Amazing Spider-Man* Nos. 39, 50, and 54. Marvel Comics: Aug. 1966 and July and Nov. 1967.

Lee, Stan (w) and Steve Ditko (p/i). *Amazing Fantasy* No. 15. Marvel Comics: August 1962.

Lee, Stan (w) and Steve Ditko (p/i). *Amazing Spider-Man* Nos. 1, 18, and 31. Marvel Comics: Mar. 1963, Nov. 1964, and Dec. 1965.

Levinas, Emmanuel. *Otherwise Than Being.* Pittsburgh, PN: Duquesne University Press, 2002.

Loeb, Jeph (w) and Tim Sale (p/i). *Spider-Man: Blue* Nos. 1–6. Marvel Comics: June 2004–May 2005.

Mackie, Howard (w), Gil Kane (p), and Tom Palmer (i). *Peter Parker Spider-Man* Vol. 1 No. 63. Marvel Comics: Oct. 1995.

Mackie, Howard (w), John Byrne (p), and Al Milgrom (i). *Amazing Spider-Man* Vol. 2 No. 13 (454). Marvel Comics: Jan. 2000.

Mackie, Howard (w), John Byrne (p), and Scott Hana (i). *Amazing Spider-Man* Vol. 2 No. 2 (443). Marvel Comics: Feb. 1999.

Mackie, Howard (w), John Romita, Sr. (p), and Scott Hana (i). *Peter Parker Spider-Man* Vol. 1 No. 98. Marvel Comics: Nov. 1998.

Mantlo, Bill (w), Sal Buscema (p), and Mike Esposito (i). *Amazing Spider-Man* No. 181. Marvel Comics: June 1978.

Marvel Comics. *40 Years of the Amazing Spider-Man*. Renton, WA: Topics Entertainment, Inc., 2004. (This is an 11 CD-Rom collection of *Amazing Fantasy* No. 15 and *Amazing Spider-Man* issues Nos. 1–500.)

Michiline, David (w), Jim Shooter (w), Paul Ryan (p), and Vince Colletta (i). "The Wedding!" *Amazing Spider-Man Annual* No. 21. Marvel Comics: 1987.

Michiline, David (w), John Romita, Jr. (p), Alex Saviuk (p), and Vince Colletta (i). *Amazing Spider-Man* Nos. 291–292. Marvel Comics: Aug.–Sept. 1987.

Millar, Mark (w), Steve McNiven (p), and Dexter Vines (i). *Civil War* No. 2. Marvel Comics: August 2006.

Millar, Mark (w), Terry Dodson (p), and Rachel Dodson (i). *Marvel Knights: Spider-Man* Nos. 1–12. Marvel Comics: June 2004–May 2005.

Niebuhr, H. Richard. *The Meaning of Revelation*. New York: Collier Books, 1960.

Oirich, Alan. "Spider-Jew." *Aish HaTorah Home Page*. 2 June 2002. http://www.aish.com/societyWork/arts/Spider-Jew.asp.

"The Religious Affiliation of Comic Book Character Peter Parker Spider-Man." http://www.adherents.com/lit/comics/SpiderMan.html.

Straczynski, J. Michael (w), John Romita, Jr. (p), and Scott Hana (i). *Amazing Spider-Man* No. 477 (Vol. 2 No. 36), 479 (Vol. 2 No. 38), 487–494 (Vol. 2 Nos. 46–53), and 500. Marvel Comics: Dec. 2001, Feb. 2002, Dec. 2002–July 2003, and Dec. 2003.

Straczynski, J. Michael (w), Mike Deodato, Jr. (p), Mark Brooks (p), Joe Pimintel (i), and Jaime Mendoza (i). *Amazing Spider-Man* Nos. 518–520. Marvel Comics: May–July 2005.

Straczynski, J. Michael (w), Peter David (w), Reginald Hudlin (w), Mike Deodato, Jr. (p), Mike Wieringo (p), Pat Lee (p), Joe Pimintel (i), Karl Kesel (i), and Dream Engine (i). *Spider-Man: The Other* (*Amazing Spider-Man* Nos. 525–528, *Friendly Neighborhood Spider-Man* Nos. 1–4, and *Marvel Knights: Spider-Man* Nos. 19–22). Marvel Comics: Dec. 2005–March 2006.

Straczynski, J. Michael (w), Ron Garney (p), and Bill Reinhold (i). *Amazing Spider-Man* Nos. 532–533. Marvel Comics: July–Aug. 206.

Waid, Mark (w), Tom Peyer (w), Salvador Larroca (p), and Danny Miki (i). *Spider-Man: House of M* Nos. 1–5. *Amazing Spider-Man* No. 163. Marvel Comics: Aug.–Dec. 2005.

Wein, Len (w), Ross Andru (p), and Mike Esposito (i). Marvel Comics: Dec. 1976.

Wisha, Victor. "Look up in the sky! It's . . . Menorah Man?" *San Diego Jewish Journal Home Page.* 4 February 2003. http://www.sdjewishjournal.com/stories/feb04_2.html.

Wolfman, Marv (w), Al Milgrom (p), Jim Mooney (i), and Frank Giacoia (i). *Amazing Spider-Man* No. 196. Marvel Comics: Sept. 1979.

Wolfman, Marv (w), Keith Pollard (p), and Jim Mooney (i). *Amazing Spider-Man* No. 200. Marvel Comics: Jan. 1980.

Wolfman, Marv (w), Ross Andru (p), and Bob McLeod (i). *Amazing Spider-Man* No. 183. Marvel Comics: Aug. 1978.

J. R. FETTINGER

The Absent Father and Spider-Man's Unfulfilled Potential

Like Lawrence Watt-Evans elsewhere in this volume, J. R. Fettinger ponders the mystery of Peter Parker's squandered potential, and arrives at a very different (and equally intriguing) explanation for the web spinner's all-too-obvious and spectacular failure to launch....

SPIDER-MAN IS A hero of mythic proportions who has used his great power to serve and protect a largely ungrateful humanity. This power has come with an equally great price that he will forever pay: his happiness, peace of mind, and the blessings of normalcy that most of us take for granted. But when his epithet is written, will he fall short of what he could have been, in both his costumed and civilian identities? And if so—why?

Are these absurd questions, considering the magnitude of his heroic deeds? Perhaps. But compare the Spider-Man of fifteen (his age when bitten by the radioactive spider) to the webslinger of the present (anywhere from twenty-five to thirty depending upon the reference). He has made few enhancements to his fighting skills, continuing to rely on sheer strength, raw intelligence, dumb luck, and the never-to-be-underestimated stupidity and lack of imagination of his foes. Except for brief flirtations with an alien symbiote designer line, and his current costume as "Iron Spidey," he has remained in his wash 'n' wear red and blue pajamas. His webbing and its delivery system has remained largely the same, superseded only by a recent physiological change that allows him to generate webbing organically, like his movie counterpart. His relations with the public he serves and the police he assists are tenuous at best. Despite occasional dalliances with team membership, his stubborn independence and feelings of inadequacy ensure that he remains a loner and, at times, a fugitive, with many considering him to be as bad as the human debris he fights.

As Peter Parker, his life is a directionless disaster. His scientific prowess should have made him the peer of Reed Richards and Tony Stark, men who became prosperous and/or well-respected for their civilian achievements, but he seems to have squandered his potential. These men are not immune from the ravages of human frailty, with alcohol being Tony's personal demon, and Reed's neglect of his wife Sue nearly driving her into the Sub-Mariner's arms more than once, but both have succeeded in balancing their superhero careers, satisfying their intellectual pursuits, and maintaining some semblance of an organized personal life. Peter Parker nearly flunked out of college, and even then failed to graduate with his own class because he forgot to take a gym credit. Two attempts at a post-graduate education failed. He made only a marginal living for years, largely as a freelance photographer because until a recent gig as a high-school teacher, he couldn't hold a steady job. His friendships often failed because he neglected them. Any success with women, including his marriage to Mary Jane Watson (who left him at least once) owes more to his partner's Job-like patience than any effort on his part (and part of MJ's devotion to Peter may be tied up in her own relationship abandonment and hero worship issues). If we didn't know that Peter was Spider-Man, we would probably consider him either "brilliant but lazy" (Dr. Connors's assessment in *Spider-Man 2*), or simply a loser.

He appears to be a chronic underachiever in both identities. But with so much in his favor, how can this be? What has kept him from putting the disparate parts of his life together and becoming an even *greater* hero? As we look back over the forty-five years of a relatively (but not completely) coherent chronicling of the life of Peter Parker, what has been the most glaring absence during that entire time? What is it that he has persistently, if unknowingly, sought all of these years, but sadly, never found?

Think about this: without question, one of the most devastating events in Peter's life was the murder of his love, Gwen Stacy, at the hands of Norman Osborn, the original Green Goblin. Gwen's death nearly destroyed him, leaving a permanent emotional scar. Yet Peter *was* able to find love again—not once, but twice, with Felicia Hardy (a.k.a. the Black Cat) and ultimately, Mary Jane. However, Peter has *never* adequately replaced Ben Parker as his father.[1] As we will see, throughout the years Peter has subconsciously searched for someone who can fill that role, repeatedly gravitating toward various older men for advice and counsel. Yet before any of them could provide permanent, positive contributions to his life, they either died—or worse—betrayed him.

This essay's purpose is not to make political statements on the impact of fathers in children's lives. We all know people who did very well with bums for fathers or no fathers at all. This essay is about Peter Parker, and how the presence of a positive male role model into his adulthood could have resulted in a very different Spider-Man than the one we know and love.

After all, being fifteen and male is scary enough. The dawning of sexual awareness, an uncooperative body chemistry, and society's continual redefinition of what is "acceptable" masculine behavior all contribute to making the journey from boy to man a harrowing one. Now toss in the complications of being your widowed aunt's sole means of support, as well as hoping that the next time you face a certain megalomaniacal super villain with four metal arms he doesn't dismember you. And it's all on your own, with no one to offer advice, guidance, support, or the benefit of their own experiences.

This does not diminish the importance of either Aunt May or Mary

---

[1] I consider Uncle Ben to be Pete's "real" father, rather than simply his "father figure." Peter's biological father died when he was a baby, but biology alone does not make one a father. Attending baseball games, engaging in snowball fights, providing advice (solicited or not) and a shoulder to lean on, infusing him with a solid base of moral and ethical values, and coming up with that immortal line "with great power comes great responsibility," are all things a true father does.

Jane, particularly once they knew his secret identity. Without them Peter, and Spider-Man, would likely have fallen apart. May's inner strength and will to live are of incalculable benefit. For all her maladies, she is almost too stubborn to die as long as she believes that someone needs her. Spider-Man's equally stubborn refusal to give up even in the face of overwhelming odds is due directly to May's influence. Mary Jane relieves some of Peter's crushing burdens, not only by listening and providing aid and comfort, but also by being his social lifeline to the rest of the non-superhuman race. Both are essential in his struggle to ensure that the "great power" that separates him from the rest of humanity does not set him above it. And while Mary Jane and Aunt May love and are proud of Peter for what he does as Spider-Man, they cannot relate to him in his capacity as either a superhuman being or a scientific genius, in his relentless pursuit of justice, or simply as a man. In fact, each privately hopes that he will one day quit the superhero business, because they would rather be comforted by his presence than his memory. Neither woman can substitute for the father figure he desires.

In the rest of this essay, we will examine the various men whom Peter has either consciously or subconsciously sought out as father figures to replace Ben Parker—what the impact on Peter's life might have been had they fulfilled that role, and the reasons that they ultimately didn't.

George Stacy

Chronicling and commenting on the death of *Gwen* Stacy has become a cottage industry over the last twenty-five years, owing equally to its perceived status by many as the defining end of the Silver Age of comics as well as to Peter Parker's relentless self-flagellation over it. However, one of the most overlooked of the myriad deaths in the Spider-Man mythos is that of her father, police captain George Stacy, the first person to actually piece together the mystery of Spider-Man's dual identity (MJ was the first to learn it, but by observation, not by deduction). Had he lived, it's likely that the career of Spider-Man would have taken a different, but perhaps not an unfamiliar, direction.

Not many people know that at the beginning of Spider-Man's career, he approached Stacy about "going legit" and becoming a special police deputy. Stacy's suggestion that Spider-Man unmask promptly killed that idea but ignited within the captain an intense curiosity about the webslinger. Later, his daughter Gwen became romantically involved with Peter Parker, the *Daily Bugle* photographer more adept at getting photos of Spider-Man than anyone else. Stacy took a liking to the responsible but mysterious and evasive young man. Peter subsequently grew wary of Stacy, but otherwise trusted him, as he had no other man except Ben Parker. It was a well-founded trust. Tragically, Stacy was in the wrong place at the wrong time, crushed by debris generated during a battle between Spider-Man and Doctor Octopus. As Stacy died in Spider-Man's arms, he revealed that he knew his secret and implored him to take care of Gwen. On that lonely rooftop, the webslinger mourned the loss of "the second best friend" he ever had (*Amazing Spider-Man* No. 90).

Had Stacy survived, I think that we would have seen something similar to the events that unfolded in Marvel's 2006 mega-event *Civil War*. While he would have kept his knowledge to himself as Peter continued to date Gwen, it is inconceivable that, had the relationship progressed to its logical conclusion—marriage—he would have remained silent. Stacy would not have allowed Peter to marry Gwen unless he came clean with her about his dual identity. It is also likely that Stacy would have reminded Peter of his earlier proposition about joining the force, and would have pressed him to pursue his crime fighting agenda within the context of the law instead of outside it. He would have worked tirelessly behind the scenes to improve Spider-Man's relationship with the civil authorities, not simply by influencing them to accept the masked man, but by helping Spidey understand *them* better, and to appreciate the limitations that public servants who don't wear masks have to face. Ultimately, I believe we would have witnessed something similar to what we saw in *Civil War* No. 2—Peter Parker unmasking and Spider-Man becoming the vanguard of a legitimate, superhuman police force. Stacy might have also tried to tutor Peter, to improve his investigative and intuitive skills and make more use of his magnificent brain rather than his superhero brawn in crime fighting.

Perhaps it is a blessing that Peter never realized what he truly lost when George Stacy died. Unfortunately, however, this tragic death led Peter's subconscious search for a father figure into the company of men who didn't always have his best interests at heart....

Miles Warren

Empire State University professor Miles Warren first took an interest in Peter Parker when his brother, Pete's high-school science teacher, introduced them during Midtown High's "College Visit Week." Impressed by the letter of recommendation his brother wrote, Miles encouraged Peter to pursue the science scholarship that ultimately funded his college education at ESU. Warren shepherded Peter through his early biology courses, marveling at the young man's brilliance but concerned about his frequent absences and increasing lack of focus on his studies. In an ironic twist of fate, Warren also chaperoned Peter's first date with a dynamic young science student when he invited Pete to a demonstration of a new defense system and encouraged him to bring a friend. This friend turned out to be none other than Gwen Stacy, who needless to say made a sad and permanent impact on both men's lives.

As being Spider-Man continued to play havoc upon Peter's life and studies, Warren was always there when Peter became dangerously close to hitting bottom, continuing to press his young student not to let his gifts and his scholarship go to waste. After George Stacy's death shattered Peter and damaged his relationship with Gwen, Warren gave Peter his home phone number and told him to call at any time. A troubled Parker took him up on this at 2 A.M., after Spider-Man had just completed a thug thrashing. Rather than being angry at Peter, Warren reminded him "I said [you could call me] anytime and I meant it." But Peter hung up, a little voice telling him that Warren was not as trustworthy as Ben Parker and George Stacy had been.

Sadly, Peter's intuition proved correct. During the Clone Saga, we learned that Warren was a lonely middle-aged man who lost his beautiful wife and daughter indirectly due to his pre-occupation with his career. It is likely that he gravitated toward Peter as a surrogate son to fill the void. The two men actually had much in common—not just their fascination with biological sciences, but also the tremendous guilt each carried due to the roles each believed he had played in the deaths of his loved ones. But unlike Peter, who used his grief to ensure that his loved ones did not die in vain, Warren's grief destroyed him. He became increasingly fixated on Gwen Stacy due to her resemblance to his late wife, and after her death became obsessed with literally re-creating her via the cloning process, not to mention exacting revenge upon Spider-Man, whom he held responsible for Gwen's death. Warren's sanity further dissipated when he discovered that the man he had come to see as a son was also the man he hated the most. And as the Professor's obsession with Gwen began taking on creepy sexual overtones, he began to see Parker as a different kind of threat: a romantic rival. In the end, Gwen Stacy's clone, Warren's own creation, turned on him, forcing him to see what a monster he had become, and Warren sacrificed his life to save a friend of Peter's whom he had kidnapped in order to lure Spider-Man to his death.

Of all of the potential father figures over the years, Warren would have been the one with the most modest impact upon the future life of Peter Parker. Unlike some of the others in our discussion, he would not have inspired Peter to take the "next step" in his vigilante career, or provided him with a business empire to oversee. But he could have given Peter something just as valuable—solid advice and counsel from a mature perspective on how to manage the myriad of conflicting priorities in life. With Warren's help, as well as his contacts, perhaps Peter would have been able to secure permanent and stable employment in a science field, a dream of both his and Ben's, and escape the instability and dysfunctional dependence upon J. Jonah Jameson for a living wage.

Ezekiel Sims

Early in J. Michael Straczynski's run on *The Amazing Spider-Man*, this bearded, middle-aged business tycoon stunned Spider-Man by demonstrating the same wall-crawling abilities and physical might our hero does. He also prompted a skeptical Peter to re-evaluate the pivotal moment of his life and of the entire Spider-Man legacy: when the radioactive spider bit him. Per Ezekiel, it was no random act of chance, but of fate, chosen for Peter by, for lack of a better term, a "spider-god." According to Ezekiel, Peter was the latest in a long line of super-powered spider people! The "Mystic Spider" storyline, as it is often called, was controversial. To many fans, the suggestion that the basis of Spider-Man's powers was anything but the intersection of chance and science was blasphemy. But that's another debate.... Throughout the period in which Ezekiel appeared, he continually pushed Peter to see himself in a larger framework, to use his powers for greater purposes than popping bad guys. Ezekiel alluded to Peter as being as dangerous as a child with a loaded gun. "It's not because the child is especially malicious.... It is because the child does not comprehend the power he holds in his hands. And neither do you" (*Amazing Spider-Man* No. 471). Later Ezekiel tells Spider-Man, "You still have a long way to go at being a true guardian in the mythic sense, even after all these years hard at work." After awhile, although still skeptical of his story, Peter began to grow more comfortable with Ezekiel, and there was a moment where Peter, MJ, and Ezekiel, over a simple dinner in the Parker home, began to feel the bonds of family.

But, of course, *we* knew that Ezekiel was eventually going to betray Peter. The older man was setting Peter up to be food for a giant spider in South America so that Ezekiel would be the one true heir to the spider dynasty. I'm not kidding. But at the last minute he saved Peter's life by sacrificing himself to said giant spider instead.

It's easy to look at the weak conclusion of this story and conclude that Ezekiel failed because, well, he was the bad guy, but that's an oversimplification. Ezekiel ultimately failed because of his own hypocrisy and short-sightedness. Throughout the story, he repeatedly chastised Peter for his inability to see beyond today's problems and the next super-villain smackdown, of failing to comprehend the true greatness that was within his grasp due to a perspective limited by science and reason. Ultimately, Ezekiel realized that *he* was the failure, not Spider-Man. While he relentlessly sought the power of the spider because of the good he believed he *could* do with it, the hero that he *could* become, he failed to realize the power that he already had—the means and the ability to do something great *right now*. Ezekiel realized that, in failing to seize the present moment, in waiting until the full attainment of great power before acting, he was wasting his abilities, whereas Peter, in his own distracted, random, and careless way, had already accomplished far more good than Ezekiel had.

Whether Ezekiel's perspective on Spider-Man's origins survives beyond Straczynski's run on the series is dubious, as it can all be easily undone or ignored by successive writers. Nevertheless, it was intriguing to meet a character who challenged Spider-Man to his very core by calling into question everything he had believed about the nature of his powers, his purpose for being, and his ultimate destiny. Perhaps one day Peter will be able to step back from his harried day-to-day existence and take up that challenge on his own.

Tony Stark

The most recent of the father figures, Stark is better known by his superhero *nom de guerre* Iron Man. In the more than forty years of stories where Spidey and Iron Man interacted (including the time where Iron Man called him a "young fool"), there was nothing to suggest the seeds were being planted for a close relationship. Peter Parker was a working-class hero who had to struggle for every cent he earned, while Stark was a corporate magnate who had inherited his wealth. As Iron Man, Stark was a highly regarded and respected hero, a member of the Mighty Avengers. Spider-Man was occasionally an outlaw, and always a misfit in the superhero community.

However, that dynamic changed when Spidey became an Avenger. Once he learned who Spider-Man was, Stark began to see him for the first time as a human being who shared common interests in science and rational thought, rather than an annoying, costumed comic foil. After the Parker home was torched by a Molten Man-wannabe with a grudge against Peter (not Spider-Man), Tony provided the family with a home in his office and apartment complex. He neutered (metaphorically) a tabloid reporter seeking to smear Mary Jane's reputation. Tony was also her primary counsel on the proper handling of Peter's apparent death during yet another controversial Straczynski

"Mystic Spider" story, *The Other*. And of course, he also designed the infamous "Iron Spider" costume, giving Spider-Man a long overdue costume upgrade.

As *Civil War* got underway, Tony asked Peter to stand with him in the troubled times to come and Peter agreed, telling Stark that he had been like a father to him. As the furor against superhuman beings increased after an accident that killed several hundred children, Tony publicly revealed himself as Iron Man, coming out in full support of the Superhuman Registration Act. In one of the most stunning moments in Spider-Man history, he compelled Peter to do the same, providing the young man with an example to follow, as any good father would do for his son. Considering Spider-Man's history with authority, this seems odd, but we have to consider that Tony was doing things for Peter that *no one* had ever done for him before. By taking Spider-Man *and* Peter Parker under his wing, Tony was giving Peter legitimacy, stature, and employment in *both* of his identities. When we consider that Peter is a young man who has spent more than half his life struggling for exactly that sort of acceptance and security, his controversial and almost unfathomable decision to reveal himself makes much more sense in this light.

If the world were perfect, the logical outgrowth would be that Spider-Man would take his place amongst the most respected and well-loved heroes of the Marvel Universe, and one day even lead his own superhero team, his own group of Mighty Avengers. But things went south quickly. *Civil War* is still playing out as I write this, but Tony carelessly overstepped the bounds of the relationship. He presumed that Spider-Man would be willing to hunt down and incarcerate superheroes unwilling to comply with the Registration Act, including none other than Captain America, the icon of Aunt May and Uncle Ben's generation. It doesn't matter how much Peter admires Stark and wants a father figure. Peter's feelings are not a priority with Tony; the mission of bringing the superhuman community into compliance with the law is. It is a mission with which Peter has become increasingly at odds. Tony wants Peter's respect and admiration, and expects it in exchange for services rendered. But he seems more interested in Peter as a "Mini-Me," a younger version of himself—a partner, but not a son.

Tony has provided Peter with almost everything—except a value system that Peter can adopt and still be able to live with himself.

Norman Osborn

We close by discussing perhaps one of the saddest, most tragic, and wasteful relationships in the Spider-Man mythos—the one between Norman Osborn and Peter Parker. Osborn himself summed it up quite succinctly when he told Peter, "We make quite a pair, don't we? You, the son without a father. Me, the father without a son." Each represents what is missing within the life of the other—what would make their lives complete, what would help them fulfill their dreams and ambitions.

But it was not to be.

Osborn first met Peter Parker when the latter was just ten years old and attending a science and technology exposition sponsored by Osborn. In the midst of the crowds and confusion, Peter's wide-eyed enthusiasm at the science on display shone brightly, capturing Norman's attention. Osborn wished that his own son demonstrated the same passion for science as Peter, and offered the young man a tour of the bio research labs. Years later, Norman discovered that this same young man was his son's college roommate, and he enthusiastically offered Peter employment with his company more than once over the course of the next several years. Of course, what Osborn only occasionally realized due to his schizophrenia was that the same young man he admired was also his greatest enemy—living under his very nose. Peter and Norman spent the next several years in conflict that ended (temporarily) only with the death of Gwen Stacy and Norman's own apparent (fabricated) demise.

Years later, Norman secretly returned from his self-imposed exile to witness the birth of his grandson, and perhaps spirit the boy away to raise himself. However, he discovered that the child had a guardian standing in the way, a self-appointed protector—Spider-Man. This common bond the two men shared—the desire to protect and watch over the child (no matter how disparately each approached it)—forced Norman to re-evaluate his relationship with Peter Parker.

Norman realized that Peter was "a son truly worthy of the Green Goblin," and decided that rather than investing his energies in destroying Peter, they would be better spent in manipulating him to join Norman in his quests (*Revenge of the Green Goblin* No. 3). This was followed by a dark and very unnerving story as Osborn, using physical and emotional torture, tried to brainwash Peter into accepting a place at Norman's side as his heir. In one sequence, during a chemically induced hallucination, Osborn attempted to literally and metaphorically substitute himself for Ben Parker in Peter's mind—and almost succeeded. While Spider-Man once again triumphed over the Goblin, Peter was left with the disturbing knowledge that he was nearly broken, a combination of the brainwashing, his own susceptibility to the charms of "the dark side," and his subconscious longing for a father.

At Spideykicksbutt.com, I have written several essays on the Green Goblin and the relationship between Peter Parker and Norman Osborn—how much they have in common and the similarity of their backgrounds. In these essays, we see that he is the only other person who is almost on the same wavelength as Peter—in their physical might, their formidable intellect, their mutual passion for the sciences, the tragedies that have befallen them, the anger that drives them, and how they play out their power fantasies. And here's the kicker, which distinguishes Norman Osborn from someone like Tony Stark (well, besides the fact that Osborn is lunatic and a super villain): Osborn *wants* a son, a family, and a legacy to pass on. While many men would have spurned the children of an accidental tryst with a woman they did not love, Norman Osborn truly wanted the children of his affair with Gwen Stacy, and raised them as his own in exile after her death.[2] He loved his son Harry, although he ultimately destroyed

---

[2] Yes, you read that right: Norman Osborn had a brief affair with Gwen Stacy. J. Michael Straczynski struck again, this time in a story arc called "Sins Past" that ran from *Amazing Spider-Man* Nos. 509–514. This affair produced twins, a boy and a girl, whose aging was accelerated due to the fact that Osborn's genetic make-up had been altered by the Goblin formula. However, in referencing the affair in a flashback as told to Peter by Mary Jane, Straczynski did not provide any context under which the affair occurred in Spider-Man history, other than it was seven months prior to Gwen's death in *Amazing Spider-Man* No. 122. I took the liberty of explaining the circumstances under which this affair likely occurred in an article at my Web site titled "DeFlowering Gwen" (http://www.spideykicksbutt.com/GreenwithEvil/DeFloweringGwen.html) back in October 2004. While the twins were revisited in a later story, the explanation of their mother's dalliance with Osborn was not. While my explanation is not considered canon, it has yet to be officially contradicted.

him in trying to force him to follow Norman's path for his life rather than allow him to pursue his own. And as difficult and egomaniacal as Osborn is, he respects the strength and courage of those who stand up to him, even as he tries to break them.

A Parker/Osborn combination would create an unrivalled business juggernaut of science, technology, and, ultimately—power. Norman is obsessed with power, and Pete is not immune to its lure, either. Many good alternative universe stories have demonstrated that a Spider-Man who ultimately obtains the financial and personal success that he has always craved is vulnerable to corruption. And Norman Osborn would definitely have been a corrupting influence. It is fascinating to imagine Peter Parker at the helm of a worldwide conglomerate. With his own genius as well as that of Osborn's behind him, we can see Peter leading a bio-engineering unit dedicated to ending hunger across the globe by developing new strains of disease and weather-resistant foods, and making deserts bloom and become life-sustaining once more. And with his and Osborn's technological prowess, we can imagine considerable advances in the development of crime-fighting techniques, and a scenario where Osborn and Parker are the primary suppliers of goods and services to the "superhuman police force" that I speculated Spider-Man leading earlier in this essay. Of all of the son/father-figure unions presented in this essay, this one certainly would have had the greatest impact upon the world at large. However, it would also have been the most combustible, and likely to end in spectacular failure. Even under ideal circumstances, Norman Osborn is too controlling, too autocratic to maintain a healthy relationship with anyone. And although he is wise enough to realize that funding the aforementioned humanitarian objectives would also be immensely profitable, he would be too prone to use them to exercise influence and control over the very people they were ostensibly helping. At best, Norman Osborn would be a less than benevolent dictator and oppressive father figure who presumed to know what was best for everyone—which would bring him into violent conflict with his chosen heir. What a story that would make.

For Spider-Man fans, the end of Mark Millar's *Marvel Knights Spider-Man* saga was a perfect coda to Norman's feelings about Peter.

In a letter mailed after the end of their latest titanic struggle, Norman expressed honest and genuine affection for his adversary, but through the perverse filter of a psychopath's mind. It was a creepy, yet defining commentary on their relationship.

In Conclusion

As noted before, Spider-Man is a great hero. But we can see that under the right circumstances and influences, he could be an even greater one, with the ability to have a much larger and more positive impact on the world—if only he hadn't lacked a positive male role model to show him the way. Sadly, there have been too few George Stacys and Ben Parkers, and too many selfish and manipulative Norman Osborns, Miles Warrens, and Ezekiel Sims (and even well-meaning, but misdirected, Tony Starks). Such is the glory and the tragedy of Spider-Man. It's still a magnificently lived life, but one perhaps doomed to be ultimately empty and unfulfilled as well.

> J. R. FETTINGER is the Webmaster of Spidey Kicks Butt (http://www.spideykicksbutt.com), and the author of all essays on the site. He lives with his wife, Karen, and children Rachel and Spencer, in Medina, Ohio. He hopes he is closer to the Ben Parker model of fatherhood than the Norman Osborn one, but his kids will have the final say on that.

References

Avery, Fiona (w), John Romita, Jr. (p), and Scott Hanna (i). "The Revolution Within." *The Amazing Spider-Man* No. 497. Marvel Comics, a division of Marvel Entertainment Group: October 2003.

Jenkins, Paul (w), Mark Buckingham (p), and Humberto Ramos and Mark Buckingham (i). "Trick of the Light." *Peter Parker: Spider-Man* Vol. 2 No. 25. Marvel Comics: January 2001.

Jenkins, Paul (w), Humberto Ramos (p), and Wayne Faucher (i). "A Death in the Family Part 1." *Peter Parker: Spider-Man* Vol. 2 No. 44. Marvel Comics, a division of Marvel Entertainment Group: August 2002.

Lee, Stan (w), Gil Kane (p) John Romita, Sr. (i). "And Death Shall Come!" *The Amazing Spider-Man* No. 90. Marvel Comics Group: November 1970.

Stern, Roger (w), Ron Frenz (p), and Pat Olliffe (i). "Surrender to the Dark." *Revenge of the Green Goblin* No. 3. Marvel Comics: December 2000.

Straczynski, J. Michael (w), John Romita, Jr. (p), and Scott Hanna (i). "Transformations, Literal & Otherwise." *The Amazing Spider-Man* No. 471. Marvel Comics: June 2001.

Weeks, Lee (w) (p), and Richard Case (i). "The Camera Doesn't Lie." *Death and Destiny* No. 2. Marvel Comics: September 2000.

ADAM-TROY CASTRO

J. Jonah Jameson
Just What the Heck Is That Guy's Major Malfunction, Anyway?

Stan Lee might say otherwise, but I've always thought he created J. Jonah Jameson, in the beginning, as a lampoon of Fredric Wertham and the holier-than-thou hypocrites who ran the Comics Code. Like Wertham, Jameson in the earliest stories saw Spider-Man through a prism of suspicion and paranoia—someone who dressed like that, behaved like that, was as insolent and socially irresponsible as that, just couldn't be a force for good. Like the Comics Code, Jonah had set himself up as a moral arbiter for society, and Spider-Man was a constant reminder that his authority, however powerful, had its limits. Of course, whatever motive Stan might have had for creating J. J., as Adam-Troy Castro points out, Jonah is one of the great paradoxical characters in modern comics, and a source of endless speculation. What the heck is that guy's problem, anyway?

NOTHING WILL EVER make him change his mind.

Logic won't do it. Integrity won't do it. The evidence of his own two eyes won't do it. The sage counsel of his most trusted advisors won't do it. The awareness that he owes his life, and his son's life, and the lives of everybody he knows, won't do it.

J. Jonah Jameson, publisher of the tabloid *Daily Bugle*, will never admit that he was wrong. He will always hate Spider-Man beyond all reason, and will always distort his headlines far out of proportion with the facts on hand to blame Peter Parker's alter-ego for everything from Electro's latest crime spree to unhappy political developments in outer Mongolia. His stand on this matter is no mere editorial position, but a genuine mania. We know this. But just what the blue blazes is the guy's problem, anyway? Why won't he see reason?

The easiest answer is that it's his story function.

Spider-Man's initial success as a character had less to do with his costume design, and his specific skill set, than it had to do with the way everything about him resonated to the specific problems of adolescence. This remains true even though the character that appears in the mainstream comic books has moved well past his high-school and college years into the realm of adulthood. In essence, the character speaks to the specific problems of puberty. Think about the sea change that rocks the world of young Peter Parker. He finds himself strong and capable and attractive to the opposite sex, while remaining clumsy in his interactions with them; he comes to recognize that he is more than what his peer group sees in him, while still craving their approval; he becomes confident and self-reliant while still subject to the infantilizing effects of Aunt May's cozying parental authority. We can even, forgive me, draw specific parallels involving the most unique among his superheroic abilities, his penchant for using the palms of his hands to squirt sticky fluid against walls. It's all about the teenage experience.

And a key element of that teenage experience is the disapproval of the powers in authority.

The early Spider-Man comics were written well before the age of Columbine, when the suspicion the old held for the young was polished to a truly poisonous sheen. But concerns over juvenile delinquency, and this strange anti-social music the kids were playing, were already common currency. The political crises of the later 1960s, driven in large part by the youth culture, were only a couple of years away. The tension was there. How appropriate, then, to present as perennial antagonist a powerful media figure who was not a blustery but generally approving figure like Perry White, but a ranting, impossibly out-of-touch blowhard who not only didn't understand, but never would understand, and was quite possibly constitutionally incapable of understanding? Especially when we saw enough of him, through Peter Parker's eyes, to recognize that he was at heart a fool, and a hypocrite, pretending moral authority when all of his pronouncements were geared toward nothing but his own enrichment?

The problem arose when Spider-Man proved a successful, long-lasting series, in which pretenses of deep, evolving characterization sometimes required heroic measures of reverse-engineering for the people surrounding him to make some kind of retroactive sense.

Aunt May was a key example. It was enough, at the beginning, for her to be just a sweet, clueless old lady who persisted in believing her nephew frail and helpless despite all available evidence to the contrary. But too much of this and readers began to wish she would just hurry up and drop dead already. Once in a great while during the Stan Lee era (and with increasing frequency, in recent years), that characterization deepened, revealing her to be a formidable woman in her own right, both tougher and more intelligent than she seemed when she had little to do beyond not keel over, baby her nephew, and completely fail to understand anything that was going on around her. The current versions of Aunt May, which include both the one appearing in the regular Marvel comics, and the Ultimate variation, are strong, capable women, with a moral center and emotional richness sufficient to explain why her nephew turned out as well as he did—and why she remains so important a part of his life.

J. Jonah Jameson, however, remains more problematic. Forget his initial reasons for distrusting a masked man with odd powers, who regularly engaged in pitched battle on the city streets. (That's downright reasonable.) Forget also his corporate greed, which initially seized on Spider-Man as a colorful figure that, demonized, would help sell more papers. (This continued long after it became clear that backing the wrong horse made Jameson look like an idiot on a regular basis.) Forget, still, Jameson's inability to admit that he's ever been wrong. (Wiser media names simply change their positions and deny that they ever espoused anything else.) Jameson's inability to recognize any virtue in Spider-Man, despite years and years and years of being proved wrong, have led him into ever-greater excesses of downright fraudulent reporting, and sometimes seem to render him worse than just a fool or a fraud: a blind, self-deluding madman. How, then, to explain him? How to make him less a cartoon, and more a believable character?

The first offered explanation is that he was living on a river in Egypt. Lee and Ditko themselves offered up a scene where Jameson, suffering what could be called a long dark night of the soul, faced his hatred of Spider-Man and admitted to himself that it was based on jealousy. Spider-Man, he confessed, in the solitude of his own office, was a far better man than he would ever be.

This is a fine provisional explanation, especially since there's never been any shortage of journalists whose entire *modus operandi* consisted of seeking out weak spots sufficient to ruin reputations in print. But let's be honest here. The comics have been deeply inconsistent on the issue of Jameson's backbone. He is often shown running from one menace or another, with all the buffoonish cowardice of a Scooby-Doo, while saying things like, "Gaaaaah." But he also led an expedition into the Savage Land, seeking photographs for his paper—an interlude that deliberately portrayed him as an analogue to King Kong's Carl Denham, which is to say vainglorious and self-aggrandizing but fully willing to march into danger if that meant protecting his own people. He also, in one memorable story, fought side by side with Spider-Man, when the *Bugle* newsroom was invaded by demons from Asgaard.[1] In other stories, he blew cigar smoke in the Kingpin's face, or faced assassins on the docks while proving he could still hit the pavements and track down stories the same way he did when he was twenty.

All of this suggests that Jameson, for all his many faults, often values and embodies a different kind of heroism than the one embodied by Spider-Man. Perhaps the single best moment he ever had, the one that most defined why he is no mere idiot, appeared during the classic Daredevil storyline, *Born Again* (85). The able but not always

---

[1] Live on Marvel-Earth, and this kind of event regularly breaks up your work day. You either deal with it, or you don't.

courageous reporter Ben Urich, an important figure in both the Spider-Man and Daredevil supporting casts, has had his fingers broken for researching a dangerous story about the Kingpin. Jameson tells him: "There are things you just don't let happen in this racket. Number One is you never get scared away from a story. Not when you've got the most powerful weapon in the world on your side." He holds up the *Bugle*. "This is five million readers worth of power. It can depose mayors. It can destroy Presidents. And it's been due to get aimed at the Kingpin for years now, but it needs you to do it." After a pause, Urich fails to respond. "You're lucky I don't fire you. Get out of my office."

I was referencing that moment when I penned this newsroom exchange between Urich and Peter Parker, in one of my own Spider-Man stories, *Revenge of the Sinister Six* (BP Books 111–112).

> Peter smiled. "I notice I've never seen him angry at you."
>
> A darkness passed over Urich's haggard features. "Well, in my case he found something that intimidates me more than his anger."
>
> "Oh, really? What?"
>
> "His disappointment." Urich rubbed his right wrist, and winced, clearly experiencing a phantom pain from long ago.

Subsequent stories, written by Brian Michael Bendis among others, establish that Urich genuinely despises his employer, considering him a monster and an awful human being. Yeah, he would. I'm sure any number of *Bugle* employees have photoshopped J. Jonah Jameson dartboards on their bulletin boards at home. But there's a great difference between hating a man's personality, and respecting him professionally. And there are also any number of indications that Jameson's employees and colleagues consider him a first-rate newspaperman from the old school, willing to stand up for the truth even if they have to tolerate the one major lapse represented by his single-minded hatred for Spider-Man.

If nothing else, there's also the example of city editor Joe "Robbie" Robertson, who serves in both the Spider-Man comic book and Jameson's life as the calming voice of reason. Robertson knows that Jameson is dead wrong about Spider-Man. He's even helped to blunt the more lunatic of Jameson's assertions against the man, sometimes by threatening to quit. But he continues working for him. Why? Because he needs the paycheck? Well, partially. But also, clearly, because he sees some virtue in Jameson's professional approach. Robertson's addition to the cast in the late '60s established a hell of a lot more than Stan Lee's desire to keep up with the changing social climate and make the series less white. It established that Jameson could not possibly be all bad—if only because a guy as fundamentally decent as Robertson was willing to stand at his side.

None of which disproves the theory that Jameson secretly hates Spider-Man for making him feel inadequate. It's no doubt still a part of the big psychological picture. But Jameson has proven so complicated, over the years, that it can't be the only explanation. There has to be more.

Part of it is that he simply can't afford to change his mind.

Military operations have a habit of becoming quagmires. You send in a few soldiers. They run into trouble. You send in more to bail them out. They run into trouble. You send in more, and more, and more, and more, each time exacerbating the problem you started out with, until all of a sudden all of your resources are on this one battlefield and withdrawal is no longer an option, because it would then be seen as a serious defeat.

The same thing is true of arguments.

The more effort you've put into claiming a ridiculous thing, the more it hurts you to pull back and say that you were wrong all along.

Jameson began his campaign against Spider-Man when the wallcrawler was just a masked professional wrestler. His position at this point was, at least in part, that Spider-Man was a poor role model for youth. Had Spider-Man remained a professional wrestler, and achieved permanent celebrity in that line, all of Jameson's railing against him would have amounted to a big fat zero. Jameson would have been able to drop the story, and move on to fresh crusades, without anybody noticing that he had been a little more full of hot air than usual.

But look what happened. Spider-Man became a superhero. Jameson tossed more words into tearing him down. Spider-Man saved Jameson's son. Jameson refused to give him credit for that. Spider-Man exposed Mysterio, the super villain Jameson had declared a hero. Jameson looked like an idiot again. Spider-Man weathered years as a fugitive after being framed for the murders of George and Gwen Stacy, and was cleared to claim his (admittedly shaky) reputation as a hero. Jameson could only doggedly stick to his old position. Spider-Man battled and defeated the Green Goblin, unmasking him as Norman Osborn after years of struggle and saving the *Daily Bugle* building within full view of Jameson and his staff. Jameson can only sputter: it's still Spider-Man.

Like the monkey who has grabbed a piece of fruit inside a narrow crevice, and cannot pull his hand free without giving up on his prize, Jameson is stuck with the one position he has spent so many years and much of his professional reputation arguing: that Spider-Man is a menace.

He's not alone in this kind of narrow-minded marching toward oblivion. The airwaves and editorial pages are filled with any number of bloviating, single-minded demagogues, who persist in repeating the same canards others have already debunked multiple times, because those are the tales that made their reputations, and admitting those tales to have been in error would eliminate their usefulness in the echo chamber.[2]

The thing is, at least twice in recent years, Jameson has proved willing to suspend the campaign when personally convenient. On one occasion, a storyline that appeared in the first twelve issues of *Marvel Knights Spider-Man*, this was in large part because Peter had succeeded in persuading Jameson that his own son, the noted astronaut John Jr., was in fact the webslinger's civilian identity. Now, granted, for Jameson to believe this even for a second, given that he's seen John and Spider-Man together, at length, multiple times, we would have to believe that he's not only stupid and deluded, but

---

[2] You're free to take this as a slur against anybody from the right's Bill O'Reilly to the left's Michael Moore, depending on your own preferences. My own position on the left is irrelevant to the smaller issue of how well J. Jonah Jameson, the fictional character, embodies the phenomenon. I take sides here only to note that O'Reilly's on-screen demeanor establishes Jameson's newsroom antics as well within the realm of real-life possibility.

quite possibly senile. (The true explanation is, of course, a script with insufficient regard for decades of past stories.) Still, if we cede Jameson the tortured maze of rationalizations necessary for him to buy that Junior and Spider-Man are the same person, we can move on to his reaction: immediately changing the editorial position of his newspaper to hail Spider-Man as the city's greatest hero. So there are indeed factors capable of budging the man from his mania—parental love being one among them.

The other incident is perhaps more instructive. It involves *The Pulse*, a *Bugle* Sunday supplement covering superhero affairs. When Jameson began this magazine to jolt the *Bugle's* long-stagnant circulation, he hired Urich and a retired superhero named Jessica Jones (once Jewel and Knightress), for its staff. Jessica, by then pregnant by superhero Luke Cage, agreed to work for the magazine on the specific grounds that she would not be party to any further libelous attacks on Spider-Man. To get the magazine off the ground, Jameson agreed. The *Bugle* kept its hands off Spider-Man for some time. But then Jameson found out that Spider-Man had joined the superhero team known as the New Avengers, which also counted such widely respected heroes as Iron Man and Captain America among its members (as well as Jones's boyfriend Cage). This affiliation, once public, promised to do wonders for Spider-Man's iffy reputation. The New Avengers even offered Jameson special access to breaking stories about their activities—which any other newspaperman would consider a major coup—in exchange for calling off his constant attacks on Spider-Man. Jameson pretended to accept these terms, but within a day used his editorial page to slime the New Avengers, expending special vitriol in a spurious attack on Cage.[3]

In short, he was so emotionally invested in continuing to hate the wall-crawler that he betrayed a promise to a valued employee, printed false accusations about the father of her child, and alienated a source most newspapermen in his position would kill to have.

No doubt about it. It was Jameson at his scummiest.

---

[3] See the comic series *Alias*, *The Pulse*, *New Avengers*, and *Amazing Spider-Man* for all the sordid details.

But it provides us the ability to triangulate his mania's precise source. We began this thesis by noting that it resisted any input from common sense, the advice of most trusted counselors, and his own personal experience. We know from the New Avengers incident that it resists open appeals to his newspaper's best interests. And we know from the John Jameson incident that it is vulnerable to his concern for those nearest and dearest to him.

Or to put it another way: Can it be that whatever factors went into his initial hatred of Spider-Man—greed, jealousy, predatory journalism, the simple stubborn refusal to admit that he could ever be wrong—he maintains his stance out for the most human of all possible reasons?

All right. I confess. I traveled this entire distance only to arrive at a conclusion I already posited in another venue. (Forgive me. I held this theory long before I wrote about it the first time, and will continue to champion it until I'm proven wrong.)

They were words I put in the mouth of a crisis counselor named Abe Saberstein, in the same novel I quoted before, *The Revenge of the Sinister Six*. Saberstein tells the wall crawler:

> For a man who's reportedly saved not only Jameson's life, but also the lives of Jameson's son, wife, friends and employees more often than I can count, the constant denial of affirmation, of approval, must have turned into a greater motivating factor than you realize. Whether or not you actually see Jameson as a father figure of sorts—and on some level I actually think you do—no sane person in your position would ever be able to avoid deep resentment about his refusal to accept you no matter what you accomplish on his behalf. And you can't help measuring yourself, if only a little bit, by that impossible standard...It may be that your need to prove yourself to this one man may be one of the factors that has kept you fighting the good fight for so long. If that's the case, then his stupid headlines deserve credit as one of the main factors that have made your continued career as Spider-Man possible.
>
> ... [leaving] the opposite side of the coin. The thorny question of just why he always seemed to hate you with special vehemence every time you saved his life.

...If I'm right, and Jameson's campaign against you is one of the factors that keeps you too stubborn to quit, then maybe some small part of him recognizes that. And maybe, just maybe...that small part of him believes that if he did stop hating you...then you might also quit saving him (416–417).

In short, Jameson can't change his mind...because Spider-Man keeps rewarding his mania by getting between him and dire peril. The wall-crawler's very success at keeping Jameson alive also keeps Jameson's hatred alive.

Their relationship is a perfect catch-22.

And is likely to remain one for as long as their stories are told.

> ADAM-TROY CASTRO's short stories have been nominated five times for the Nebula, two times for the Hugo, and once for the Stoker. He has contributed to previous Smart Pop volumes about King Kong, Hitchhiker's Guide, *Alias*, and Harry Potter, among others. His book *"My Ox is Broken!"*, a guide to the TV series *The Amazing Race*, came out in late 2006, and he has been assured that the paperback version of his collection Vossoff and Nimmitz will be out sometime in 2007. He lives in Miami with his long-suffering wife Judi and a rotating assortment of cats that now includes Maggie, Ralphie, Uma Furman, and Meow Farrow.

PAUL LYTLE

Power, Responsibility, and Pain
The Price of Being Spider-Man

What makes a hero? The great deeds he performs? The foes he overcomes? The power he wields? Or is it the size of the burden he's forced to carry? If you haven't guessed by now, I'm in the burden-he-has-to-carry camp. So is Paul Lytle, if the essay below is any indication....

"O, I am fortune's fool!"

—*Romeo and Juliet*, Act III, scene i

I HADN'T BEEN BORN when *Amazing Fantasy* No. 15 hit the newsstands in 1962. I didn't read it until it was reprinted decades later. By that time, the early Spider-Man comics were being collected in the *Essential Spider-Man* series, and volumes were being released quickly. I devoured them. I knew a little about Spider-Man beforehand, but I found something in those early stories that I was not expecting.

After about 100 issues, I had to the put the books down. I was *depressed.*

I couldn't take it anymore! The world just dumped on Peter Parker every issue, and he *never* got a break. I wanted to go back in time to have a word with Spidey creator Stan Lee, and convince him to give the poor guy a date that was *not* interrupted by a super villain. (Don't give me that look; time-travel is a frequent solution in comic books.)

Peter finally did have a date or two. And then he had a girlfriend, and a serious one at that. I was happy for the kid. I was excited for him. But at the same time, I was wary. You see, this girlfriend of his was not Mary Jane Watson, and everyone knows that he ends up with MJ.

Sure enough, the Green Goblin kills this girlfriend, causing Spider-Man to battle the Green Goblin to the death and (you guessed it!) be blamed for the murder of Norman Osborn, who was the alter-ego of the great maniacal murderer. This causes Harry Osborn, Pete's best friend, to go on a mission to hunt down and kill Spider-Man—who is, of course, Peter Parker. All the while, Aunt May has fallen in love with Doctor Octopus, who keeps being harassed by that mean ol' Spider-Man. Aunt May misinterprets Spider-Man's efforts to save her and actually tries to kill him!

Yes, I'm serious.

All in all, life as a superhero has not been good for Peter Parker.

And the thing is, he didn't ask for any of it. The price a superhero must pay is usually related to that hero's powers or actions. Not so with Spider-Man. The hurt brought on Parker seems vindictive and arbitrary, as though the world has decided to make an example of him for no other reason than fate needing somebody to kick around. A quick look at those early issues would make anyone wonder at how Spider-Man has lasted so long.

An Eye for an Eye

Okay, maybe I was a touch hasty before. If we are going to be honest, Peter Parker does deserve *some* of what he gets. In *Amazing Fantasy* No. 15, which is the comic that introduces Spidey, Pete has the chance to capture a thief, but he does not. He has his own problems, he says. That thief then chooses to hide out in the Parker home and kills Uncle Ben.

The first *Spider-Man* movie compounds the problem. This time, Ben is killed as he is waiting in his car to pick up Pete. Ouch! If we did not get the point that this was really Peter's fault before, we get it now!

This is a rather ignoble way of starting things off, for sure, but the event is as important to Spider-Man's origin as the radioactive spider itself. This is the one true failing in Parker's life for which he must atone. But the question then becomes: Has he repaid that debt, and if so, how much more has he paid in addition?

The toll he must pay begins with his image and his job.

No superhero gets quite the same media coverage as Spider-Man does. The press just goes ga-ga over Superman. And why not? Superman himself is writing some of the stories! The media are rather awed by the mystery of Batman. They hate the X-Men, but the X-Men are so secluded at their mansion that they only occasionally notice. Captain America is nearly worshipped, the Fantastic Four are treated as celebrities, and I'm not sure that the Hulk is even aware of what is being said about him.

But Peter is only just getting started when J. Jonah Jameson begins his quest to squash our friendly neighborhood Spider-Man. It all begins in *Amazing Spider-Man (ASM)* No. 1, when Jameson first uses his newspaper, the *Daily Bugle*, to besmirch Spidey's image. Seriously, it happened that quickly. And nothing Spider-Man does seems to help. Later in that same issue, Spidey saves the life of John Jameson, J. Jonah Jameson's son! Does this mend things between the wall-crawler and the newspaper publisher? No, Jameson becomes convinced that Spider-Man was trying to *kill* John rather than save him.

Spider-Man has even saved Jameson himself on several occasions. Personally, if a superhero saved me, I would probably become a fan for life. But Jameson is not one to relinquish his core beliefs, and those beliefs are: 1) money solves everything and 2) Spider-Man is a menace.

Jameson's obsession does benefit Parker in one way. Peter is already desperate for cash. Jameson is always looking for new pictures for his philippics, and he is willing to pay any photographer who can get the shot. Parker, of course, is able to provide. At first, Jameson even pays pretty well. He eventually gets stingy, but those first payments allow the Parkers to live comfortably.

But even here we should point out the psychological effect of having someone's own work used against him. Pete's photos are constantly used to illustrate the threat Spider-Man poses. It's like those political books where a really hideous picture of a President is used.

300 pictures are taken of this person every day, and the publishers pick the one where he is just about to sneeze. It's sort of like that, only Peter takes the pictures himself, and he does it every day.

Pete makes it clear that the only reason he takes this abuse is because of his money problems. Spider-Man is the only major superhero I can think of who is poor, and there is a reason that comic-book creators avoid writing poor heroes. How do they pay for their gadgets? How do they make the rent when they spend all night fighting crime? How do they keep a job while saving the world every five seconds? It's easier for the writers just to make the hero rich from the start so they don't have to deal with the problem. But Pete is constantly in need of money, and he makes that money by denigrating himself. He would never do that to another person, but he would do it to himself because he has obligations to an ailing aunt.

And what about that aunt? Are things any better at home?

Peter Parker is an orphan, but his aunt and uncle took him in. Rereading *Amazing Fantasy* No. 15, it is hard to imagine two people who could be more loving to a boy. They did not appear much in that comic, but they were more giving and attentive than most parents.

The film version of Uncle Ben is even better. In the comic he was great, but in the movie he was everything he was in the comics and more—he was concerned. The famous line about power and responsibility appeared only in narration in the original comic, but in the film it comes from Ben's mouth, and it fits well there.

And then came the event that would haunt Peter forever, the one great sin in Pete's life.

What happened to Uncle Ben was tragic, but it did not stop there. Ben's death did something to Aunt May. She became weak where she had not been so before, and the bills began to pile up. Grief had struck her in the most horrible of ways. Money was a real problem, as we had already learned, but May's judgment began to slip as well. It began with a real hatred of Spider-Man, but it progressed to a sympathy and even love for Doctor Octopus. She could not understand the threat he posed, and her trust in him was only strengthened every time he and Spider-Man faced off.

In an epic three-way battle between Doc Ock, Hammerhead, and

Spider-Man, Doc Ock used Aunt May as a human shield, and May still could not see what was really happening. Spidey finally gets to Doc Ock, but the battle was not yet won. Peter Parker's family life hit perhaps its lowest point as Aunt May found a pistol and fired it at Spider-Man. It was only her frail state that saved Pete, because she shot wide, allowing Spider-Man to escape. But the fight did not end there.

It ended at a wedding, of all places. Right after the most terrible event of Pete's life (discussed next), May agreed to marry Doc Ock. It was not Spider-Man who stopped the proceedings here, but Hammerhead again. The interruption was all that was needed, for the melee seemed to bring about the death of the good doctor. May was free, for a time.

Well, at least he had that great girlfriend, right? I mean, Mary Jane has always been by his side, even from the very beginning. Right?

That's how I assumed things went. Mary Jane is always in the cartoons or movies. If you pick up a new comic, she is there. Every new revision of his origin has MJ standing just a few feet away when that spider bites into Peter. Hadn't she always been around in one way or another?

Those people who go back to the early comics after getting to know the modern Spidey (as I did) are in for a surprise. First of all, MJ is not even in the story for the first few years.

Spider-Man's first serious love interest was *Bugle* employee Betty Brant, though their relationship never really even got started because Spider-Man (as usual) was always in the way. When she started dating a *Bugle* reporter, Pete started chasing larger prey. Mary Jane Watson was first mentioned in *ASM* No. 25, though it was not until No. 42 that she finally met Pete. (As a side note, Stan Lee must have realized even then how important she would become since he alluded to her consistently for more than a year before finally revealing her.)

Consider those issue numbers. *ASM* No. 42 came out in November of 1966, more than four years after Spider-Man was introduced. Not long, considering that Spidey has now been around for more than forty years, but it goes to prove that MJ was not part of the original vision of the story.

Between those critical issues of No. 25 and No. 42 came No. 31, obviously. In No. 30, Pete left behind Betty Brant forever (sort of), and No. 31 introduced Gwen Stacy.

At first, Gwen Stacy thought Peter was self-righteous and aloof. That opinion did not last terribly long. She and MJ competed for Pete's affections for a time, but Peter chose Gwen, and MJ ended up with Harry Osborn (son of the Green Goblin, of course—nobody said this was going to be simple).

Gwen's father was police captain George Stacy, who began to figure out Spider-Man's true identity. In a battle between our favorite webslinger and Doc Ock, Captain Stacy was mortally wounded while saving a child from falling debris. His dying words revealed that he knew that it was Pete under that mask, and he asked the young superhero to take care of Gwen.

Meanwhile, Gwen blamed Spider-Man for the death (naturally), and no amount of evidence would shake that belief (are we seeing a trend here?). Surprisingly, that didn't seem to put too much of a strain on their relationship. She didn't know who Spider-Man really was and Pete doesn't seem to care all that much. They became more and more serious about each other.

At this juncture in my reading, I was bewildered. After all, Peter ends up with Mary Jane, and I had never heard of Gwen Stacy!

I would soon come to understand how important Gwen Stacy was (and is) to Spider-Man, for the single most important event in Peter's life centered around her. The Green Goblin took Gwen hostage and, in a battle with Spidey, flung her off the George Washington Bridge. Spider-Man used his webbing to catch her, but it was too late. She was dead.

What is really interesting here is a small notation found, almost overlooked, in the frame where Spidey's webbing catches Gwen's legs. Her body reacts to the sudden jerk, contorting unnaturally backward. And there, right beside her neck, we see the small sound effect: "Snap!"

Now, later evidence suggested that it was the fall that killed her and not Spider-Man, but that does not really matter. There was enough doubt at the time to haunt any man for the rest of his life. Her death alone would have been loss enough, but his involvement in that death and his feeling of responsibility for it still weigh on him.

The importance of this event cannot be overstated. To put it in context, when Kurt Busiek and Alex Ross retold those years of the Marvel Universe in their essential book *Marvels*, they ended each issue with a catastrophic event, such as the attack by Galactus. Their final event, the climax of the series, and the one that finally destroyed the will of the main character, was the death of Gwen Stacy. Not half of New York being ripped apart, not some threat of aliens—the death of one single woman. It was the defining moment for Spider-Man, and it will never be forgotten.

The death of the Green Goblin did not console Pete, and he turned to the best friend he had left: Mary Jane Watson.

Ah, yes. We're on track now, aren't we? Well, no, not quite. You see, while Peter would propose sixty issues later, Mary Jane refused him and disappeared for five years. After her return, she finally accepted his proposal, and they were married in 1987, twenty-five years after Spider-Man first appeared in *Amazing Fantasy* No. 15.

At one point, Mary Jane got pregnant, though she seemed to miscarry the child. In fact, there was plenty of evidence to suggest that the Green Goblin (yes, he's back) kidnapped the infant. But even after ten years, that plot has yet to have a satisfactory conclusion.

And in the course of their marriage, Pete and MJ have separated more than once, and Mary Jane once seemed to die in a place crash. (Well, they have all seemed to die at least once, including Aunt May and Spider-Man himself. Gwen's death was heartbreaking, but each additional death—especially when they come back to life—has been less moving. It's hard to get emotional about them anymore.)

Putting MJ at the beginning of the first movie or in the first episode of the cartoon really undermines the emotional turmoil Peter Parker has had to deal with to be Spider-Man. Nothing in the films reach the emotional level of watching the Green Goblin kill his girlfriend.

And thus we arrive forty years later. Death and heartbreak have followed Parker around since the murder of Uncle Ben. Does he deserve it because of that one initial sin? We can hardly say that he has been repaid in kind. He has dealt with poverty, ridicule, dishonor, the madness of a loved one, the death of another, and a stormy relationship with his wife, including having to mourn her death prematurely. How many lives must be lost for Uncle Ben's to be paid?

But we must understand that none of these things can pay for the death of Uncle Ben. What has paid for it is the good that Spider-Man has done because of that death. He has saved countless lives and protected countless people. That is the payment of the debt. The pain he has experienced is something different.

A Merciful Rebirth

Superheroes never die, of course, especially in the Marvel Universe. But recently Marvel caused a rebirth amongst its heroes that differs from the normal "fake death." This time, in its Ultimate line of comics, the entire Marvel universe was reborn in the modern day with a new continuity, new origins, and new battles. *Ultimate Spider-Man* was the first of these re-envisioning, and writer Brian Michael Bendis, over the last several years, has been rewriting the web crawler into something familiar, but different also. Bendis is a fine writer, and his books are well worth the read, but there is no comparing Stan Lee's Spidey to the new one. The Ultimate Spidey, quite frankly, has it easy in comparison.

The first of many places where Bendis pulls his punches with Pete is in the boy's job. In this version, Peter does not take photographs for the *Bugle*, but instead runs their Web site. Probably more realistic (no one now would hire a fifteen-year-old photographer), but passing along an anti-Spider-Man story and helping *create* that story are two separate things.

Even his family life is better now. Here May is an aging hippie who hardly misses a step when Ben dies. Not that she is not in grief, for she is, but her emotional and physical strength keep her afloat. She remains a strong character and a strong influence throughout the series, or at least what has been written so far. If there is to be a wedding for her and Doc Ock in the future, I cannot imagine how it will come about.

The love triangle between Pete, Gwen Stacy, and MJ? Hardly a footnote. Gwen did not seem to have any interest at all, even if Mary

Jane did get a little jealous. Gwen had to live with the Parkers for awhile, but on the whole it was pretty innocent.

Bendis put Pete and MJ together almost from the start. They have their problems, but they seem to always come back together. What had been serious romances in the original comic are either nonexistent or frivolous in this new universe.

And the death of Gwen in this version was much more merciful to Peter than it was in the original. This time, Carnage got her. That's it. No dropping off a bridge, no rescue attempt by Spidey. She just died. Terrible, of course, but hardly the same thing. Certainly Pete felt guilty over it, but there is something about that little "Snap!" in the original death scene that has had us wondering for decades. The death of the Ultimate universe's Gwen Stacy will not be long remembered.

I feel better for Peter reading these comics, but when young Parker starts complaining about how hard his life has been, I'm not much on sympathy. In this comic, the only event that has forced Peter to grow is the death of Uncle Ben. It is little wonder that he acts like a spoiled teenager at times. That's what he is. The original Peter Parker lost that a long time ago.

I like the Ultimate version of Spider-Man, but I am not in awe of him as I am with the "classic." Bendis has created a Spider-Man that has summoned a great deal of inner strength to keep doing the job he does. That is impressive. Stan Lee, Steve Ditko, and the creators who came after them formed a Spider-Man who has been utterly broken 100 times and keeps coming back for more, even if the job takes his very soul. That is something incredible.

Perhaps this is why we like him so much. After about 100 issues I put the books down, depressed. But I came back to them. The sacrifices that Peter Parker makes cause us to truly care for him. No other superhero commands in me quite the same sort of affection because no other superhero would give quite so much.

Back to Work

There have been some great artists working on Spider-Man titles, but none of them have matched one particular scene, drawn by Steve

Ditko, in *Amazing Spider-Man* No. 30. It was before Mary Jane Watson and just before Gwen Stacy, when Parker's heart belonged to Betty Brant. Like all of Parker's relationships, however, Spider-Man kept getting in the way, and Peter broke it off with Betty without her ever knowing why. The image I have in mind is of Peter walking away with Betty looking at him, bewildered. The specter of Spider-Man, an outline only, is standing between them, his head bowed in sorrow and his arms outstretched, holding the two apart. It is Ditko's best illustration, and my favorite of any Spider-Man comic book I've read.

In the end, that one image tells the story of Peter Parker more fully than any story arc. Peter wants to live his life, and Spider-Man will not let him. With great power comes great responsibility, yes, but for Peter Parker, responsibility is not the half of it. It is sacrifice, heartache, and loss. It is his entire life destroyed, and the lives of those around him.

In *ASM* No. 98, the last frame is a wonderful drawing of Peter and Gwen kissing. The tenderness of the image is touching, the text around it is more than a little foreboding: "Who says we never give Spidey a happy ending?"

Well, we know how that turned out now. Spider-Man stories simply do not end happily. Knowing this much about Peter Parker's life, I greet each new issue with concern over his future.

Maybe this is part of what keeps me coming back. He is the greatest of the heroes because he does it for the least. Everyone else gets fame or love or friends or *something*. They get something out of it. Spider-Man gets nothing back. In fact, he must continue to *give*. We cannot accuse him of having a motive other than a sense of mission.

Things have been looking up for Spider-Man lately. He did, of course, marry Mary Jane. They had a couple of separations, but they are together now, and they seem happy.

In *The House of M*, the world was transformed to give each hero exactly what he wanted. For Parker, it was a life with Uncle Ben, Aunt May, a son, and, yes, Gwen Stacy—*not* Mary Jane Watson. We must never forget that Gwen is the one he wants, but still, he's no longer alone, and that has made a big difference. When your whole life is nothing but hurt, a little triumph will sustain you for a lifetime.

And recently, he was made a member of the Avengers. This turn of events may change everything. I said before that Spider-Man is the only poor major hero, but living in Stark Tower has freed him up financially. Also, what was truly terrible about Peter's life in the '60s was how utterly alone he was, and in a way that no major superhero has ever been alone. We may say that Batman is alone, but Batman has Robin, Alfred, Batgirl, Nightwing, Catwoman, Commissioner Gordon, Oracle and her Birds of Prey, and countless others. Even the X-Men have each other as company, even if the world hates them.

Pete's marriage cured that loneliness to an extent, but now he is with people who really understand his powers and what it means to be a hero. At last he can go out to a movie with people who will not think it rude when, after hearing police sirens, he suddenly leaves.

And in all of this, we should be happy for him. Parker has spent enough time in this solo battle. He has earned his rest.

But then, he's Peter Parker. Even as I am writing this, Marvel's *Civil War* is changing everything yet again, and changing everything so quickly that each issue could potentially change this analysis of Spider-Man's life. It may be the event to start another run of bad luck for Pete. If not this, then *something* will.

"Who says we never give Spidey a happy ending?" Unfortunately, we suspect that all of Spidey's endings will be mournful.

PAUL LYTLE is an author and musician living on the southwest side of Houston, with his wife Anastasia. He earned a bachelor of arts from Houston Baptist University in English and political science with a specialization in creative writing, and is currently working toward a master of liberal arts degree. He is an editor and writer for the bi-monthly webzine *Primum Mobile* (http://www.Primum-Mobile.net) and is currently amassing quite a collection of comic books and gently used paperbacks. This is his second essay for the Smart Pop series, the first appearing in *The Man from Krypton*. More of his writings, as well as news and other projects, can be found at www.PaulLytle.com.

Annotated Bibliography

The following comic books represent critical events in the life of Peter Parker/Spider-Man. Almost all are from *Amazing Spider-Man (ASM)*, and are generally available reprinted on CD-ROM and in trade paperbacks.

Conway, Gerry (w) and Gil Kane (i). *ASM* Nos. 121–122. Marvel Comics: Jun.–July 1973. The most critical of Spidey comics, where Green Goblin kills Gwen Stacy. The battle that follows brings about the death of the Goblin.

Conway, Gerry (w) and Ross Andru (i). *ASM* Nos. 130–131. Marvel Comics: Mar.–Apr. 1974. The surprise wedding between Aunt May and Doc Ock, and so soon after the death of Gwen.

Lee, Stan (w) and Steve Ditko (i). *Amazing Fantasy* No. 15. Marvel Comics: Aug. 1962. In my opinion this remains the best Spider-Man comic of all time. Explains Spidey's origin and the death of Uncle Ben.

Lee, Stan (w) and Steve Ditko (i). *ASM* No. 1. Marvel Comics: Mar. 1963. The course of Peter's life is forming quickly. Aunt May's money trouble is discussed on page two, and J. Jonah Jameson begins his infamous tirades on page four!

Lee, Stan (w) and Steve Ditko (i). *ASM* No. 25. Marvel Comics: June 1965. Mary Jane Watson is first mentioned, but not completely seen.

Lee, Stan (w) and Steve Ditko (i). *ASM* No. 30. Marvel Comics: Nov. 1965. Pete and Betty Brant separate for good.

Lee, Stan (w) and Steve Ditko (i). *ASM* No. 31. Marvel Comics: Dec. 1965. The first appearance of Gwen Stacy.

Lee, Stan (w) and John Romita (Sr.) (i). *ASM* No. 42. Marvel Comics: Nov. 1966. MJ is first introduced to Peter.

Lee, Stan (w) and Gil Kane (i). *ASM* No. 90. Marvel Comics: Nov. 1970. Gwen's father, George Stacy, is killed. Gwen blames Spider-Man for the death, solidifying her hated for the web crawler.

Lee, Stan (w) and Gil Kane (i). *ASM* No. 98. Marvel Comics: July 1971. If only it had ended here. Gwen Stacy and Pete share a much deserved kiss that proves to be the high watermark of their relationship.

Michelinie, David (w), John Romita, Jr. (p), and Alex Saviuk (i). *ASM* Nos. 290–292. Marvel Comics: Jul.–Sept. 1987. Parker proposes again and is finally accepted.

Romita, John (Sr.) and Gerry Conway (w). *ASM* No. 115. Marvel Comics:

Dec. 1972. Aunt May shows her loyalties when she shoots at Spider-Man to protect Doc Ock.

Shooter, Jim (plot), David Michelinie (script), and Paul Ryan (i). *ASM* Annual No. 21. Marvel Comics: 1987. The marriage, twenty-five years after Spider-Man first appeared.

Stern, Roger (w) and John Romita, Jr. (i). *ASM* No. 243. Marvel Comics: Sept. 1983. Mary Jane's long-awaited return.

Wolfman, Marv (w) and Ross Andru (i). *ASM* No. 182. Marvel Comics: Jul.–Aug. 1978. Peter first proposes to Mary Jane, and she refuses in the next issue, only to disappear for another five years.

DAVID HOPKINS

Secrets and Secret-Keepers

Why the mask?

Sooner or later, it's a question every storyteller who deals in super-heroes has to ask him or herself: Why does our hero keep his identity a secret? Sure, there are the obvious reasons—or excuses—as anyone who's ever watched an episode of E! The True Hollywood Story *can easily imagine: a fear of celebrity; a desire for privacy, anonymity; a need to escape the public spotlight, if only for a few hours. So, okay, that might answer the question in a public sense. But why wear a mask with your loved ones? Your friends, your family? Why hide from them?*

David Hopkins is happy to suggest a few possible answers....

AFTER NEARLY A decade of writing Spider-Man, creator Stan Lee decided to inject Peter Parker with a dose of maturity in *Amazing Spider-Man* No. 100. Spider-Man beats up a team of bank robbers, and realizes it doesn't give him the same thrill it used to. He bounces along the rooftops: "Maybe I'm finally growing up, at last!" Peter laments his life as a "corny costumed clown," and thinks of the alternative, a normal life with then-girlfriend Gwen Stacy. What would married life be like as Spider-Man? "It's tough enough to keep my secret identity from her now. But once we were married, the strain could be too great."

Wait. Hold on.

He plans to keep his secret identity from his own wife?! Yep. He decides his only option is to either quit being Spider-Man entirely or forgo any hope of marriage. Now *this* is a superhero who's serious about maintaining a secret identity!

The superhero's story, like all heroes' stories, is a journey of self-discovery. As part of this, the alter ego has always been a central motif in the superhero genre. Superman, Batman, Captain Marvel, the Hulk, Daredevil, Thor, and Iron Man, all of them and numerous others have hid behind a fabricated identity. Even Odysseus, in Homer's *The Odyssey* (which I would consider to be the first true superhero story[1]), made use of the alter ego. When Polyphemus the one-eyed giant asks Odysseus his name, he responds with "Outis," meaning "Nobody." And then after escaping the giant, when his ship is almost out of range, he shouts out to the giant, "I am Odysseus, son of Laertes." These bold "I am" statements are popular in superhero films, always delivered with a healthy dose of melodrama. These lines exist to emphasize that the mild-mannered civilian is merely a facade for the primary identity of the true hero. The first Spider-Man film starts with the line "Who am I?" while the last line confidently answers the question, "I'm Spider-Man."

Many of these superheroes have a confidant, someone to share the secret of their true identity. For instance, Superman has Ma and Pa Kent. No matter how difficult things get in Metropolis, he can always fly home to Smallville to sit with his parents on the front porch and share some fresh-baked apple pie. Batman, the brooding dark hero, who never seems too conflicted about living "a normal life," could at least drive back to the bat cave and chat with Alfred, who'd probably have a martini waiting for him. The Hulk has Rick Jones. Daredevil has Foggy Nelson. The X-Men have each other. The Fantastic Four never bothered with secret identities, and are treated like celebrities because of it. But Spider-Man has suffered more, fought harder, and held tighter to his secret identity than any other superhero. For twenty-two years, Peter Parker was without a true confidant.

So Why the Secrecy?

Peter Parker's answer is straightforward and well rehearsed: I keep my identity secret to protect my loved ones from those who would

---

[1] While Odysseus may not be able to fire a lethal optic blast or possess the enhanced traits of some irradiated animal, he operates on a level that exceeds normal human ability, and his enemies are certainly supernatural.

hurt them to get at me. The movie beats this rationalization into the ground. "No matter what I do, no matter how hard I try, the ones I love will always be the ones who pay." Okay, we understand—this is the big reason. But in comic-book continuity, Peter has several other reasons that have made his secret much more than just a secret.

1. UNCLE BEN

When Peter Parker first gained his powers, his first impulse was not to go home to tell Aunt May and Uncle Ben. Peter figured he could earn some money as a masked wrestler with his unfair super-powered advantage. He probably would have gotten grounded if Aunt May and Uncle Ben found out what he was doing. So originally, the secret was due to good old-fashioned teenage mischief. Borrowing the car without permission. Sneaking off to a party. Or using your radioactive spider powers to moonlight as a professional wrestler. You know, the usual stuff.

As the origin goes, Spider-Man comes face to face with a criminal on the run. Spider-Man steps aside and lets him escape claiming it's not his responsibility. Later, that same criminal kills Uncle Ben. Peter's inconsolable guilt became the primary motivation for taking his masked wrestler persona and transforming it into a superhero—forever atoning for his sin. I see Spider-Man as an act of transference. Spider-Man must bear the responsibility for the sin on behalf of Peter, thus shielding Peter from ever having to deal directly with the guilt and tell Aunt May what he's done. Spider-Man is his secret. And that secret is no longer a matter of teenage mischief—it is a sacred responsibility. To end the secret, in Peter's traumatized psyche, is to end Spider-Man. And in a sense, allow him to be free from guilt.

2. AUNT MAY

Peter lost his parents at the age of six; Red Skull killed them when he blew up their airplane. With Uncle Ben's violent death, Aunt May is the only parental figure he has left. If Peter told her he was indirectly responsible for his murder, would she blame him? Especially since Aunt May shares the general public opinion about "that horrible Spider-Man." Would he lose the rest of his family? It's something Peter is not willing to risk.

In the early years of the comic-book series, Aunt May was continually in ill health. Numerous storylines involved Spider-Man having to search for the cure to save her and finding it just in the nick of time. Peter is certain he has the touch of death. If he came out about being Spider-Man, she might have a heart attack. And Stan Lee did his best to perpetuate the theory that Aunt May's failing health could not stand the words, "I'm Spider-Man," coming from Peter's mouth.

To complicate matters, Aunt May has had a particular fondness for Dr. Otto Octavius, Spider-Man's nemesis Doctor Octopus. He kidnapped her once, but Aunt May was treated so well, she was completely oblivious to being a hostage. Later, seeking a new hideout from the law, Doctor Octopus rented the spare bedroom in Aunt May's house. Most surprisingly, in *Amazing Spider-Man* No. 131, Doctor Octopus and Aunt May almost got married. Kids don't want to think about their parents in the bedroom. I can only imagine the horror Peter felt whenever his mind wandered too far, to sweet old Aunt May and Doc Ock (with the physique of Mr. Potatohead) on their wedding night. Yeesh. Who needs kryptonite when you have that hanging over your head? If Peter shared his secret identity with Aunt May, might she pick Dr. Octavius over Peter?

3. J. JONAH JAMESON

Must be difficult to work for a newspaper with an editorial policy to destroy you. Peter Parker has the definitive soul-sucking job. He takes pictures of himself as Spider-Man and sells them to the *Daily Bugle*, so they can further discredit and demoralize the webbed menace. Is this a means of further punishment to cope with his secret identity guilt? Or is he once again finding ways to exploit being Spider-Man, beyond a career as a masked wrestler? Or maybe he simply tries to keep his friends close, and his enemies closer?

If he were to reveal his secret identity, losing his job would be the least of his concerns. J. Jonah Jameson would ruin Peter's life as only a corporate media-power can. Jameson would sue Peter Parker for millions.[2] Jameson would crucify Peter on the front cover of his pa-

[2] As Jameson does in *Amazing Spider-Man* No. 533.

per. The *Daily Bugle* is a daily reminder as to why he should keep his secret. Each new edition of the paper reinforces the paranoia. Yes, everyone *is* out to get the friendly neighborhood Spider-Man, and J. Jonah Jameson leads the charge.

4. CAPTAIN GEORGE STACY

In what has to be one of the saddest moments in Spider-Man's history, retired Police Captain George Stacy, Gwen's father, dies in *Amazing Spider-Man* No. 90. Spider-Man and Doctor Octopus were fighting along the rooftops, as superheroes and super villains are wont to do. A crowd gathers below, including Captain Stacy. Doc Ock's mechanical arms had gone out of control, and they knock a chimney off the roof. The debris is about to fall on a boy too petrified to move, but Captain Stacy acts quickly and pushes the boy out of the way. Instead, the bricks land on Captain Stacy. He is fatally wounded. With his dying words, Captain Stacy tells Spider-Man, "It's Gwen! After I'm gone there'll be no one to look after her, no one, *Peter*, except you! Be good to her son! Be good to her. She loves you so very much." Peter's first reaction is surprise at Captain Stacy knowing his secret identity! "You...you know who I am! You must have always known!" Another father figure dies as a result of Spider-Man, and again his identity takes center stage.

Gwen Stacy blamed Spider-Man for her father's death, which partially explains why ten issues later in *Amazing Spider-Man* No. 100, Peter insisted on keeping his secret from her even if they were to get married. He couldn't let her know that he was responsible.

5. GREEN GOBLIN

Captain Stacy wasn't the only person who knew Spider-Man's secret. There's Green Goblin. In *Amazing Spider-Man* No. 39, Green Goblin used a special gas to numb Spider-Man's spidey-senses, then followed Spider-Man home to discover his secret identity. Fortunately, in the next issue, Spider-Man knocked Green Goblin into live wires, causing Green Goblin to have amnesia. (I can't explain the science. It's comics!) However, this amnesia was not permanent, and over the next few years Goblin's memory came and went at the worst possible moments. As Peter feared, Green Goblin used this knowledge of Spider-Man's true identity to hurt those closest to Peter, specifically Gwen Stacy in *Amazing Spider-Man* No. 121.

The damsel-in-distress is as old as *The Odyssey*; it's the most over-used plot device since the ticking time bomb. The hero must always save the beautiful girl from the clutches of evil men. And certainly the superhero genre has had its share of damsels-in-distress. Lois Lane could win a lifetime achievement award. And as Spider-Man's own plucky love interest, Gwen Stacy, possessing both beauty and vulnerability, certainly seemed primed for the role. With this dramatic device so overused, no reader at the time suspected such a character would actually die. Green Goblin kidnaps Gwen, who he knows is Peter Parker's girlfriend, luring Spider-Man into a fight on the Brooklyn Bridge.[3] During the melee, Gwen is knocked off the bridge. Spider-Man shoots a web-line to save Gwen and stop her fall. The webbing grabs her ankle, and she stops suddenly, with a "snap!" coming from her neck.[4] Again, the guilt overcomes Peter Parker. He tells a police officer, "She's dead, and Spider-Man killed her" (*Amazing Spider-Man* No. 122).

Gwen Stacy died because she knew Peter Parker, and Green Goblin knew Peter Parker was Spider-Man. If other villains were to find out Peter's secret, surely Gwen wouldn't be the last love of Peter's to die at the hands of a psychotic, vengeful villain. So no one else must know his true identity.

But one more person did know. It wouldn't be revealed until many years later, but Mary Jane Watson knew from the very beginning. While critics would call this revisionist history, when looking over the entire continuity, it works with surprising consistency. Particularly, it makes the final page of *Amazing Spider-Man* No. 122 that much more meaningful, adding a touch of dramatic irony. Distraught

---

[3] The original caption on *Amazing Spider-Man* No. 121 says it's the George Washington Bridge, but Stan Lee (as editor) has said he labeled it in error. Some reprints of the issue have had the text amended.

[4] There's been some controversy over what actually killed Gwen Stacy, and Professor James Kakalios answers this question in his book *The Physics of Superheroes*. Kakalios claims the sudden stop would've been the cause of Gwen Stacy's death as "traveling at such a speed (an estimated 95 mph), coming to rest in such a short time interval [would be] ... no real difference between hitting the webbing and hitting the water."

and grieving Gwen's death, Peter yells at Mary Jane, verbally striking out and pushing his friend away. In a silent three-panel sequence that still gives me chills, Mary Jane stands at the door for a moment, all too aware of the guilt Peter feels as Spider-Man. Mary Jane could reveal what she knows, but chooses not to and instead shuts the door, staying there with him—to comfort him and allow him to hold onto the security blanket of his secrecy.

How Does One Keep a Secret?

Peter Parker keeps his secret because he has been traumatized by the unintended consequences of his own lack of responsibility. Like most traumatized persons, he needs a sense of control. The secret identity is his control. And this deep psychological need to maintain his secret identity, ironically forces him to go to elaborate and dangerous lengths to keep it. His secret identity is the proverbial "finger in the dike" holding back a potential flood of further tragedy. As he says in *Amazing Spider-Man* No. 100, "Why must everything I touch end in tragedy? And those I love are always hurt the most." But has the secret caused him more pain than comfort? What are the psychological effects of long-term secret keeping?

In *Emotional Longevity*, Dr. Norman Anderson explores how emotions affect health and well-being. Part two of the book deals specifically with the results of secrecy, and concealing and revealing trauma. Dr. Anderson offers unique insight, which could be applied to understanding Peter Parker and the effect his secret has had on him.

Keeping a secret involves the mind being able to control thoughts. It does this by using two complementary but oppositional processes—the *intentional operating process* (the operator) and the *ironic monitoring process* (the monitor):

> The operator works on the conscious level, helping us think about what we want to think about. The monitor, on the other hand, works unconsciously, telling us when we're having or are about to have thoughts that we do not want, so we can immediately correct them (Norman 71).

For example, if Spider-Man swings through the city looking for criminal activity, the operator keeps a collection of "criminal looking" images (menacing guy with ski mask and gun) at the forefront of his mind, while the monitor registers and rejects everything that doesn't look "criminal" (police officer directing traffic) or distracts from the task at hand (pretty girl in red dress). If Peter tries to come up with a witty response to a villain's banter, the operator searches for the most amusing response while the monitor tells Peter all the other options are lame, and urges him to pass over those.

The monitor and operator also work together in helping to avoid doing things, such as revealing your secret identity. The operator helps Peter talk about matters besides the identity, offering a distracter, while the monitor looks for anything that might get too close to "I'm Spider-Man" so it can tell his brain to skip over those things. According to Dr. Anderson, this monitoring process—by focusing so closely on the very thing the person is trying ignore—makes it nearly impossible not to fixate on that very subject. It's difficult to act normal around someone you aren't supposed to tell something to while the "something" is bouncing around in your head.

For Peter Parker, it's no different. Here's how it might work during an average day (circa Stan Lee era):

7:30 A.M.: Wake up in the morning. Go downstairs. Aunt May is fixing breakfast. She says good morning.
Monitor: Do not tell her you are Spider-Man.
Operator: Instead, talk about how good her cooking is.
8:45 A.M.: Go to Empire State University for first class of the day, Dr. Connors's science class. On the way, see best friend Harry Osborn.
Monitor: Do not talk about Spider-Man.
Operator: Make fun of him about something.
11:00 A.M.: Early lunch. Hang out with Flash, Mary Jane, Gwen, and Harry.
Monitor: Do not tell them about plans to change into your Spider-Man costume and swing through the city looking for crime.
Operator: Say you're going to the library.
12:00 P.M.: After lunch, change into Spider-Man costume and swing through the city looking for crime. Lo and behold, there's a thug

robbing some poor old lady. Beat him up, and web him to a light post for the police to get him.

Monitor: Do not tell the thug you are Peter Parker.

Operator: Engage in witty banter instead.

12:15 P.M.: Time to get to work at the *Daily Bugle*.

Operator: For the love of God, make sure to change back into your normal clothes.

12:30 P.M.: Enter the newsroom. Say hi to Betty Brant.

Monitor: ...but do not say, "I'm Spider-Man."

12:35 P.M.: Get chewed out by J. Jonah Jameson for taking crappy photos of Spider-Man.

Monitor: ...who you are, so don't tell him.

6: 00 P.M.: After work, spend rest of the evening saving more old ladies from thugs, who seem absolutely obsessed with purses.

Monitor: But do this as Spider-Man, *not* Peter Parker.

1:00 A.M.: It's late. Try to sneak in the house quietly. Aunt May is still up, wondering where you've been.

Monitor: Don't say you've been swinging around as Spider-Man.

Operator: Say you were at the library studying.

1:05 A.M.: Somehow the library excuses still work after all these years. Aunt May pats you on the head, and tells you what a good boy you are, and that dinner is in the fridge.

Keep in mind, Peter has had to keep this secret every day for several years. Dr. Anderson notes, "Chronic thought suppression might be a risk factor for depression and anxiety" (72). This might explain Peter's sour demeanor. Studies have shown that keeping a secret has great emotional consequences, particularly when the secret keeper is "left with nothing to think about but the secret itself" (Anderson 74). Any attempts to further suppress only "causes intrusive thoughts about the secret to manifest themselves in the psyche of the secret keeper" (Anderson 74).

Around friends and Aunt May, Peter tries to put on a happy face and pretend no problems exist. Dr. Anderson would categorize this behavior as trademark for a repressor.[5] "Repressors generally cope with feelings of anxiety by denying that such feelings exist and sup-

---

[5] From Freud's theories on anxiety-avoidance, the two coping styles are active (sensitizers) and avoidant (repressors). More information can be found here: http://www.utdallas.edu/~kprager/chpt%206.htm.

pressing disturbing thoughts" (76–77). Their avoidance leads to physiological trouble:

- higher heart rates and blood pressure
- larger biological responses to stress
- elevated cholesterol, cortisol, and glucose levels
- reduced immune-system functioning (77)

Peter's enhanced spider-powers have probably shielded him from the majority of these problems. I'm sure his cholesterol level is on the low end of things to worry about. However, it's interesting that in *Amazing Spider-Man* No. 87, Peter had the flu. Not the result of an evil bacteria gun or mutant flu-powered villain. Instead, Spider-Man caught the regular old normal-person bug.[6] To my knowledge, he's the only superhero to have gotten sick without kryptonite or radioactivity being involved. In Peter Parker's flu-induced delirium, he actually confessed to everyone that he was Spider-Man. Later, after coming to his senses, he recanted on the confession. He convinced Hobie Brown (a.k.a. the Prowler) to pose as Spider-Man with Parker in the room to further validate the idea that Peter was simply out-of-his-mind with the flu.

Dr. Anderson's studies also show that disclosing trauma and secrets has remarkable benefits with both mood and health, which leads us back to Mary Jane—the one person who's known his identity from the very beginning. When she finally confronts Peter about his secret, it marks his first step toward dealing with the trauma surrounding his secret identity.

Mary Jane Saves the Psyche

Before Mary Jane returned as a serious romantic prospect, there was Black Cat. Black Cat was a long-time admirer of the webbed menace, and knew nothing of his true identity. For the writers, this relationship posed an interesting reversal. She was the only costumed

---

[6] Yes, pun intended.

character Peter ever seriously dated, and consequently she's the only person Peter has ever revealed his identity to...without being deliriously sick or without them figuring it out first (*Spectacular Spider-Man* No. 87). If Peter said he's Spider-Man, it would shock and surprise his friends. However, when Spider-Man revealed he's Peter Parker, Black Cat was hardly impressed. This relationship was over before it started. Black Cat could not accept Spider-Man's ordinary life. "To her, Peter Parker was such a bore and a drag that she couldn't bear to look at him unless he was dressed as Spider-Man" (Fettinger). This hardly makes Black Cat a true confidant, someone to ease Peter's troubled mind. From her perspective, Peter Parker is nothing impressive without his mask. And so, there's very little empathy for him dealing with his secret.

Only Mary Jane[7] could play the hero and rescue Peter Parker's psyche. In *Amazing Spider-Man* No. 257, Peter Parker is in his apartment, recovering from a grueling battle with the Puma. Mary Jane arrives unannounced to celebrate her modeling job. She brings the wine. She inquires about his injured arm, but Peter lies saying he sprained it playing racquetball. Peter's spidey-sense goes off, and he hurriedly shoves Mary Jane into the bathroom and jams the doorframe so she can't escape. Then Puma crashes through his window (having sniffed Spider-Man out, of course). True to form, Peter covers his face so Puma won't see his identity while he changes into Spider-Man. Mary Jane is trapped, banging on the door, as all hell breaks lose on the other side. Spider-Man takes the fight outside, and eventually Mary Jane busts down the door to reveal a completely thrashed apartment. After the fight, Peter Parker returns home having completely forgotten about Mary Jane. Once he enters the room, she hugs him, greatly relieved that he's okay. But how does Peter explain this one? The *intentional operating process* in his brain must have short circuited as he struggled to find a new lie:

---

[7] In his Web article "Why Did It Have to be You, Mary Jane?" (http://spideykicksbutt.com/WhyYouMaryJane/WhyYouMaryJanePart1.html) J. R. Fettinger writes the most comprehensive essay on the subject of Peter Parker and Mary Jane. Fettinger removes all doubt that Mary Jane is the one Peter was meant to be with, despite Marvel's fickle editorial policy toward her character.

MARY JANE: You don't have to make up another one of your phony excuses, Peter! Not now! I know the truth! The *real* truth!
PETER: What are you talking about?
MARY JANE: I've known your secret for years! Up until today, I always thought I could cope with it if I ever had to experience it firsthand, but I can't! I can't! I just can't cope with the fact that Peter Parker is secretly Spider-Man!

The story continues in the next issue, where Peter tries to explain. Mary Jane cuts him off, giving a most honest assessment of Peter Parker's life: "What's the use, Peter? You're only going to lie to me!" and two panels later "I care about you, Peter! I really do! But you come with so much baggage!" Later, Peter has a moment alone with his thoughts: "Sometimes I feel like I have absolutely no control over my own life!"

In *Amazing Spider-Man* No. 259, Mary Jane and Peter are able have a talk while in Central Park. Poor Peter is still trying to think of a way to cover up his secret identity. He thinks: "What am I going to do? How can I ever convince Mary Jane that she's wrong about secret identity? Should I even try?!" I guess the Hobie Brown strategy can only be used once. Mary Jane laments they've known each other such a long time, and yet they don't really know each other at all. Instead of interrogating Peter about his secret life as Spider-Man, she tells him about her own secret life growing up with an abusive father, how she worked extra jobs to pay for her mother's hospital bills, and how she eventually deserted her sister to start her own life. Mary Jane shows vulnerability as a way to reassure Peter it's okay to confide. We all have our secrets, but still Peter is worried. "I still don't know what to do about Mary Jane knowing my secret identity. The girl just bared her soul to me! How can I lie to her now?!" Finally, he yields and admits that Spider-Man can count Mary Jane as a friend.

The most significant and important aspect of this disclosure is that the world didn't end, nobody died, nothing bad happened as a result of Peter having a confidant. If anything, it improved the friendship between Peter and Mary Jane, leading to their marriage. He had proposed to Mary Jane before No. 257, and she had turned him down. Clearly, she couldn't marry someone who couldn't be honest with her. Eventually, after a second proposal and (temporary) rejection the marriage Stan Lee hinted at with Gwen Stacy in *Amazing Spider-Man* No. 100 comes to fruition in *Amazing Spider-Man Annual* No. 21 with Mary Jane. Peter has begun to cope better with the trauma of his past.

Whereas Peter worried about how he could keep his secret from Gwen Stacy if they married, with Mary Jane, he didn't have to. She already knew. In fact, she wouldn't marry him until he was honest about it. Gwen Stacy will always be idealized with some Spider-Man fans as what could have been. As a result, Mary Jane is often reduced to a token character, a pretty redhead model who Peter somehow ended up with. These fans fail to see Mary Jane's much larger role as the confidant—something Gwen Stacy never was. Mary Jane is a woman strong enough to deal with Peter Parker's roller coaster existence. Venom, Carnage, and the Clone Saga—through it all, they survived. With the married Spider-Man, instead of just watching him bounce along the rooftops woefully philosophizing, occasionally we see him talk to Mary Jane about his problems.

Coming Out about Spider-Man

More recently, Aunt May also discovered his secret identity. At first, she was shocked, hurt, and confused—but no heart attack as Peter anticipated long ago. Her response was similar to Mary Jane's: "You don't have to explain and you don't have to lie to me anymore. I know your secret. I know you're Spider-Man." Aunt May is a stronger woman than Peter gives her credit for.

Peter's secrecy hurt Aunt May deeply. He could not trust her with something so central to his life. Once the secret was out, Peter was able to confess his actions that caused Uncle Ben's death, and from their conversation, Peter found the emotional healing he had needed for so long: someone to forgive him. Aunt May accepted Peter Parker as Spider-Man—and then promptly canceled her subscription to the *Daily Bugle*.

In both cases, the two women in Peter's life had to confront him, disclose the secret themselves, and forgive his lies. The two most important people in his life, and they had to pull it out of him, while he resisted every step of the way. Who me? Spider-Man? Such resistance on his part would make a reader think that Peter Parker would be incapable of revealing his secret to the public. After all, being honest with Mary Jane and Aunt May is one thing. For every villain he's ever fought to suddenly know his home address is another thing altogether. He would never be that reckless and tell everyone. Obviously. But that's exactly what he does.

While writing this essay, a major event happened with Peter Parker that relates directly to this essay. (Have I got good timing or what?) In *Civil War* No. 2, Peter Parker reveals his identity to the entire world during a press conference! "I'm not wearing my old mask because I'm ashamed of what I do. I'm proud of who I am, and I'm here right now to prove it. My name is Peter Parker, and I've been Spider-Man since I was fifteen years old. Any questions?" Maybe he did it because he felt safer, having recently moved with Mary Jane and Aunt May to the New Avenger headquarters. Maybe he did it because confession is good for the soul. Either way, he understood this as a breakthrough moment. Then immediately after the press conference, in the next issue of *Amazing Spider-Man*, he threw up in the nearest restroom. Time will tell if Peter's announcement will stand as a permanent fixture in his continuity, or if things will magically return to status quo, as they sometimes do in comics. For the moment, he's done what he never thought was possible. Peter Parker resolved the matter of his secrecy and the burden it entails without letting go of his responsibility to be Spider-Man. He said in the press conference, "I'm proud of who I am." This statement would have never come from the Stan Lee era webslinger, a character who viewed himself as a "corny, costumed clown." Maybe he's finally growing up at last.

DAVID HOPKINS is a high-school English teacher and comic-book writer (*Karma Incorporated*, *Emily Edison*, and *Antigone*). He lives in Arlington, Texas, with his wife Melissa and their daughter Kennedy. If anyone from Marvel reads this, he'd like a job writing Spider-Man—thank you very much. Visit David's Web site at www.antiherocomics.com

References

Anderson, Norman B. and P. Elizabeth Anderson. *Emotion Longevity: What Really Determines How Long You Live*. New York: Viking, 2003.

Conway, Gerry (w), Gil Kane (p), John Romita Sr and Ton Mortella (i). "The Night Gwen Stacy Died." *Amazing Spider-Man* No. 121. Marvel Comics: June 1973.

Conway, Gerry (w), Ross Andru (p), Frank Giacoia and David Hunt (i). "My Uncle…My Enemy?" *Amazing Spider-Man* No. 131. Marvel Comics: Apr. 1974.

Conway, Gerry (w), Alex Saviuk (p), and Andy Mushynsky (i). *Spider-Man: Parallel Lives*. Marvel Comics, 1989.

DeFalco, Tom (w), Ron Frenz (p), and Josef Rubinstein (i). "Beware the Claws of the Puma!" *Amazing Spider-Man* No. 257. Marvel Comics: Oct. 1984.

DeFalco, Tom (w), Ron Frenz (p), and Josef Rubinstein (i). "The Sinister Secret of Spider-Man's New Costume." *Amazing Spider-Man* No. 258. Marvel Comics: Nov. 1984.

DeFalco, Tom (w), Ron Frenz (p), and Josef Rubinstein (i). "All My Pasts Remembered." *Amazing Spider-Man* No. 259. Marvel Comics: Dec. 1984.

Fettinger, J. R. "Why Did It Have to be You, Mary Jane?" May 2001. http://spideykicksbutt.com/WhyYouMaryJane/WhyYouMaryJanePart1. html.

Kakalios, James. *The Physics of Superheroes*. New York: Gotham Books, 2005.

Lee, Stan (w), John Romita (p), and Mickey Demeo (i). "How Green was My Goblin!" *Amazing Spider-Man* No. 39. Marvel Comics: Aug. 1966.

Lee, Stan (w), John Romita (p), and Jim Mooney (i). "Unmasked at Last!" *Amazing Spider-Man* No. 87. Marvel Comics: Aug. 1970.

Lee, Stan (w), Gil Kane (p), and John Romita (i). "And Death Shall Come!" *Amazing Spider-Man* No. 90. Marvel Comics: Nov. 1970.

Lee, Stan (w), Gil Kane (p), and E. Giacoia (i). "The Spider or the Man?" *Amazing Spider-Man* No. 100. Marvel Comics: Sept. 1971.

Straczynski, J. Michael (w), John Romita Jr. (p), and Scott Hanna (i). "Interlude." *Amazing Spider-Man* No. 478. Marvel Comics: Jan. 2002.

Straczynski, J. Michael (w), John Romita Jr. (p), and Scott Hanna (i). "The Conversation." *Amazing Spider-Man* No. 479. Marvel Comics: Feb. 2002.

Straczynski, J. Michael (w), Ron Garney (p), and Bill Reinhold (i). "Part 2 of The War at Home." *Amazing Spider-Man* No. 533. Marvel Comics: Aug. 2006.

ROBERT BURKE RICHARDSON

Spider-Man Saves the World

The recognition of the absurd: For some of us, that recognition is a moral and ethical reaction to the existential crisis of the modern world, the essential state of unreason in which mankind finds itself today, as dramatized in the theater of Beckett and Stoppard, and the art of Dali and Ditko. Me, I just find some things funny, though like Robert Burke Richardson, I, too, recognize the fundamental absurdity of the superhero's dilemma....

FOR PETER PARKER, and for each of us who reads, watches, or plays his story, Spider-Man saves the world.

The means by which Spider-Man achieves this feat is by getting hopelessly tangled in his own contradictory duties. Most ethicists distinguish at least two kinds of duties: duties to oneself and duties to others. For Spider-Man, the duty to himself conflicts with his duties to others, others interfere with his duty to himself...and others also interfere with his duties to (other) others. It's a tangled web that cannot be untangled by rational or logical means—it can only be resolved through an act of faith. Peter Parker's creation of Spider-Man is that act of faith.

In order to delineate the sources and threads of Spider-Man's ethical duties, it is helpful to distinguish Peter Parker as a separate, pre-existing entity from his heroic alter ego. In the two major modern retellings of Spider-Man's story—Sam Raimi's film version introduced in the 2002 *Spider-Man* movie, and Brian Bendis and Mark Bagley's *Ultimate Spider-Man* comic-book series, launched in 2000—Peter finds himself to be a promising young man long before the radioactive spider crosses his path. Peter has a talent for science that attracts the attention of people like Norman Osborn (and, later, Otto Octavius) and also suggests that Peter has a bright future ahead of him.

With the possible exception of Mary Jane Watson, Peter's odd ways and potential for future greatness do not endear him to his classmates. In *Ultimate Spider-Man*, in particular, eternal jock nemesis Flash Thompson seems to know that Peter is going places (contrary to Flash himself, who has peaked in high school) and is therefore intent on making Peter's life a living hell. Peter is someone who could potentially grow up to change the world for the better, yet it is this very potential to serve humanity that puts him at odds with his classmates.

An interesting dilemma had therefore already developed long before the spider made its appearance, though not one that was irresolvable per se. Peter has a duty to himself to see that his scientific gifts are realized, but in so realizing his gifts, he would also enrich the world he lives in, thus satisfying his duties to others, and resolving the initial dilemma.

One radioactive spider-bite later, this elegant solution was no longer feasible. It could even be argued that Peter met the spider, a product of super science, specifically *because* of his natural gifts, meaning these supernatural complications were implicit and unavoidable consequences of his basic essence, and that Peter's initial dilemma could never have naturally resolved in the manner considered above. Inevitable or not, however, Peter's dilemma remains the same. But when one has the proportional speed and strength of a spider, what effect does that have on one's duties to others? How does it change one's duties to oneself?

Peter was still a high-school student when the spider bit him, and probably not overly concerned with abstract ethics of the kind we're examining here. As most of us would in Peter's situation (and this relatable and psychologically real aspect of the character is intrinsic to both Spider-Man's enduring popularity and, as we shall see, his ability to save the world), Peter used his newfound powers to increase his own happiness. This begs the question—is personal happiness a credible ethical duty?

John Stuart Mill, one of the main voices in the school of thought known as Utilitarianism, might argue that it is. In books like *On Liberty, Representative Government and Utilitarianism*, Mill argues that individual interest and happiness is the starting point for all considerations of the institutions of government and society. He even goes so far as to say, "In proportion to the development of his individuality, each person becomes more valuable to himself, and is, therefore, capable of being more valuable to others" (120).

I think Mill would argue that there is nothing wrong with the teenaged Peter Parker using his powers to (for example) play sports. Peter's sudden athletic ability would bring much joy to Peter and to his classmates. The only person who wouldn't be happy about it would be former star Flash Thompson, and no one's going to shed a tear for that jerk. The theory of utilitarianism holds that the good is whatever maximizes pleasure for the greatest number of people, while simultaneously minimizing pain. Mill and utilitarianism pave the way for Peter to be a sports star, earn lots of money, get the girl, and to live happily ever after. There is one slight problem, however: utilitarianism is *not* the ethical system that determines Peter's world.

Peter became a wrestler to make some money—money desperately needed by his aunt May and uncle Ben—and didn't use his powers to stop a criminal who was running off with a corrupt promoter's money. Utilitarianism tells us that this behavior is perfectly acceptable: Peter wasn't actively hurting anyone, and was helping himself (by not putting himself in harm's way), as well as his aunt and uncle (by earning money). As we all know, however, tragedy resulted from these supposedly ethical actions.

Unfortunately for Peter Parker, his world is not governed by utilitarian principles. Peter's uncle was killed by the same criminal Peter failed to stop that day, and it was as if the universe itself was punishing Peter for not doing more with his powers. With power comes responsibility, and Peter was correctly taking responsibility for the financial well-being of his family—but with *great* power comes *great* responsibility, and he had not, apparently, exercised *that*. Not only does Peter's universe lack the modern sensibility of Mill's thinking, but it feels almost Elizabethan in flavor. The Elizabethans viewed the cosmos as highly structured (often represented as a series of concentric spheres), and going against this natural order (disrupting the harmony or music of the spheres) by, say, failing to adequately live up to one's ethical obligations, elicited very real and severe consequences (as demonstrated in Shakespeare's tragedies such as *King Lear* and *Macbeth*).

For Peter Parker, then, personal happiness is either not a duty at all, or one so overbalanced by his duties to others as to be virtually non-existent. Peter's external duties are exaggerated to the point where he must go above and beyond any reasonable requirement just to break even—even fighting on behalf of those who have wronged him, or seek to do him or others harm. Peter is expected to be proactive while crime-fighting—to go out of his way to stop crimes before they even happen—no matter what vengeance it may bring down upon his head (or the heads of his loved ones).

This puts him in an irresolvable ethical crisis. In order to satisfy his exaggerated duties to strangers, he must compromise his duties to himself, and to the people he loves most. Here, then, Peter's dilemma is reminiscent of the biblical Abraham's, whom God ordered to kill his own son on top of Mount Sinai. Abraham, in addition to loving his son, had sworn to follow God's teachings—including the commandment, *Thou Shalt Not Kill*—yet God told him, directly and with no room for interpretation, to kill his only son.

Most ethicists today follow Immanuel Kant in believing that ethics applies to all rational beings. Ethical duties therefore apply to all humans (and maybe dolphins and chimpanzees, though that's really a topic for another essay); as a rational being, Abraham is expected to behave ethically (and, conversely, as an ethical being, he is expected to behave rationally—the two go hand-in-hand). In a work called *Fear And Trembling*, the philosopher Søren Kierkegaard—or, technically, Johaness de Silentio, the pseudonymous name under which Kierkegaard penned the book—suggests that Abraham resolves his crisis by abandoning reason altogether. Could a similar maneuver work for Peter Parker?

The first thing to understand about Kierkegaard's solution, which he calls a teleological suspension of the ethical (in which the ethical is set aside in favor of a temporarily higher purpose), is that it is not a regressive act: it's not as if, faced with the profound absurdity of God's test, Abraham simply abandons reason—rather, he *transcends* reason. Faith, Kierkegaard argues, does not supersede reason except in the extreme case of someone (like Abraham) who finds himself in spiritual crisis; in this (and only this) rare instance, the individual in crisis may, by virtue of the absurd, teleologically suspend the ethical and become a Knight of Faith—someone for whom faith is a higher calling than reason.

Is it possible that a philosopher who lived 300 years ago (or, rather, the imaginary personality the author created, through whose fictional principles we might better consider the biblical Abraham) might hold the key to Peter Parker's ethical salvation? While I think the letter of Kierkegaard's theory might fit Peter Parker's dilemma, I find the tone of it all a bit too dark. Spider-Man, particularly in his flagship comic-book series, *The Amazing Spider-Man*, is a character who sometimes goes to dark places: there was the death of Gwen Stacy at the hands of the Green Goblin, and more recent depictions of a very troubled Peter in Marvel's *House of M* and *Marvel Zombies* mini-series. Usually, though, Spider-Man is funny—a guy who cracks wise while cracking heads, quipping his way through adversity that would be a heartbreaking downer if it happened to anybody else. And it is, perhaps, overstating things to claim that Peter Parker is in the same sort of spiritual crisis as the biblical Abraham. Peter's in a tough spot, sure, but God hasn't contacted him with a set of contradictory demands (at least, not yet).

One thing that is common to both Peter Parker's universe and to Abraham's situation, however, is a healthy dose of the absurd: neither finds himself in a universe that makes much sense. For Peter, the absurd manifests itself most keenly through his wonderful rogues' gallery: in all of comics, only Batman faces a sillier bunch of villains. Spidey not only regularly squares off against weirdoes like Electro, the Vulture, the Scorpion, the Lizard, Doctor Octopus, the Green Goblin (with exploding pumpkins!), the Sandman, and the king of all absurd villains, Mysterio—but also takes on lesser-known baddies like Paste-Pot Pete (whose weapon of choice is glue), and the giant flower from the classic '60s cartoon.

Spider-Man's story shares not only a sense of the absurd with Abraham's, but a sense of redemption as well: God lets Abraham off the hook at the last minute by providing a lamb for him to sacrifice in place of his son. Spider-Man ultimately hunts down and catches the criminal who killed Uncle Ben. The fact that Peter doesn't kill his uncle's murderer suggests that more than mere vengeance is at play—he is balancing the cosmic books, and redeeming himself in the eyes of the universe which demands so much of him.

Considering again the Elizabethan flavor of Peter's universe, but adjusting for tone, perhaps Peter isn't living out a tragedy, but rather an Elizabethan comedy. Shakespeare's classic *A Midsummer Night's Dream* has more than a whiff of the absurd to it as well, with its donkey-headed buffoon, Bottom, and the hopelessly tangled relationships of young lovers Hermia, Helena, Demetrius, and Lysander. And there is something else here of relevance to our discussion of Spider-Man as well. Take Duke Theseus's musings at the beginning of Act V:

Lovers and madmen have such seething brains,
Such shaping fantasies that apprehend
More than cool reason ever comprehends.
The lunatic, the lover, and the poet
Are of imagination all compact:
One sees more devils than vast hell can hold;
That is the madman: (259)

Theseus here conflates lovers, poets, and the insane. With his wife Mary Jane, we've gotten frequent glimpses of Peter Parker the lover, and we've even seen him, on rare occasion, delve into the poetic, but Spider-Man, with his unending supply of devils to battle, is surely the madman. Spider-Man is a fantasy who can move beyond the reason that so constrains poor Mr. Parker (apprehending more than cool reason comprehends, as it were).

A Midsummer Night's Dream, like the stories of Abraham and Spider-Man, confronts its characters with a world that doesn't make sense. When *A Midsummer Night's Dream* opens, the young lovers find themselves in a state of disharmony that reflects the disharmonious world they've inherited. In Elizabethan thinking, the celestial sphere informs the mortal world, and the heavens—symbolized by the ongoing fight between the faerie king Oberon and his wife Titania—are out of harmony. The characters in *A Midsummer Night's Dream*—and the audience—move through the play encountering all manner of absurdity, and then—absurdly!—everything works itself out in the end. It is my contention that stories of this kind function to redeem the world: they take the frustrating, irrational, and wholly wonky reality we're all born into and render it, for a brief moment at least, comprehensible.

The story of Spider-Man does the same thing, but for a more modern audience. Peter Parker is an everyman faced with an implacably absurd universe who—by donning homemade tights and punching people in the face—renders the world temporarily comprehensible for everyone else.

Let's look again at Peter as he was before the spider bit him. He had conflicting duties that ought to have resolved as he grew into and successfully utilized his potential. Then the spider bit him, and his responsibility grew proportionally with his power. Now Peter is in a real dilemma—one that he can't solve on his own. Like Abraham when God makes his demand, or the young lovers at the start of *A Midsummer Night's Dream*, Peter is faced with a world that doesn't make sense, and a no-win situation. His solution is the creation of a new entity, Spider-Man, whose true power (beyond sticking to walls and spinning webs) is the ability not only to reconcile the contrary obligations placed upon Peter Parker, but to excel at doing so: Spider-Man makes the absurd into the wonderful. Whether on the movie screen, the TV, or in the pages of a comic book, anyone who has seen Spider-Man swinging through the urban landscape recognizes the thrill of pure joy Peter takes—and we, vicariously, take—in rising above it all. Like Abraham before he teleologically suspends the ethical, Peter struggles with the logical constraints of his new condition until he reaches a crisis point; then, through an act of faith, he transcends those limitations (apprehending through faith what cool reason could not comprehend).

It's up to each person both individually, and as part of a generation, to go out there and redeem the world—it's part of what mythic stories of heroes setting off to find their fortunes, slaying absurd creatures, and journeying (literally or metaphorically) to the underworld only to return with new knowledge about how to live are all about.

Since the character first appeared in *Amazing Fantasy* No. 15 in 1963, and even more so since the launch of the phenomenally successful film franchise in recent years, Spider-Man has been one of these stories. But can Peter Parker and Spider-Man, now that we've taken such pains to separate them, ever be put back together again? If Spider-Man became conflated with Peter Parker, rather than existing as a separate creation that fulfills Peter's responsibilities as Peter himself cannot, wouldn't Spider-Man then also suffer from the same irresolvable ethical dilemmas which led to his creation in the first place?

It looks like we're about to find out. At the time this essay is being written, Peter Parker has just publicly unmasked at the end of *Civil War* No. 2. Peter's side of the story, which details the feelings and motivations that led him to make this potentially deadly public reveal, is told in writer Joe Michael Straczynski's *Amazing Spider-Man* No. 532, and shows that, like the meditation we ourselves are currently engaged in, Peter's decision is an expression of his potential. Peter has moved up in the Marvel Universe: he's a member of premier super-group the Avengers, he's found a mentor and surrogate father in Iron Man, and is married to a model. Clearly, Peter Parker is no longer the nerdy loner we first met forty-three years ago.

It was Peter's unusual potential that led to his ethical crisis, and then to the act of faith that created the Spider-Man persona. Thus far, Peter Parker has been a psychologically fractured character—two personalities in a single skull—and I can't help thinking that this was very much in character with the century that spawned him, given the dominant role Freud and concepts like the ego and the id have had on our conceptions of the psyche. Does the new Peter Parker/Spider-Man unity indicate that the new millennium is moving toward a more stable, unified state? Unfortunately, that hasn't seemed to be the case during these first six years (in fact, the world has seemed even *more* in need of saving of late).

If Peter can successfully integrate his two disparate halves, it will tell us something about the world today. If he cannot, it will tell us something else. Perhaps the necessity of an anonymous Spider-Man was merely an intermediary step on Peter's journey, and his improved social situation has finally resolved the crisis that necessitated the creation of Spider-Man when he was a teen. Or, maybe, he's going somewhere the like of which we haven't seen before, and finding an all new, all different way of saving the world.

One thing is certain, though: with the success of the Spider-Man film franchise, and the vitality of the comics, it's a good time to be a Spider-Man fan.

ROBERT BURKE RICHARDSON hunts Snark in Edmonton, Alberta. He is the author of the elderly superhero saga *Old School*—"These aren't your father's superheroes...they're your grandpa's!"—from Arcana Studio, as well as stories, essays, and pointless posts on his weblog, elf-help.blogspot.com.

References

Mill, John Stuart. *On Liberty, Representative Government and Utilitarianism*. Great Britain: Wordsworth Classics, 1996.

Shakespeare, William. "A Midsummer Night's Dream." *Complete Works of Shakespeare*. Great Britain: Wordsworth Editions, 1999. 299–300.

MICHAEL MARANO

Inner Demons, Outer Heroes, Outer Villains

A Look at Monstrosity in *Spider-Man* and *Spider-Man 2*

And so, in a way, we come full circle. In our opening essay, Darren Hudson Hick proposed we look at Spider-Man as a kind of monster-made-hero, a symbol of the atomic age, a reflection of our unspoken fear and anxiety. In this concluding essay, Michael Marano suggests that the monster is less a symbol of fear, perhaps, than of greatness—a portent of possibilities, a speaker of wisdom, offering us a glimpse of the transcendental. Perhaps so. For me, the superhero, and this hero in particular, will always be a kind of mirror, showing us visions of who we wish to be and who we fear we are....

"**I** WILL NOT A DIE A MONSTER!"

Those are the last words of Dr. Otto Octavius in *Spider-Man 2*. There's an echo of the tragic to them, like something said by a ruler of Thebes at the end of a play you had to read in junior high. Cadmus, Pentheus, Athamas, Oedipus...these were guys who really knew how to suffer, back in the days when misery was an art.

But by the time that Otto utters those defiant words, it's too late. In the classical and the tragic sense, Otto has, against his will (or as a result of his *mis-directed* will) already been a monster and has served his function as one. As J. Jonah Jameson, editor-in-chief of the *Daily Bugle* points out, it was Otto who made Doctor Octopus, "Doc Ock," the Hyde to Otto's own Jekyll:

> It's all over town, Robbie. Gossip. Rumors. Panic in the streets, if we're lucky! Crazy scientist turns himself into some kind of a monster. Four mechanical arms welded right onto his body. Guy named Otto Octavius winds up with eight limbs. What're the odds? Hoffman! What're we gonna call this guy?

Maybe what Otto really means with his dying words is that he'll subvert, redefine, and reclaim his role as a monster, take it back from the city-wide-panic-inducing function that Jonah has assigned to the role and to him via splashy *Daily Bugle* front pages. Whom is Otto really defying by refusing to be a monster? Himself? Fate? Bad luck? Those pesky mechanical arms that seem to have minds of their own, even as he uses those arms to reclaim his humanity and drown the out-of-control fusion reaction he's created? Maybe he's defying a long tradition of monsters going back...well...as far back as the first cracks in the egg of the Western tradition itself.

Before he became "Doctor Octopus," Otto may have learned a few things about monsters from T. S. Eliot while courting his poetry-loving, English Lit major wife, Rosalie. ("T. S. Eliot is more complicated than advanced science!" Otto said, as much to young Peter Parker as to his beautiful and doomed wife in the second *Spider-Man* film. "If you want to get a woman to fall in love with you, feed her poetry!") Eliot was no slouch when it came to monsters—check out "The Hollow Men," "Gerontion," and "The Wasteland" for starts—and if Otto is trying not to die as a monster, Eliot's definitions of monstrosity may be the very thing Otto is trying not to be. Eliot's monsters are not just hollow; they are morally paralyzed, like denizens of Joyce's Dublin. Eliot's monsters, by echoing tragic figures from the classical era, remind us that it might just be our tragic flaw to think that we modern people are so different from those ancient, classical guys (and gals like Medea) that we're not susceptible to the kinds of tragic falls they suffered. Something that maybe needed to be said in the "Wasteland" of post-WWI Europe. When Eliot tells us to "Consider Phlebas," it's *us* we're supposed to think about. Otto may have not only learned *about* Eliot's monsters while trying to impress Rosie, but *from* Eliot's monsters, because that's what monsters are for...*learning*. Usually monsters teach us really harsh and kick-in-the-teeth brutal lessons at that, like how hubris and the structure of tragedy can rise up from dusty marble ruins and bite you in the ass.

Becoming a monster. Defying becoming a monster. Learning from monsters. These are common threads through the first two Spider-Man movies, and as such, they provide a thematic backbone for the films and also tie the movies to some of the most fundamental and primal concerns of Western Lit that have made college freshmen chug coffee and sweat on the nights before term papers are due.

But what does it mean, to be a monster? As J. Jonah points out, a monster is a disruptive force that can cause upheaval in a community—just think of Godzilla or Kong or Frankenstein's monster or the Green Goblin or the Vulture or the Rhino or the Grizzly or the Jackal or...uhhhmmm...Jonah's son, Man-Wolf. Disruption is the defining factor. The shark in *Jaws*, for instance, is just a big dumb fish...it's a marvel of evolution...it eats, swims, and makes little sharks. It only becomes a monster when it intrudes on the nice casual flow of human affairs by chomping down on skinny-dipping hippie chicks and little boys on inflatable rafts.

There's a specific context to the disruption caused by monsters that makes them implements of learning. If you trace the word "monster" to its origins, something kind of remarkable reveals itself, and that's the revelatory nature of monsters. "Monster" comes from the Latin word *monstrum*, meaning "a portent or a showing"—as in the word "demonstrate." And it is also related to "monument," and the Latin verb *monere*, meaning "to warn." The disruption that a monster causes in human affairs is a *monition* that humans are supposed to take to heart. Monsters are a revelation of higher spiritual or aesthetic reality, portents sent from On High that indicate that all is not well on earth, and that some heavenly disruption is in order to show us dumb mortals what's wrong so we can make things right.

Monsters, as portents, tend to have a political dimension; they deal with wrongs that are not so much personal and private (even though they may begin in the home or family), but that have an impact on the community and what the Romans would call the *Res Publica* as a whole. This is something that a real-life conservative journalist named Jonah has pointed out on several occasions, Jonah Goldberg of the *National Review Online*, in the essays "Monsters, the Good and Damned" and "A Word About Monsters."

The unnatural birth of a *person* as a "monster" (in the pre-PC days, when congenital conditions were supernatural-seeming deformities to be feared) was thought to reflect the unnatural course of that person's life and the impact that unnatural life would have on entire communities…cities…kingdoms…dynasties. The monstrous birth was thought of as the first domino flicked in a chain reaction of disasters. Monstrous births, the advents of monsters, were like movie trailers of what was to come, only without the annoying car ads and the barrage of *Tron*-like animations urging us to go to the snack bar. Yanking this idea of the monster into the realm of Shakespeare and the Bard's use of history, we can see by digging (through biased chronicles) that Shakespeare's greatest monster, Richard III, had a portentous, monstrous birth—up there with something out of Larry Cohen's killer baby pic, *It's Alive*—that reflected his later impact on England. According to Sir Thomas Moore's 1513 account, Richard came misshapen into the world a hunchbacked breech baby that had to be delivered via cesarean:

> Richarde the third sonne, of whom we nowe entreate, was in witte and courage egall with either of them, in bodye and prowesse farre vnder them bot, little of stature, ill fetured of limmes, croke backed, his left shoulder much higher then his right, hard fauoured of visage, and suche as is in states called warlye, in other menne otherwise, he was malicious, wrathfull, enuious, and from afore his birth, euer frowarde. It is for trouth reported, that the Duches his mother had so muche a doe in her travaile, that shee coulde not bee deliuered of hym uncutte: and that hee came into the worlde with the feete forwarde, as menne bee borne outwarde, and (as the fame runneth) also not vnto-thed, whither menne of hatred reporte aboue the trouthe, or elles that

nature chaunged her course in hys beginninge, whiche in the course of his lyfe many thinges vnnaturallye committed. (*The History of King Richard the Third* 4)

In the Greek traditions of the tragic and that really depressing town of Thebes (what did the line of Cadmus do to property values and HOA fees?), displeasure from the gods (like that which is shown via monstrous births) over the death of the previous king Laius is shown to Oedipus and his subjects in the form of famine, disease, and the sterility of women and livestock. Nasty portents brought about by human sinfulness are a staple of tragedy. In *Macbeth*, heavenly displeasure over the murder of Duncan is revealed by night-like darkness during the day, the killing of a falcon by a mousing owl, and by Duncan's war-horses devouring each other. Icky. These portents aren't specifically monsters, per se, but they function in the same way that the advent of monsters does in ancient and pre-modern cultures. Iulius Obsequens, a Roman writer who compiled all the prodigies and omens in Livy's *History*, made a direct connection between the monstrous happening of a mule (a hybrid animal that's supposed to be sterile) giving birth and civil discord, the rampant births of bastards, much of Rome burning down, and war between Caesar and Pompey.[1]

Iulius also makes a connection between Caesar's sacrifice of freakish animals with no hearts and a certain unpleasantness we associate with the Ides of March of which Shakespeare made dramatic use. Iulius rattles off a P. T. Barnum shopping list about the catastrophic births of deformed beings such as: a boy with four feet, hands and ears burned to death at the instruction of seers, a birth that seems connected to the defeat of the Roman army by the Vaccaei; a four-footed girl; a two-headed calf; lambs born with horses' feet and one with the head of a monkey; women giving birth to live serpents; and quite a few hermaphrodites who were killed and thrown into the sea at the instruction of priests. If all this seems remote and "other," with no relation to the modern world, well...in their February 10, 1947

---

[1] "Mula pariens discordiam civium, bonorum interitum, mutationem legum, turpes matronarum partus significavit. Incendium quo maxima pars urbis deleta est prodigii loco habitum. Inter Caesarem et Pompeium bella civilia exorta" (*The Book of Prodigies*).

issue, *Life Magazine* reported on a pair of "Siamese" twins (as they were called back then), the product of what *Life* calls a "monstrous birth" in China, who were left to die on a village dump because they were considered a "bad omen."

We, most especially the "we" of a city like Athens, Corinth, Rome, or the canyon-like maze that is the New York of the Marvel Universe and the Spider-Man films, are expected to *learn* from monsters as portents. And just as the personal conflicts of tragic figures like Oedipus and Macbeth can affect entire communities (revealing monsters and portents as they do so), *inner* conflicts of monstrosity in the first two Spider-Man films move outside of the personal sphere and become matters that affect all of Manhattan. The monstrosity and freakishness of the three main "super" beings of *Spider-Man* and *Spider-Man 2*— Doctor Octopus, the Green Goblin, and Spider-Man himself—while personal and private in origin, are classical revelations, old-school portents, from which the entire is city is expected to learn.

How's everyone's favorite webslinging crime fighter *monstrous*? Spidey's a good guy, and doesn't look freaky like Ben Grimm or The Hulk. But look at Spidey's origin. Back in the Cold War era, Peter Parker was made a hero, given strange and...well...portentous powers, through the bug-a-boo that was making monsters throughout the 1950s: radioactivity. Radioactivity, which makes monsters in the Cold War pop-culture mythology, can also make you a hero in the Marvel Universe: Daredevil, the Hulk, the Fantastic Four...none of them had any problems with hair loss, lymphoma, radiation sickness, or any of the other nasty things you might see in medical reports concerning a certain August day in Hiroshima.

Radioactivity, though a real and deadly thing, had a mythic dimension in Cold War pop culture, because it created monsters: the ants of *THEM!*, the big lizard of *The Giant Behemoth*, Godzilla...the list goes on. Even alien menace of 1951's *The Thing*, though not a mutant, was heralded by the ominous crackle of a Geiger counter. Similarly, in the post-Love Canal era, industrial waste, though a real and deadly thing, had a mythic function making monsters: *Humanoids from the Deep*; giant *Ticks*; those Cannibalistic Humanoid Underground Dwellers of *CHUD*; the lake monster of *Monstroid*, even roving bands of *Redneck Zombies*. While toxic waste made a slew of monsters, it only made one hero I can think of: the Toxic Avenger. Funny to think that back in the good ol' days, if you wanted to be a hero, your mom just had to bang Zeus...no poisons were involved, just mythic mojo.[2]

The thing that makes monsters in the twenty-first century isn't radiation, toxic waste, or lovin' from Olympus, anymore. What's taken over that mythic role is genetic manipulation. In 2002, *USA Today* ran an article on the shift in pop culture from the monster-making potential of radiation to those of genetic engineering:

> *Spider-Man* director Sam Raimi says the radioactive spider that gave birth to the 1962 comic-book webslinger no longer seemed relevant in the age of the human genome project. "It was in James Cameron's original script treatment back when he was originally going to direct," he explains. "He altered the legend of Spider-Man a bit by making the radioactive spider into one that is genetically altered. It seemed a logical change from 1962 to 2002."

Spidey's origin, in its 1960s comic-book/Cold War context and its 2002 movie/genetics context, could have made him a bad guy monster or a hero. His powers are portentous because, as the result of their mythic origins, they are directly tied to Fate, the same force that was working behind the scenes at Thebes in *Oedipus*, with the downfall of Caesar according to Iulius, and by implication, the birth of Richard III as recorded by Thomas Moore. Heck, Fate, if you think about it, makes monsters better than those new-fangled teratogens radiation, toxic waste, and genetic engineering could any day. Macbeth would have been just a regular guy without the intersection of Fate, and Peter would have been just a regular guy without it, too.

There's a hint of the monstrous to Spidey. He, more than even the rampaging Hulk, is easily painted as a menace by the *Bugle*. And by

---

[2] True, some of Zeus' kids may have a bit of the monstrous about them. Pentheus may not have been crazy about Zeus' kid Bacchus in *The Bacchae*, and having a god for a daddy didn't win Polyphemus the Cyclops any beauty contests, but the reps of Hercules, Perseus, and Theseus (who, like Polyphemus, may have had Poseidon for a poppa) as heroes outweigh the reps of monster demi-gods.

Amazing Spider-Man No. 100, Peter had begun to consider himself a menace to his own life as well. In order to live happily as Gwen Stacy's husband, Peter chose to take a serum designed to negate his spider powers. But in doing so, Peter was forced to face his inner monstrosity even further, when, as a side-effect of the serum, he grew four extra arms. It's telling that Peter developed the serum in case the radioactivity that gave him his powers became dangerous, in the way that the "monster-making" radiation of Cold War pop culture is dangerous. The subsequent story arc involved both the Lizard and Morbius, the Living Vampire— two overt monsters. At the end, both Spidey and Curt Connors, the Lizard in human form, discussed their own monstrousness and their need to fight their inner demons (dovetailing the story arc with the one previous, in which Harry Osborn, Peter's roommate, had been dealing with his inner demon of drug addiction).

The first two Spider-Man films clearly indicate this inner conflict of Peter's. Right off the bat in *Spider-Man*, Peter warns us in a voiceover that, "The story of my life is not for the faint of heart. If somebody said it was a happy little tale...if somebody told you I was just your average ordinary guy, not a care in the world...somebody lied." He'd rather be even a big fat jerk like Flash Thompson than the person he is. The bulk of *Spider-Man 2* deals with Peter's deep-seated ambivalence about being Spidey. Peter's ambivalence grows to the point that he loses his powers and has to go to an old Dead Head doctor for advice. (What medical certification board would trust a Dead Head with a prescription pad?) Peter, in longing to cast off his heroic mantle, wants also to cast off that which is, in a very traditional sense, divinely imposed on him: his spider powers; his monstrosity. Heroic stature, like the revelation of a monster, comes from On High...via displeasure from Olympus or from Zeus' mojo, transmitted by his fondness for smokin' hot mortal chicks.

Yeah, the status of being a monster or a hero comes from On High. But that might just be half the job. If monsters are portents, it takes a priest or an oracle to interpret the portent that the monster is, and in so doing, fully actualize the monster as a disruptive force. In *Oedipus*, the job of interpreting portents falls to the Oracle of Delphi and the seer Tiresias. In the world of the Spider-Man movies, it's J. Jonah Jameson who tells the city what to think of its super beings.

Jameson? Functioning as a holy man? Well, yeah. It's Jonah who names the Green Goblin, barking, "Hoffman! Run down to the patent office! Copyright the name, 'Green Goblin.' I want a quarter every time someone says it!" He names "Doc Ock," as mentioned above. About Spider-Man, he snarls, "He doesn't want to be famous? I'll make him *infamous*!" The process of naming, of interpreting the arrival of a portentous being, is the ascribing of menace, and even though Jonah doesn't name Spidey, he devotes incredible energy and influence to interpret him as a "wall-crawling freak." Peter wants to give up the status of "menace" imposed on him along with the "great powers and great responsibility" he's been shouldered with as Spider-Man. "No, Uncle Ben," says Peter in a fantasy flashback, "I'm Spider-Man no more." And like Tiresias, who in *Seven Against Thebes*, interpreted the need for a savior of the Theban city state, Jonah can also ascribe the status of "hero" onto a public figure...which he does to Captain John Jameson. "An American hero! My son...the astronaut!" he beams. Seer, priest, and newspaper editor serve a lot of the same functions (though the Columbia School of Journalism, to my knowledge, has never taught seminars on reading entrails).

There's a thin line, then, between "hero" and "monster." Norman Osborn as the Green Goblin exploited this when he tried to strike a corrupting alliance with Spidey...something he did at the behest of his own inner monster, which had already had a corrupting influence on Norman's own better nature. In a split personality scene that would do Sally Field's Sybil proud, the Goblin talks to Norman from within a mirror, calling himself Norman's "greatest creation, granting you what you always wanted—power beyond your wildest dreams! There is only one who could stop us! Or, imagine if he should join us!"

Doc Ock, the Goblin, and Spidey, knowingly or not sharing the same kind of origin that begets heroes and monsters, their roles in society interpreted by the same kind of defining authority wielded by Jameson, have more in common with each other than they do with the regular folks of New York. The Goblin has his own view of the closely aligned roles of the monster and the hero, which Peter/Spidey doesn't buy. "You're an amazing creature, Spider-Man. You and I are not so different." Peter points out one teensy difference: "I'm not like you; you're a murderer!" Whereupon the Goblin launches on a tirade worthy of any badass from Shakespeare:

> Well, to each his own. I chose my path, you chose the way of the hero. And they found you amusing for a while, the people of this city. But the one thing they love more than a hero is to see a hero fail, fall, die trying. In spite of everything you've done for them, eventually they will hate you. Why bother...? Here's the real truth: there are eight million people in this city. And those teeming masses exist for the sole purpose of lifting the few exceptional people onto their shoulders. You? Me? We're exceptional. I could squash you like a bug right now, but I'm offering you a chance. Join me! Imagine what we could accomplish to-gether...what we could create. Or we could destroy! Cause the deaths of countless innocents in selfish battle again and again and again until we're both dead! Is that what you want? Think about it, hero!

But what *is* the defining difference between a monster and a hero? Aside from the minor technicality about...y'know...not killing people?

The difference reveals itself at the point of origin for both the hero and monster, at the point of *birth*, which can reveal the monstrosity of a guy like Richard III or the heroic nature of a guy like Hercules, who killed two serpents in his crib. What decides whether or not the advent of an "amazing creature" brings forth a hero or a monster are the crucial ingredients of tragedy (the genre that gives us monsters, heroes, and portents a plenty): hubris (a kind of blasphemous arro-gance), and *hamartia*, (the tragic flaw of a great person).

In the case of both the Goblin and Doc Ock, the moments of their creation from out of the lives and identities of two ambitious and basically good men are fraught with classical hubris, the defying of the divine by placing oneself on the level of the divine. Hubris *is* the *harmartia*, the tragic failing that brings about a downfall...the transformation of a man into a monster. As monsters, the Goblin and Doc Ock are *showings* regarding the sins that brought about the creation of the monsters themselves. (As mentioned above, the Goblin calls himself Norman's creation; Otto, according to Jonah, has made a monster out of himself.) And in this context, it's interesting to note that in pop culture, the teratogens that make monsters—radiation, toxic waste, and genetic manipulation—are themselves typically portrayed as products of human hubris.

Norman sees his work as a commoditization of human nature itself. "Forty thousand years of evolution, and we've barely even tapped the vastness of human potential!" he says, as if such a thing can be tapped for use and export, like oil from a well. His employee Doctor Stromm is the voice of reason and learning free of hubris, urging caution and going "back to formula."

Otto, filled with wonder and pride at the power of his fusion reactor, marvels at his own work, uttering the Promethean cry, "The power of the sun! In the palm of my hand!"—forgetting that the power of the sun belongs to Apollo, who is a pretty harsh customer when it comes to perceived trespasses on his purviews. Just ask Marsyas, whom he flayed for being a better musician than he. Contrast Otto's Promethean cry with that of laid-off electrician Uncle Ben while he changes a light bulb in the first film: "And the Lord said, 'Let there be light!' And voilà! There is light. Forty soft, glowing watts of it!" To which Aunt May, keeping Uncle Ben even more humble, replies: "Good boy! God will be thrilled. Just don't fall on your ass! "

Monsters are about learning…and that just might be the reason why monsters are so intimately tied to the quest for knowledge, from the occult studies in the Prague ghetto that begat the Golem to Frankenstein's lab to the gene-splicers of *Jurassic Park* and the botched teleportation devices of *The Fly*. The *learning* that begat Doc Ock and the Goblin is tainted. To riff on Goya, it is the sleep of a moral reason that brings forth monsters. Peter became Spider-Man without any hubris. Yeah, his trip to the Columbia lab where he crossed paths with that genetically modified spider was couched in learning, but Peter himself had no heaven-defying pride about him.[3]

While monsters show heavenly displeasure, heroes have a lot to show, as well, but in a different way. They *demonstrate*, as do mon-

---

[3] Although Arachne, the woman changed into a spider by Athena after she challenged the goddess to a weaving contest, got her "spider powers" from hubris.

sters, but not what's morally wrong with us—they demonstrate what's right and what we can be if we realize our full potentials. It's implied in the movies that Peter learned about what it meant to be a hero not only from his uncle Ben, but from comic books, too. Remember how upset he was in *Spider-Man 2* when he asked his aunt May about his comic-book collection as she was moving out of her Forest Hills home, and she said that she "gave away those dreadful things." Peter may have been a DC Comics fan, something which can be inferred from Aunt May's hospital bed scolding in the first film: "You do too much—college, a job, all this time with me. You're not Superman, you know."

Comic-book heroes *showed* Peter what he could be, and he in turn, as Spider-Man, showed others. As Aunt May said about Peter's former neighbor, little Henry Jackson, who wants to grow up to be Spider-Man:

> He knows a hero when he sees one. Too few characters out there, flying around like that, saving old girls like me. And Lord knows, kids like Henry need a hero: courageous, self-sacrificing people setting examples for all of us. Everybody loves a hero. People line up for them. Cheer them. Scream their names. And years later, they'll tell how they stood in the rain for hours just to get a glimpse of the one who taught them to hold on a second longer. I believe there's a hero in all of us that keeps us honest, gives us strength, makes us noble, and finally allows us to die with pride. Even though sometimes we have to be steady and give up the thing we want the most. Even our dreams. Spider-Man did that for Henry and he wonders where he's gone. He needs him.

The Goblin understands, too, that both the hero and the monster are defined by the city at large, the community for which both hero and monster are showings. But the Goblin has the inverted view of Aunt May, thinking that the community will turn on the hero, loving to see him fall like a tragic character brought low by the hubris that brought The Goblin himself into being. But just the opposite is true. The hero shows New York how to stand up for what is right, even if it means pelting a horribly beweaponed freak with garbage and tire irons, as happens when New York comes to Spidey's aid at the Roosevelt Island tramway: "Leave Spider-Man alone! You're gonna pick on a guy trying to save a bunch of kids?" "Yeah! I got something for your ass! You mess with Spidey, you mess with New York!" "You mess with one of us, you mess with all of us."

The city learns from the hero, coming together in a display of post-9/11 cohesion and community spirit. The folks on the elevated train that Peter saved in *Spider-Man 2* also prove Aunt May right, standing up to Doc Ock. Says one bruiser to Ock: "You wanna get to him, you gotta go through me!" And the other New Yorkers fall in line to protect Spidey. It's worth noting that no one on the train turned on Spidey the way the Goblin predicted, by whipping out his or her cell-phone and snapping pics of a mask-less Peter for a nice chunk of change from Jameson and the *Bugle*.

Despite what Spidey shows the city, as a hero with traits that can be called freakish or even monstrous, the most important things that are learned are internal. Peter, as a hero, shows *himself* what he can be. His internal conflict between being a regular guy and being a hero (and maybe a monster) is solved by what he can show New Yorkers, from Henry Jackson to the folk who stood up to the Goblin and Doc Ock. By showing himself what he can show others, Peter embraces, or at least accepts, his identity as Spider-Man, as does Mary Jane. He is completed *internally* through this other-directed showing, and it's only as a complete man that he can find a moment of happiness as both Peter and Spidey with Mary Jane: "Go get 'em, Tiger!"

Norman, shown his own monstrosity in his dying moment, forsakes being a monster, reaching out to his ersatz son, Peter, for the sake of the son he's let down. "Don't tell Harry!" he says with his last breath.

Otto had to be shown his own monstrosity through Peter's heroics. With his dying defiance of his fate as a monster, he became a hero, saving the city he had been willing to destroy in order to hubristically hold "the power of the sun" in his hand. Personal hubris is counteracted by becoming other-directed, by being shown what it is that you show the world in your role as a monster. This brings you back from being a monster. *Hamartia*, the self-directed flaw of hubris, once it is *shown* for what it is, can be cast off in favor of the heroic. A showing of an inner flaw frees the city of its monsters by freeing the *self* of what has made it monstrous. It's the awakening of sleeping reason. Personal completion, the making whole of the self, like that which Peter achieved, is that which slays monsters. And slaying monsters is the duty of the hero, a tradition that could be argued started with Zeus' half-mortal sons, Hercules and Perseus. The inner monster is overcome by the inner hero through the heroic concern for others.

Peter could only embrace his own heroic status at the end of *Spider-Man 2* through his concern for the city and for Mary Jane. There was no hubris or *hamartia* to his gaining his powers, but he, like the Goblin and Doc Ock, could only be complete by the forsaking of hubris. Peter has hubris? Well, yeah. The monstrously hubristic thing in Peter, that he overcame to become a whole person, was his *self-directed* desire to be free of what he saw to be monstrous in himself... the powers that make him a wall-crawling freak. His hubristic act was to shun both his great power and great responsibility, in effect shunning the lessons of his uncle Ben. Peter was shown his hubris in this desire to shun being a hero by the people of the city to which he, Doc Ock, and the Goblin were all themselves showings. The city, made heroic monster-fighters by what Spider-Man showed them, functioned as heroes by showing Peter the hubris embedded in his choice to forsake his identity as Spider-Man and freeing him from it, just as Peter frees Norman and Otto by his own example. The personal realm and the public realm are collapsed. Inner flaws, like those of Oedipus and Macbeth and other tragic/public figures, that affect the community as a whole, when *resolved* through the community, facilitate the kind of inner harmony that Norman, Otto, and Peter all attain. Shown, and inspired, the city becomes its own hero by allowing heroes to exist among its citizens. It's in this way that inner demons and public monsters are slain.

For the past fifteen years, MICHAEL MARANO's work has appeared on the Public Radio Satellite Network program *Movie Magazine International*, syndicated in more than 111 markets in the U.S. and Canada. His commentary on pop culture has appeared in venues such as *The Boston Phoenix, The Independent Weekly, The Weekly Dig, Science Fiction Universe,* and *Paste Magazine.* Marano's short fiction has been published in several high-profile anthologies, including the Lambda-winning Queer Fear series, *The Mammoth Book of Best New Horror 11* and *Outsiders: 22 All-New Stories from the Edge*; his first novel *Dawn Song* won the Bram Stoker and International Horror Guild Awards. He can be reached via www.myspace.com/michaelmarano.

References

Goldberg, Jonah. "A Word About Monsters." *National Review Online.* 9 February 2005. http://www.nationalreview.com/goldberg/goldberg200502090800.asp.

———. "Monsters, the Good and the Damned." *National Review Online.* 9 July 1999. http://www.nationalreview.com/goldberg/goldberg070999.html.

More, Thomas. *The History of King Richard the Third.* Whitefish, Montana: Kessinger Publising, 2004.

Obsequens, Iulius. *The Book of Prodigies.* Archived at http://www.gmu.edu/departments/fl d/CLASSICS/obsequens.html.

Vergano, Dan and Susan Wloszczyna, "Genetics Take Starring Role on Silver Screen." *USA Today,* 17 June 2002. Archived at http://www.usatoday.com/news/science/2002-06-18-genetics-movies.htm.